ARIS AND PHILLIPS CLASSICAL TEXTS

JULIUS CAESAR

The Gallic War Books V–VI

Edited with an Introduction,
Translation and Commentary by

Jennifer Gerrish

LIVERPOOL UNIVERSITY PRESS

First published 2022 by
Liverpool University Press
4 Cambridge Street
Liverpool
L69 7ZU

www.liverpooluniversitypress.co.uk

This paperback edition published 2024

British Library Cataloguing-in-Publication data
A British Library CIP record is available

ISBN 978-1-80085-629-5 hardback
ISBN 978-1-80207-468-0 paperback

Typeset by Tara Evans

Printed and bound by CPI Group (UK) Ltd, Croydon CR0 4YY

Cover image: *People and places in* The Gallic War *Books 5–6 (detail)*

CONTENTS

INTRODUCTION

I. Caesar's Life and Political Career

Caesar's Early Life

Gaius Julius Caesar (hereafter Caesar) was born in 100 BCE to an old but recently undistinguished patrician family. The *gens Iulia* traced their origins to the goddess Venus and her son, the Trojan War hero Aeneas, and the family took its name from Aeneas' son Iulus (also known as Ascanius). Caesar's father (also Gaius Julius Caesar) never reached the consulship, but served as praetor (the rank below consul on the *cursus honorum*, the progression of offices) and was later proconsul of Asia, probably in the late 90s BCE. Caesar's aunt Julia married Gaius Marius, a distinguished politician and general. Marius was a *novus homo* (a 'new man', the first in his family to attain senatorial office) who had risen to prominence through military victories in Spain and Numidia and was elected tribune of the plebs once and consul seven times. Marius' family was of respectable but not noble standing; his marriage into the *gens Iulia* at once bolstered his own aristocratic credentials and burnished the reputation of the Julians, who had no great recent accomplishments to speak of.

Caesar was a youth in 88 BCE when war broke out between Marius and his rival L. Cornelius Sulla. The proximate cause for the war was a dispute over Sulla's command against Mithridates VI, the king of Pontus, a lucrative assignment for the year of his consulship. Marius, twenty years older than Sulla, was loath to see his last chance at a glorious campaign fall into his rival's hands, and conspired with the tribune of the plebs P. Sulpicius Rufus to reassign the Mithridatic command to himself. Six years of factional violence peaked with Sulla's second march on Rome in 82 BCE and the subsequent bloody program of proscriptions (though Marius died of natural causes in 87). Caesar was fortunate to escape serious harm when he refused Sulla's order to divorce his wife (the daughter of the Marian Cinna) thanks to the intervention of distinguished relatives.

More generally, the conflict between Sulla and the Marians exemplified the increasingly polarized nature of Roman politics in the first century BCE. The *optimates* and *populares* were loose political factions who

used particular approaches to gain power rather than organized political parties in the modern sense. Broadly speaking, the *optimates* supported policies that appealed to ancestral tradition and expanded the powers of the senate; they tended to conserve power in the hands of a few old, aristocratic families. The *populares* proposed legislation that appealed to the general populace, such as generous land reform policies; they generally sought to strengthen the powers of the plebeian tribunes and preserve the tribunate as a bulwark against senatorial overreach. The conflict between these two approaches would be a contributing factor in the later civil war between Caesar and Pompey (Gnaeus Pompeius).

Caesar spent much of the 70s BCE in Asia and enjoyed some success campaigning against the forces of Mithridates VI, king of Pontus. The year 69 BCE marked an important moment in the young Caesar's burgeoning political career. In addition to serving in his first senatorial office, the quaestorship, Caesar delivered the eulogy for his aunt Julia, wife of Marius, and took the opportunity to praise the nobility and divine descent of the *gens Iulia.* Caesar also took the bold move of displaying the *imago* (death mask) of Marius at Julia's funeral, thus defying the memory of Sulla and perhaps giving some indication of his future *popularis* inclination.

In 63 BCE, Caesar won the office of *pontifex maximus*, the highest priesthood in Rome, through exorbitant bribery; he was also elected praetor for the following year. During this same year the disaffected young aristocrat L. Sergius Catilina (Catiline) assembled a band of conspirators intending to spark an armed popular revolution. When the consul M. Tullius Cicero uncovered Catiline's plot, he proposed that the conspirators be given the death penalty through a decree of the senate (*senatus consultum ultimum*) and without trial. Caesar, who had previously supported Catiline in his candidacy for the consulship, spoke against this measure, but the speech of M. Porcius Cato in favor of execution carried the day. Cato also tried to implicate Caesar in the conspiracy; Cato had little evidence and found no success, but the episode established him as one of Caesar's most intractable foes.

After his praetorship in 62 BCE Caesar received Further Spain as his pro-praetorian assignment. By this point Caesar was deeply in debt (not atypical for an ambitious politician); it was only through the intervention of the wealthy former consul M. Licinius Crassus that Caesar escaped

prosecution by his creditors and took up his post in Spain. He spent most of his governorship attacking Iberian settlements under specious pretexts with the aim of refilling his coffers. This effort was so successful that Caesar was not only able to recoup his losses but also to make significant donations to the state treasury. For this the senate voted him a triumph – a lavish victory procession regarded as one of the highest public honors – but a technicality in Roman election law created a dilemma for Caesar. He had intended to run for the consulship of 59, and candidates were required to register in person by a certain deadline. In order to enter the city, Caesar would have to cross the *pomerium* (sacred border) and resign his *imperium* (military command). However, a commander receiving a triumph was not permitted to re-enter the city until the day of the triumph. Caesar requested permission to register for the election *in absentia*, but was denied; he would have to choose. Much to the surprise and concern of his rivals and critics, Caesar declined the tremendous honor of the triumph and returned to the city to register for the election.

Caesar's Consulship and The First Triumvirate

To first win the consulship and then to be able to use the office effectively, Caesar needed support. His political audacity had earned him the suspicion, if not the outright hostility, of many of Rome's more conservative senators, and he anticipated that his candidacy and consulship would be hindered by optimate opposition. In order to bolster himself, Caesar brought together Crassus and Pompey, whose long-standing mutual antagonism made cooperation seem unlikely. However, like Caesar, Crassus and Pompey stood to gain from a potential coalition; Pompey's eastern conquests had yet to be ratified by the senate, and Crassus was wealthy but not especially powerful. Their arrangement (called the 'First Triumvirate' by modern historians) was informal but influential; their combined wealth and political sway secured Caesar's election and enabled all three partners to advance their individual political goals. Caesar's consular colleague M. Calpurnius Bibulus found himself so thoroughly steamrolled that by mid-spring he refused to attend meetings of the senate. Pompey's settlements were ratified and land was granted to his veterans, and Crassus recouped the enormous sums he had spent on political campaigns (including his support for Caesar's election as pontifex maximus and consul). Caesar used his influence not only to pass legislation that increased his popularity

among the *populus Romanus*, but also to secure for himself a potentially lucrative proconsular assignment. The tribune Vatinius proposed that Caesar be granted Cisalpine Gaul and Illyricum for a five-year term and three legions to command. Soon after the *lex Vatinia* was approved by the plebeian assembly, Pompey proposed that the senate also grant Caesar Transalpine Gaul; although this request was met with resistance by the *optimates* (particularly Cato), it eventually passed, and he was granted an additional legion.

The strong-arm tactics of the triumvirs and Caesar's general self-aggrandizement fomented bitter resentment among Caesar's opponents and rivals. Cato, whom Caesar had opposed in the debate about the fate of Catiline's co-conspirators, was particularly hostile. A staunch *optimate* and self-proclaimed defender of traditional values, Cato had long been alarmed by Caesar's exceptional career and sought to obstruct him at every turn, and by the end of Caesar's consulship Cato's frustration had reached a fever pitch. However, Caesar's enemies would have to wait and watch from Rome as he embarked on his proconsular assignment, since Roman law protected sitting magistrates from being brought to trial; so long as he was proconsul, Caesar was immune from prosecution. Cato and his allies could gather their ammunition in anticipation of the end of Caesar's term, but for the time being, Caesar was untouchable.

The Gallic War

In winter of 58 BCE Caesar set out for Transalpine Gaul, which would serve as 'home base' for his operations as proconsul. In Caesar's day, Roman Gaul was made up of several distinct entities. Cisalpine Gaul (or 'Nearer Gaul') covered the Po river plain and stretched from the Apennine mountains of Italy to the Alps, and was the earliest part of Gaul to be brought under Roman rule; Rome conquered the major city of Mediolanum (Milan) in 222 BCE and after the Social War Cisalpine Gaul was carved out of Italy as a separate province. Transalpine Gaul (sometimes called simply 'the Province') lay beyond the Alps, in the region of modern Provence, in southern France. Beyond Transalpine Gaul was 'Hairy Gaul' (*Gallia Comata*), so called by the Romans in derision of the Gauls' perceived wild, unkempt appearance.

According to Caesar (*BG* 1.1), the peoples of *Gallia Comata* could be divided into three groups: the Belgae, the Aquitani, and the Gauls

(or Celts). The *BG* also chronicles Caesar's interactions with the Britons (who were related to the mainland Celts) and the Germans, who dwelled beyond the Rhine. A brief discussion cannot fully represent the diversity of the people Caesar encountered in his Gallic campaigns. Although Caesar identifies some differences in language and custom among various peoples, Caesar's account is somewhat lacking in subtlety and there was probably more diversity among those grouped as 'the Gauls' or 'the Germans' than Caesar presents; the summary here is constrained somewhat by this limitation of our main source. Speaking in very general terms, the Gauls of the Transalpine and Cisalpine provinces lived in towns (*oppida*; Caesar uses this word to describe fortified settlements as well as military forts) and were ruled by some form of oligarchy; they relied heavily on Roman imports and in turn profited from the export of various metals, agricultural products, and slaves to the Romans.[1] Of the Gauls' social structure, Caesar identifies the Druids and 'knights' (*equites*) as holding special status (*BG* 6.13–15). He describes the Gauls as deeply religious and possessing a draconian view of justice (6.16). Relationships between the Gallic peoples varied widely, as the narrative of *The Gallic War* demonstrates; while they might unite for a common cause (for example, in the revolt of Vercingetorix) and shared certain cultural features, the groups remained politically independent. Caesar provides brief ethnographies of the Britons (*BG* 5.12–14) and the Germans (6.21–28), both in this volume. The Britons and Germans subsist on milk and meat, he says, and are ignorant of agriculture (5.14, 6.22). Caesar reports that the Britons dyed themselves blue for battle and practiced polyandry (5.14), while the Germans dressed in scanty reindeer pelts and had only a rudimentary sense of religion (6.21). Overall, the Britons and Germans are depicted as more 'savage' and 'uncivilized' than the inhabitants of Transalpine and Cisalpine Gaul, and the Germans are explicitly contrasted with their more 'civilized' Celtic neighbors; it is perhaps no coincidence that these groups presented Caesar some of his fiercest challenges.

Caesar's victories in Gaul probably had additional significance to those with some sense of Roman history. The Gallic invasion and sack of Rome in the early fourth century BCE still haunted the Roman consciousness

1 A. King, *Roman Gaul and Germany* (Berkeley: University of California Press, 1990), 25–33.

in Caesar's day (and received elaborate description in Livy's history of Rome, written more than a generation after Caesar's campaigns). Many Gallic peoples had supported Carthage during the Second Punic War, when Hannibal procured supplies and troops from towns in Cisalpine Gaul as he marched toward Italy. More recently, Caesar's uncle Marius had campaigned against the Cimbri and Teutones, Germanic peoples who had raised concerns in Rome by migrating through Roman territory and attacking her allies. This history of Gallic threats to Roman security provided Caesar ample pretext for war, although it is less than clear that the Gauls posed a comparable danger in the mid-first century.

What we often refer to as 'the Gallic War' was not a single protracted war, but a series of conflicts and campaigns of varying magnitude. The first issue in which Caesar involved himself upon his arrival in 58 BCE was a dispute over the migration of the Helvetii, who sought to march through Transalpine Gaul on their way to seek a new settlement in the west, away from the harassment of German peoples. Caesar denied them permission to cross through the province. Although the Helvetii turned north away from the province, Caesar nevertheless pursued them, perhaps aiming to set the tone for his tenure in Gaul (*BG* 1.1–30). Later in that year, Caesar intervened on behalf of several states against the German king Ariovistus, who had been encroaching on their territory and whose forces Caesar routed (*BG* 1.31–54). In 57 BCE, a report that the Belgae planned an insurrection against Rome offered a convenient pretext to expand into modern Belgium; during the same year, with his lieutenant Publius Crassus acting as intermediary, Caesar forced the coastal people of western Gaul to surrender to Roman authority. As this news spread, envoys came from far and wide, including from beyond the Rhine, to signal their recognition of Roman rule. For these achievements, the senate declared Caesar a fifteen-day thanksgiving (*BG* 2.35).

Despite the apparent completion of his assignment in Gaul, Caesar's command was nevertheless extended for five more years following his meeting with Pompey and Crassus at Luca in 56 BCE. The peace he had achieved the previous year was short-lived, broken by an uprising of the Veneti and others who inhabited the Atlantic coast (*BG* 3.1–27). 55 BCE began with the invasion of Gaul by the German Usipetes and Tencteri; Caesar not only drove them into retreat, but for the first time led his forces across the Rhine (*BG* 4.1–19). Caesar claims that the

Germans suffered 430,000 casualties in his victory, including women and children who had been cut down in flight (4.14–15). Following the German campaign, Caesar set his sights on a new target. The Celtic peoples of Britain had been offering support and encouragement against Rome to their counterparts on the mainland, which provided Caesar the pretext to cross the Channel (a more compelling pretext, that is, than the pursuit of glory). The expedition to Britain launched late in the year, probably in August. Storms drove the fleet off course and inflicted significant damage, and by the time Caesar landed in Britain the Britons were prepared. The fighting was largely indecisive, and little was accomplished, other than the achievement of the crossing itself. The senate nevertheless awarded Caesar another thanksgiving for his German and British campaigns, this time for twenty days (*BG* 4.20–37). Cato unsuccessfully opposed the thanksgiving on the grounds that Caesar's conduct against the Germans (particularly the slaughter of women and children in flight) was disqualifying, even treacherous.

54 and 53 BCE, the years covered in this volume, are discussed in more detail below (pp. 26–29). This period saw mixed results for Caesar as he attempted to expand his reach in Britain and Germany. A second expedition to Britain was cut short when he was recalled to the mainland to respond to a Gallic revolt. Caesar imposed tribute on the British groups and took a number of hostages, but did not establish a permanent Roman settlement (*BG* 5.5–23). Back in Gaul, Caesar confronted an uprising led by the Eburones. Although the Romans eventually gained the upper hand, it was not before the ambush and destruction of an entire legion (*BG* 5.26–37). Moreover, the rebellion, which involved many groups, revealed the extent of Gallic resentment toward the Roman occupation, foreshadowing the great revolt of 52 BCE. Caesar's second foray across the Rhine (in the following year, 53) was even more of a disappointment than the British expeditions; his attack succeeded in deterring the Germans from offering the Celtic Gauls further support against the Romans, but failing supplies prevented a longer campaign or settlement. The balance of the year was spent exacting retribution for the revolt of 54.

The culminating conflict of both the Gallic War and *The Gallic War* was the widespread uprising led by Vercingetorix, leader of the Arverni, in 52. Although the Gauls were not politically united, they found common cause in their hatred of Roman rule and fears for their future prosperity and

security. Even groups like the Aedui, who had long enjoyed special favor from Caesar in exchange for their support, defected to Vercingetorix' cause. Vercingetorix took advantage of Caesar's inability to obtain supplies from former allies like the Aedui by focusing his attacks on the Romans' supply train and foraging parties. Caesar successfully besieged the town of Avaricum (Bourges; *BG* 7.13–28), but Vercingetorix escaped to Gergovia, the Arvernian capital. The Gauls successfully defended Gergovia, and the Romans were forced to abandon the siege; Caesar's claim that 46 Roman centurions and 700 legionaries died in the fighting may well be an undercount (7.36–51). Caesar pursued Vercingetorix to the town of Alesia. While the Gauls believed they were prepared to withstand another siege, they were unprepared for the elaborate siege works constructed by the Romans, who aimed to starve out the Gauls rather than take Alesia through direct combat. The Roman fortifications were arranged in two lines; one allowed the Romans to attack those defending the city while the other created an additional barrier against reinforcements from the outside. When it became clear that the Romans were equipped to carry on the siege longer than the Gauls could survive, Vercingetorix surrendered, and was eventually paraded through Rome as part of Caesar's triumph before being executed (7.68-89). The rest of Caesar's time in Gaul was spent snuffing out any embers of resistance and bringing his former allies back to heel (*BG* 8).

All told, during Caesar's proconsulship millions of Gauls and Germans were killed, and many of those who were not slaughtered still suffered tremendous losses of resources (and in some cases, their autonomy). It is clear that Caesar profited handsomely from his conquests, not only in absolute economic terms but also in the support of his soldiers and his reputation among the Roman people. The extent to which Caesar's interventions were *necessary* is less clear, and depends largely on how one defines necessity (and from whose perspective). Our understanding and interpretation of the events in Gaul are colored by the fact that our most complete source for these campaigns is Caesar's own account, *The Gallic War*.

Breakdown of the Triumvirate and Civil War

Although Caesar was not physically present in Rome he remained a forceful player in the political scene during the 50s, maintaining his

influence in public life through various subordinates as well as fellow triumvirs. However, the interests of the triumvirs soon began to diverge. Supporters of rival tribunes Publius Clodius and T. Annius Milo formed gangs whose street violence disrupted the normal functioning of the city; politics was no longer dangerous for politicians only. Pompey encouraged the supporters of Milo, while Crassus seems to have tested the waters of an alliance with Clodius. Pompey and Cicero were reconciled upon the latter's return from exile, and Cicero was instrumental in securing Pompey's election as *praefectus annonae* (the official in charge of the grain supply) to respond to a worsening food crisis. Pompey quickly remedied Rome's grain shortage, which provided a much-desired boost to his waning popularity; once again it was Pompey, not Caesar, being cheered as the champion of Rome's people. Pompey's return to the spotlight was dimmed, however, by Caesar's exploits in Gaul, the reports of which thrilled the public and troubled Caesar's enemies.[2]

Aware that both the appearance and the reality of internal discord would weaken their collective influence, the triumvirs convened at Luca (just within the borders of Caesar's province) in the winter of 56 BCE. The meeting was surely tense, but it was productive nevertheless. Pompey and Crassus would stand for the consulship of 55, and the election would be postponed until the end of the current campaign season so that Caesar's soldiers would be able to return to the city to vote in person (as was required). As consuls, Pompey and Crassus quickly extended Caesar's proconsular command in Gaul for several years and assigned lucrative provinces to themselves, as well (the Spains for Pompey and Syria for Crassus).

The final unravelling of the triumvirate might be said to have begun with the death of Julia, Caesar's daughter and Pompey's wife, during childbirth in 54 BCE. In order to preserve the family connection that bolstered their political bond, Caesar suggested that Pompey marry his grand-niece Octavia, while he himself would divorce his wife and marry Pompey's daughter. Pompey rebuffed this offer and instead married Cornelia, daughter of Metellus Scipio, a notable supporter of the optimate cause, perhaps signaling his ambivalence toward a continued partnership with his fellow triumvir. The third partner was removed from the equation when Crassus was killed on campaign in Parthia in the next year in a

2 See pp. 19–26 on the publication and distribution of Caesar's commentaries.

catastrophic defeat that claimed the lives of over 30,000 Roman soldiers. Soon the conditions in the city deteriorated as the hostility between Clodius and Milo's gangs was inflamed by the elections of January 52, in which Clodius and Milo both stood for office. Clodius himself was murdered at Milo's command in the ensuing violence, and the senate was compelled to adopt an extraordinary measure: Pompey was made sole consul to address the crisis. Acting with uncharacteristic decisiveness, Pompey brought charges against Milo and the most egregious of his supporters; Milo went into exile in Massilia (modern Marseille). When order was restored, Pompey selected his new father-in-law Metellus Scipio as his co-consul for the remainder of the year and renewed his own governorship of Spain for an additional five years. Crucially, this allowed Pompey to retain possession of his legions.

Meanwhile in Gaul, Caesar's proconsular term was nearing its end, and he faced a dilemma similar to that which he had faced during his propraetorship in Spain. So long as he held *imperium,* Caesar would be immune from prosecution; he thus hoped to run for the consulship of 49 BCE, so that he could maintain unbroken *imperium* between his proconsulship and a new office and forestall the attacks of Cato and his other enemies who had no doubt been eagerly awaiting the expiration of his Gallic command. However, in order to register as a candidate, he was required to enter the city as a private citizen, rendering him vulnerable to legal attack. Caesar calculated that his best option was to seek an exemption to be registered for the election *in absentia* so that he could transition directly from his proconsular province into the consulship. Cato and the *optimates* vehemently opposed the idea, and Pompey prevaricated. In 51 BCE, a group of *optimates* suggested that Caesar's mandate in Gaul had been fulfilled and that he should be immediately recalled. Caesar was able to defer the matter by investing heavily in the elections for the following year, and in 50 BCE had some measure of protection in the form of friendly tribunes and the consul L. Aemilius Paulus (the brother of M. Aemilius Lepidus, a longtime Caesarian partisan). However, it was increasingly clear that Caesar and the senate (including his erstwhile triumviral partner Pompey) were moving toward a major confrontation.

The continuing Parthian threat brought matters between Caesar and the senate to a head in 50 BCE. The senate resolved to send a force of two legions to protect Syria from Parthian incursions. Caesar and Pompey

were each required to relinquish one legion for the cause. Pompey had sent Caesar one legion as reinforcements several years prior and ordered that this legion be his contribution to the Syrian defense. On paper, their sacrifice was equal, but in reality, Caesar was doubly disadvantaged; he was no doubt further irritated by the fact that the two legions remained stationed at Capua rather than being sent on to Syria. Later that year, the issue of terminating Caesar's Gallic campaign was once again raised. The tribune C. Scribonius Curio, one of Caesar's supporters, proposed a compromise: both Pompey and Caesar would give up their provinces. A majority of senators supported Curio's proposal, but under pressure from Cato and his optimate allies, Pompey agreed to take a stronger stance against Caesar; he assumed command of the two legions at Capua and awaited Caesar's response.

On the first day of the new year Curio presented the senate with a letter from Caesar with one final proposal: once again, Caesar suggested that he and Pompey both lay down their commands. Over the course of the next week, the senate debated this and other proposals to avert war, but ultimately Caesar's enemies prevailed, and on 7 January 49 BCE the senate passed the *senatus consultum ultimum* against him. While the outcome was fully predictable, if not wholly inevitable, Cato and his allies were nevertheless surprised at the alacrity of Caesar's response. On 10 January, he marched with his army across the Rubicon, the river which formed the boundary between his province and Italy. This was illegal – *imperium* was to be surrendered at the moment one set foot outside one's province – and was interpreted as a declaration of war.

From the Rubicon Caesar moved swiftly south down the peninsula, accepting the surrender of the Italian towns he passed through. Pompey and the senate abandoned the city, retreating first to Campania and then to Brundisium, whence they sailed on to Greece to muster reinforcements. Cicero, who accompanied him, described the retreat in his letters as a source of great shame. Before pursuing Pompey himself, Caesar took aim at his rival's (now enemy's) forces in Spain. After a lengthy siege the Pompeian stronghold of Massilia (in Gallia Narbonensis; modern Marseille) surrendered in late summer. After concluding this campaign, Caesar returned briefly to Rome. The absence of senate leadership from the city had delayed the consular election for 48 BCE, and Caesar was appointed dictator by the remaining senators for the purpose of holding

the vote; perhaps unsurprisingly, Caesar himself was elected consul (with long-time supporter P. Servilius Vatia Isauricus). He resigned the dictatorship after the election and pursued the Pompeians in Greece. Pompey and his supporters briefly gained the upper hand with a victory at Dyrrachium in July 48 BCE, but failed to capitalize on their success. In August, Caesar and Pompey met once more in battle at Pharsalus, in central Greece. The Caesarians were victorious. While Pompey himself fled, many of the Pompeians surrendered. Throughout the civil war, Caesar maintained a policy of liberal *clementia* (forgiveness); he offered forgiveness to any of Pompey's supporters who surrendered to him, and the promise that their estates would be untouched and that they were still welcome to hold public office. This strategy was not wholly altruistic. The contrast with Sulla's behavior was pointed; Caesar had waged war against fellow citizens, but his opponents had been defeated, not conquered. Furthermore, the pardoned would thereafter be indebted to Caesar; this rendered them politically useful (or, at the very least, neutralized any potential threats). While this policy allowed Caesar to maintain some continuity in government and avoid the reputation of a vengeful warlord, it left room for resentment to fester, something he would eventually have cause to regret.

Pompey fled to Alexandria, where he may have expected safe harbor due to his patronage of the former king Ptolemy XII. However, the current king, Ptolemy XIII, was entangled in a civil war against his sister Cleopatra VII and under the sway of ambitious advisors. Pompey found not refuge but treachery, and was slaughtered upon arrival, his head preserved as a token of goodwill for Caesar, who was in swift pursuit. According to Plutarch, Caesar reacted to the news of Pompey's assassination with horror and sadness.[3]

Dictatorships and Death

Caesar's grief (whether real or feigned) soon gave way to his ambition. In the Alexandrian civil war, he saw the opportunity to ally himself with a powerful royal family and took the side of Cleopatra. However, Caesar had not come prepared for a major war, and he and Cleopatra were besieged by the forces of Ptolemy and Arsinoë IV, Ptolemy's co-ruler and other sister. Reinforcements eventually arrived and Caesar escaped

3 Plut. *Caes*. 48.2.

disaster. Ptolemy drowned while trying to evade capture and Arsinoë was taken hostage; Caesar installed Cleopatra and her other brother Ptolemy XIV as co-rulers. Cleopatra's claim to the royal succession was bolstered by the birth of Caesarion, her son with Caesar, conceived during the long siege.

Although Caesar and Cleopatra achieved victory in early 47 BCE, Caesar did not return to Rome permanently until the fall of 45. From Alexandria he travelled east to confront the king of Pontus, Pharnaces II, who had been installed by Pompey and who was exploiting the Romans' internal discord by invading neighboring regions that were under Roman control. Caesar's victory over Pharnaces was swift; Caesar was said to have advertised the victory in his triumph with an inscription of the simple phrase "*Veni, vidi, vici*" ("I came, I saw, I conquered").[4] From Pontus Caesar returned briefly to Rome, but quickly turned back to Africa, where some of the Pompeian holdouts who had refused Caesar's *clementia* (including Cato and Metellus Scipio) had taken refuge. Rather than surrender to Caesar after their defeat in the battle of Thapsus, Cato and Scipio committed suicide.

In 46 BCE Caesar celebrated his victories with a quadruple triumph in Rome; around this same time, the senate conferred upon him annual dictatorships for a ten-year period. This was, of course, antithetical to the conventional function of the dictatorship and evoked Sulla's dictatorship, which had been granted with no expiration date (although Sulla resigned it within a year). However, Caesar still did not have the opportunity to settle in. Even after Thapsus, several Pompeian leaders remained in Spain and had raised a substantial army. In late 46, Caesar went to Spain in hopes of exterminating the Pompeian cause once and for all. One of Pompey's sons, Gnaeus, was killed, as was Titus Labienus, who had served under Caesar in Gaul but changed his allegiance during the civil war.[5] Another of Pompey's sons, Sextus, managed to escape, but otherwise Caesar's victory was total, and he returned to Rome for the last time in October of 45.

During his brief time as dictator, Caesar enacted several reforms and measures, some more controversial than others. He commissioned a

---

4 Suet. *Caes*. 37.

5 Labienus appears frequently in Books 5 and 6; see biographical note on his first appearance at Comm. 5.8.1.

number of building projects, including the Forum Julium and the Saepta Julia; both of these were completed during the rule of Augustus, Caesar's grand-nephew (adopted as Caesar's son in his will) and Rome's first emperor. Caesar sought to address Rome's debt crisis and moderate the conflict by making concessions to both borrowers and lenders. He increased the senate membership from around 600 to 900, filling its ranks with supporters and allies, including several from Spain and Gaul. This naturally alienated Caesar's critics from Rome's aristocratic family lines, who viewed the senate as their exclusive birth right. Caesar also rewarded his provincial allies by extending citizenship rights, particularly to towns and regions in Gaul and Spain that had supported him during his various campaigns. In addition to these reforms, Caesar also looked to address Rome's foreign threats. The Parthians had continued to menace the border regions after Crassus' defeat and death in 53 BCE, and Caesar planned to lead a campaign against them, with his departure date set for 18 March 44 BCE.

It is difficult to know Caesar's ultimate plans for the dictatorship. It seemed unlikely that he intended to follow Sulla's lead in resigning it once his aims were accomplished. The possibility of one man holding absolute power indefinitely was antithetical to the Roman constitution, and it concerned many senators grievously. On the other hand, Caesar had also eschewed another, more troubling aspect of the Sullan precedent by rejecting proscriptions and land confiscations in favour of *clementia* and settling his veterans outside Italy. Whatever he had in mind, Caesar's recognition as dictator *in perpetuum* in February 44 BCE may have been what provoked his critics to take drastic measures. On the 15th of March (the Ides), as the senate convened for business in the Theatre of Pompey, Caesar was assassinated by a mob of senators. As many as sixty senators were part of the conspiracy; they considered themselves tyrannicides rather than assassins, and saw their act as the liberation of Rome from autocracy. Caesar's murderers included Marcus Junius Brutus, who had long enjoyed Caesar's favor; Brutus had been pardoned by Caesar after Pharsalus, having joined the Pompeian cause in the belief that Caesar had irreparably harmed the Roman constitution. Having been stabbed twenty-three times, Caesar fell before a statue of Pompey and died; he was fifty-five years old.

II. Caesar as Author

Caesar's Literary Output

Caesar's most famous literary works are those that have survived intact to the modern era: *The Gallic War* and *The Civil War*.[6] Their renown is not merely a reflection of their good preservation; as eyewitness accounts written by one of the most consequential politicians in Roman history (let alone the first century), they represent a unique and invaluable perspective and, particularly on the Gallic campaigns, provide information unavailable from other sources. *The Gallic War*, Caesar's account of his proconsulship, is discussed in more detail below. *The Civil War* narrates the war between Caesar and Pompey in three books, beginning with the senate meeting of 1 January 49 BCE and breaks off awkwardly in 48 BCE, covering the beginning but not the full course of the siege of Alexandria. Scholars generally assume that Caesar abandoned the work unfinished, and unlike *The Gallic War* (the dissemination of which is discussed below), *The Civil War* was not published in Caesar's lifetime.[7]

The war commentaries represent just a small fraction of Caesar's literary portfolio; unfortunately, most of his prolific output has been lost, although the titles and subject matter of his many projects are fairly well-documented. The diversity of Caesar's *oeuvre* attests to an ambitious and creative mind; he demonstrates proficiency in areas ranging from poetry to oratory to linguistic analysis. There is some justification, then, to the remark made by the interlocutor of Tacitus' treatise *Dialogus de Oratoribus* that Caesar possessed a "divinely-inspired genius" (*divinum ingenium*, 21.5), the full cultivation of which was limited by his preoccupation with politics and warfare.[8]

Still, Caesar found time to pursue his literary projects despite the burdens of his 'day job'. While in Gaul, Caesar wrote a two-book

6 Three other works narrating Caesar's campaigns – *The Alexandrian War, The African War,* and *The Spanish War* – were handed down under Caesar's name, but scholars today do not believe Caesar himself actually wrote them. While these works are similar in content and form to the genuine Caesarian works (*The Gallic War* and *The Civil War*), they lack the rhetorical polish and elegance of Caesar's authorial style and are generally ascribed to unknown officers from Caesar's campaigns.

7 W. Batstone and C. Damon, *Caesar's Civil War* (New York and Oxford: Oxford University Press, 2006), 29–32.

8 Cf. Quint. *IO* 10.114.

treatise on the Latin language (*De Analogia,* 'On Analogy') that was praised by the grammarian Fronto as "incredibly meticulous", (*libros scrupulosissimos*, *Parth.* 9) and by Cicero as having been written "with outstanding precision" (*accuratissume, Brutus* 253). Around forty fragments of this work survive, preserved in the form of quotations by ancient grammarians and other commentators. According to Cicero, *De Analogia* was dedicated to him, and it may have been written in response to Cicero's own treatise *De Oratore* ('On the Orator').[9] Caesar covered a number of topics in *De Analogia*, including prescriptions for linguistic standardization and word choice. Regarding the latter, he advised simplicity; authors should choose clear and common language when possible, and avoid unusual words "as you would avoid a cliff" (*scopulum*).[10] Caesar's own adherence to these principles is discussed in more detail below.

Caesar was also admired as a great orator; even Cicero could not begrudge him praise on that count (*Brut*. 252; cf. Quint. *IO* 10.114, Suet. *Jul.* 55). We possess several fragments of his speeches, including a portion of the eulogy for his aunt Julia (Suet. *Iul*. 6.1); many sources also single out for praise his prosecution speech against Cn. Cornelius Dolabella, a supporter of Sulla.[11] Although it is difficult to reconstruct how Caesar might have amplified the text of his oration with his delivery, the small sample we have does give some indication that his style was carefully constructed to fit each occasion, ranging from reverent and lofty in Julia's eulogy to forceful and energetic in his court speeches.[12]

Caesar seems to have enjoyed writing poetry, as well. He composed a poem called 'The Journey' (*Iter*) on his way to Spain in pursuit of surviving Pompeians in 46 BCE. The imperial biographer Suetonius reports that Caesar also authored a number of other works including a tragedy about Oedipus and a poem on the 'Praises of Hercules', but their publication was forbidden by Caesar's heir Augustus (Suet. *Iul* 56). Fewer

---

9 G. Pezzini, 'Caesar the Linguist: the Debate About the Latin Language' in L. Grillo and C. Krebs (eds), *Cambridge Companion to the Writings of Julius Caesar*, 173–92 (Cambridge: Cambridge University Press, 2018), 185–87.

10 Gell. *NA* 1.10.4.

11 See, for example, Tac. *Dial.* 34.7, Suet. *Iul.* 55.1, Plut. *Caes.* 4.

12 H. van der Blom, 'Caesar's Orations' in L. Grillo and C. Krebs (eds), *Cambridge Companion to the Writings of Julius Caesar*, 193–205 (Cambridge: Cambridge University Press, 2018), 201–204.

than ten lines of Caesar's poetry survive, but, as that same interlocutor of the *Dialogus* archly remarks (21.6), this may be to the benefit of Caesar's literary reputation; Caesar's poetry does not receive the same praise as some of his other works (like the war commentaries, as discussed below).

Caesar produced several other works which do not fit neatly into the categories above, including many personal letters (some preserved with Cicero's correspondence), a collection of memorable quotations, and an invective known as the *Anticato*. The latter seems to have taken the form of an epideictic speech in two books, although it was surely not delivered aloud in public. Caesar's *Anticato* was written in response to Cicero's *Cato*, an encomium of Cato written after his suicide in 46 BCE. In this work Caesar employed the familiar *topoi* of invective; he assails Cato's character and faults him for his drunkenness, abuse of family members, and excessive and hypocritical moral rigidity. This work may not have had the intended effect, as insulting the memory of the deceased optimate champion probably only galvanized those who had begun to view Caesar as a tyrant; indeed, the twentieth-century biographer Gelzer refers to this text as Caesar's "most disastrous mistake".[13]

Caesar's Prose Style

The clarity and precision of Caesar's prose style were noted by his contemporaries and in the modern era have made *The Gallic War*, in particular, a permanent fixture in the Latin classroom. It has been the gateway to Roman literature for generations of Latin students around the world, and today it still comprises the prose portion of the US Latin Advanced Placement curriculum. Although modern students of Latin may perceive the language as 'dead' or fossilized in its regularity, in Caesar's day the language was very much alive and evolving. Caesar's writing has been hailed as "correct" by modern readers, but there is a certain circularity to this judgment, for Caesar's work played an important role in establishing the parameters of 'correct' *Latinitas* as it is conceived and taught today.[14]

13 M. Gelzer, *Caesar: Politician and Statesman*, P. Needham, transl. (Cambridge, MA: Harvard University Press, 1968), 332.

14 For more detailed discussion of Caesar's prose style with many examples, see C. Krebs, 'A Style of Choice' in L. Grillo and C. Krebs (eds), *Combridge Companion to the Writings of Julius Caesar*, 110–30 (Cambridge: Cambridge University Press, 2018).

Regarding vocabulary, Caesar followed his own advice from *De Analogia*, in which he argued that word choice (*dilectus verborum*) was the foundation of eloquence (*origo eloquentiae*, Cic. *Brut*. 253). As was mentioned above, he advised writers to avoid unusual or unfamiliar vocabulary, and he himself adhered to this prescription in the war commentaries. Caesar opted for consistency over variety, avoiding synonyms when the same word would do; for example, he shows a strong preference for *flumen* ('river') and avoids the variants *fluvius* and *amnis*.[15] It has been estimated that he used only 3,200 distinct lexemes across both texts, which total some 83,000 words.[16] Caesar further limited his lexicon by avoiding poetic and archaic language; he also eschewed excessively technical military vocabulary, except a few words that he frequently employed (e.g., *aquari*, 'to collect water' or *pabulari*, 'to forage').[17] Caesar's choices on the smallest scale, orthography (the spelling of words) and morphology (the formation of words through declension or conjugation) echo the principles of his lexical choices. Caesar aimed for regularity and standardization in his word forms; as with vocabulary, he avoided archaic or unusual spellings and morphology. We can observe the same consistency and clarity in Caesar's syntax as we see in his lexical choices and word forms. Caesar shows a strong preference for certain constructions, like the ablative absolute and indirect speech, whose use is characteristic of official or senatorial records, and he frequently employs certain repetitive or redundant words or phrases borrowed from the language of bureaucracy.[18] Some scholars have taken this to mean that Caesar's war commentaries were based on his formal annual reports to the senate, which would have been characterized by formulaic language and a similar economy of expression.

Composition, Publication, and Purpose of The Gallic War

15 M. von Albrecht, *A History of Roman Literature: From Livius Andronicus to Boethius* (Leiden: Brill, 1997), 416.

16 J. F. Gaertner and B. C. Hausburg, *Caesar and the Bellum Alexandrinum: An Analysis of Style, Narrative Technique, and the Reception of Greek Historiography* (Göttingen: Vandenhoeck and Ruprecht, 2013).

17 Krebs, 'A Style of Choice', 124–25.

18 M. von Albrecht, *Masters of Roman Prose from Cato to Apuleius*, N. Adkins (transl.), (Leeds: Francis Cairns, 1989), 59–60 and *A History of Roman Literature*, 416–17.

Caesar's most famed literary projects are his two war commentaries, on the Gallic War and the Civil War. However, the popularity and familiarity of these texts belie their complexity, particularly in the case of *The Gallic War*. The apparent simplicity of Caesar's writing is deceptive; for a work that many casual readers assume is a straightforward glorification of Caesar's Gallic conquests, *The Gallic War* is elusive in many respects. Basic questions cannot be answered with certainty: When was *The Gallic War* written? How was it published or distributed? Higher-level interpretive questions have provoked debate and varying levels of consensus: What was Caesar's purpose for writing *The Gallic War*? Who was its intended audience(s)?

The text itself does not supply explicit answers. Many ancient historians reflected on their philosophies of history and the nature of their projects in prefaces or asides. For example, the historian Sallust (a contemporary and supporter of Caesar) considered history-writing a form of public service, while Livy, who wrote under Rome's first emperor, viewed history as morally instructive.[19] *The Gallic War* famously opens with a geographical description ("All Gaul is divided into three parts…") and proceeds directly to the narrative. There is no introductory preface or introduction of the author and his aims as we might expect to see in the work of a historian.

But *was* Caesar a historian, and should we expect him to follow the conventions of ancient historiography? The earliest references to Caesar's works on the Gallic War and the Civil War refer to them not as 'histories' (*historiae* or *res gestae*) but as *commentarii* ('commentaries').[20] *Commentarius* derives from the verb *comminiscor* ('to invent') and shares its root (*-men-*) with words related to the idea of memory (e.g., *mens* 'mind', *memini*, 'to remember'); its etymology thus suggests that a *commentarius* is something created to aid memory. The name is applied to a wide variety of written documents from antiquity, including a booklet on electioneering by Cicero's brother Quintus, a treatise on aqueducts by Frontinus, and the *Attic Nights* of Aulus Gellius, an extensive collection of anecdotes and notes on philosophy, language, history, and other topics. The diversity of ancient texts described as *commentarii* precludes a simple definition of the genre (if, indeed, it can even be called that), but

19 Sall. *Cat.* 3 and Livy preface.

20 Aulus Hirtius, *The Gallic War* Book 8 preface; Cicero, *Brutus* 262.

a few general observations can be made. Commentaries were written records, and seem to have emphasized content over form; that is, there was no expectation that a commentary be artful or entertaining, but rather that it would supply the information that the author deemed important about a given topic. They often served a utilitarian purpose, as, for example, memory aids or reference texts; contemporary remarks about Caesar's commentaries suggest that commentaries could also provide 'raw material' for the work of professional historians (more on this below). Beyond this, generalizations are difficult.

The fact that Caesar's commentaries are our earliest surviving examples of works called *commentarii* further complicates the picture and makes it difficult to know the extent to which *The Gallic War* would have matched or defied the expectations of Caesar's audience. Contemporary evidence suggests that *The Gallic War* was already recognized as exceptional at the time of its publication. Both Hirtius and Cicero imply that Caesar's work was more elaborate and fully developed than contemporary expectations held for a *commentarius*:

> Everyone agrees that nothing was ever finished so perfectly by another author that it is not surpassed by the polish of these commentaries. These commentaries have been published so that historians will not be ignorant of such great achievements, but everyone agrees that those historians have actually been robbed of an opportunity, not granted one
>
> (Aulus Hirtius, *The Gallic War* Book 8 preface).

> While he intended that those who wished to write history would use what he had prepared, it seems he has only done a favour to the incompetent, who are content to apply the curling iron, and he has deterred anyone with any sense from writing. For there is nothing more pleasing in a work of history than clear and lucid brevity
>
> (Cicero, *Brutus* 262).

Ultimately, whether *we* call *The Gallic War* a 'history' or a 'commentary' is irrelevant to our understanding of its contemporary reputation (and, at any rate, the ancient conception of genre was somewhat more fluid than in modern literary studies). Whatever *The Gallic War* was, the work's artistry and craft were recognized and admired by Caesar's contemporaries (including Cicero, one of the great literary minds of Caesar's day).

In the preceding discussion I have referred both to the 'publication' of *The Gallic War* and also to the 'time of its publication'. However, the details of *The Gallic War*'s dissemination are contested by scholars, and there is no firm consensus on when and how the commentary reached the form in which we have it today. Cicero's mention of *The Gallic War* in his treatise *Brutus* indicates that at least some part of Caesar's commentary must have been circulating in some form before 46 BCE. Book 8 was written by Caesar's lieutenant Aulus Hirtius soon after Caesar's death (*BG* 8 pref.; Hirtius died in 43 BCE, providing a *terminus ante quem*). Beyond this, scholars have been left to develop arguments about the date and format of publication based on the internal evidence of the commentary itself.[21] There are two main schools of thought. Some argue that Caesar wrote and distributed *The Gallic War* in its entirety in one instalment. Unitary composition was the default assumption for many years, and its advocates included prominent Caesarian scholars like Gelzer and Rambaud.[22] Some proponents of this view argued that the likely time of composition and publication was around 51 BCE, when Caesar was struggling to convince the senate to either extend his proconsulship or allow him to run for consul *in absentia*; a neatly-packaged record of his glorious deeds in Gaul might have been persuasive to those who had not yet made up their mind about Caesar (if any such senators existed).[23] Others argue for serial composition and publication; in this view, Caesar probably wrote up each year during the winter break from campaigning and sent it immediately to Rome.[24] The argument for *seriatim* publication rests heavily on the apparent development of Caesar's style and literary techniques over the course of the seven original books. Scholars have specifically noted the increased use of direct speech, as well as shifts in vocabulary and the grammatical

21 A. Riggsby provides a useful overview of the debate (*Caesar in Gaul and Rome: War in Words* (Austin: University of Texas Press, 2006, 9–15).

22 Gelzer, *Caesar: Politician and Statesman* and M. Rambaud, *L'art de la deformation historique dans les Commentaires de César*, 2nd edn. (Paris: Les Belles Lettres, 1966).

23 See, for example, Gelzer (1968) 170–72.

24 Arguments for serial composition include Wiseman, 'The Publication of *De Bello Gallico*' and C. Krebs, 'Caesar, Lucretius, and the Dates of *De Rerum Natura* and the *Commentarii*', *Classical Quarterly* 63 (2013) 772–79. F. E. Adcock tried to carve out a middle path, suggesting that Caesar may have written the books year-by-year, but polished and published them all together (*Caesar as Man of Letters*, Cambridge: Cambridge University Press, 1956, 89).

structures commonly employed. As Riggsby points out, serial publication also would have better served Caesar's need to maintain his connection with Rome and to remain in the public eye even at a distance.[25]

Beyond the limited suggestions in the text itself, we might look to Caesar's intended audience and purpose for writing *The Gallic War* for clues about its publication, since these factors surely influenced Caesar's decisions about how and when to disseminate the books of his commentary. At least two distinct audiences may be identified: a senatorial audience to whom he was pressured to justify his continued involvement in Gaul and the *populus Romanus*, whose loyalty and affection he worked to maintain during his years away from the city. Among the senate, Caesar had both partisans and enemies. The annual distribution of a new installment of *The Gallic War* provided an opportunity for Caesar to make the case each year for his continued involvement in Gaul. The expansion of Rome's territory was always enticing, but Caesar's enemies would not have been enthused at its achievement in Caesar's name. Instead of portraying his campaigns solely as expansionist endeavors, Caesar repeatedly emphasizes the internal instability of the Gallic states he encounters and characterizes the Gallic aristocracy as deeply factionalized and prone to rebellion. Caesar highlights the danger posed to the *res publica* by those who exploited internal conflicts in an attempt to galvanize support for throwing off the mantle of Roman rule.[26] In turn, Caesar depicts himself as the restorer of order and harmony; through his leadership, possible usurpers are put in check and peace and stability are returned to the province.[27] Of course, there would also be conquests and booty, but Caesar depicted his immediate goals as more practical (and thus harder to argue against). While Caesar's staunchest enemies (like Cato) were unlikely to be swayed, at least during the early years of the Gallic campaigns it is likely that some remained more open-minded.

---

25 Riggsby, *Caesar in Gaul and Rome*, 11.

26 Vercingetorix accomplished this on the largest scale in 52 BCE, but he had many predecessors. For example, in the opening chapters of Book 1 the Helvetii, at the instigation of one Orgetorix, decide to migrate through Roman territory in defiance of Caesar's orders. Caesar responds swiftly and forcefully on the grounds that the presence of these "warlike men, hostile toward the Roman people" (*homines bellicosos, populi Romani inimicos*) would pose a serious threat to the province (*magno cum periculo provinciae*, 1.10). Further examples from Books 5–6 are discussed below.

27 See pp. 29–30 on the prevalence of this theme in Books 5–6.

When Cato and the *optimates* sought his recall or obstructed his requests, Caesar's supporters could thus point to *The Gallic War* for evidence that, despite Caesar's repeated and glorious victories, parts of Gaul remained unstable and required his continued presence. In turn, Caesar used the narrative to flatter and reward his supporters, who maintained the crucial connection between Caesar and Rome while he was in Gaul, by highlighting their roles or the achievements of family members (such as Publius Crassus, son of the triumvir, who receives a star billing in Book 3).[28] On the whole, Caesar was careful and generous in describing the activities of his legates, who were generally of high social rank. While the dramatic, exemplary vignettes were more often reserved for centurions or low-ranking (even anonymous) soldiers, Caesar's officers receive favorable depiction;[29] he particularly emphasizes their loyalty and obedience as virtues.[30] While Caesar is careful not to let his legates outshine himself, these portraits were surely flattering both to his officers themselves and also to their political allies, friends, and families back in Rome.

While Caesar's partisan operatives maintained the channel of communication between Caesar and his senatorial peers, he also sought to ensure his accomplishments in Gaul were celebrated and glorified among the Roman people. Caesar's long absence from the city created a precarious situation for the *popularis* politician. While Pompey and other politicians could curry political favor with public festivals and handouts, proposing popular legislation, or funding lavish building projects (like Pompey's theatre, completed 55 BCE), Caesar had to seek alternative means of cultivating his base. The annual distribution of *The Gallic War* provided an opportunity to speak to the people themselves and not just the political elite. Not only did Caesar use *The Gallic War* to impress the people by highlighting his accomplishments, he also used clever rhetoric and literary techniques to align his own achievements with the success and good fortune of the Roman people themselves. As Krebs points out,

---

28 K. Welch, 'Caesar and His Officers in the Gallic War Commentaries' in *Julius Caesar as Artful Reporter: The War Commentaries as Political Instruments*, K.Welch and A. Powell (eds), 85–103 (London: Duckworth, 1998), 91–93.

29 The notable exception is Sabinus in Book 5, on which see p. 33.

30 Welch, 'Caesar and His Officers'.

the phrase *populus Romanus* appears forty-six times in Book 1 alone,[31] and a majority of the total appearances of the phrase are made in close conjunction with Caesar's name or reference to himself.[32] Caesar thus underscores both his indebtedness and service to the *populus Romanus*. Furthermore, many of the most colorful and exciting scenes in *The Gallic War* featured junior officers and even anonymous common soldiers, who are frequently praised for bravery and self-sacrifice.[33] It is possible that members of Caesar's audience were able to imagine themselves (or a family member or a friend) in these vignettes and thus feel a personal connection with Caesar's victories. Perhaps Pompey was building them theatres, but Caesar was securing a more lasting legacy for the Roman people; Caesar was the conqueror of the known world and a pioneer on behalf of the *populus Romanus*, expanding Rome's authority to the ends of the earth.

The traditional view of *The Gallic War* is that it was disseminated in written form and that it was meant to be read. This view takes Rome's political class (including senators and prominent equites) as Caesar's primary audience. However, as was discussed above, the Roman people also comprised an important segment of Caesar's target audience. Dissemination in written format alone would have excluded a significant percentage of that intended audience, either due to limited literacy[34] or the economic and practical challenges of obtaining a physical text.[35] Recent scholarship has explored the possibility that *The Gallic War* reached a

31 C. Krebs, 'More than Words: The *Commentarii* in their Propagandistic Context' in *Cambridge Companion to the Writings of Julius Caesar*, L. Grillo and C. Krebs (eds) 29–42 (Cambridge: Cambridge University Press, 2018), 38. Krebs reckons 80 overall mentions of the *populus Romanus* in *The Gallic War*.

32 E. S. Ramage, 'The *populus Romanus, imperium*, and Caesar's Presence in *De Bello Gallico'*, *Athenaeum* 90 (2002) 125–46, 133.

33 Welch, 'Caesar and His Officers', 90. See below for examples from Books 5 and 6.

34 See W. A. Johnson, *Readers and Reading Culture in the High Roman Empire: A Study of Elite Communities* (Oxford and New York: Oxford University Press, 2012) for an overview of literacy, reading, and book culture; although Johnson's study focuses on the early empire, many of his observations will obtain for the late republic as well.

35 According to the imperial poet Martial, books sold for anywhere between 24 and 80 bronze asses, depending on the quality of production. In Martial's day, an ordinary soldier's pay was 10 asses per day, suggesting that this was an unattainable luxury (or at least a steep investment) for the non-wealthy. Cf. T. P. Wiseman, *The Roman Audience: Classical Literature as Social History* (Oxford: Oxford University Press, 2015) 5.

wide public audience through oral performance in public venues.[36] The Roman elite often indulged in *recitationes*,[37] private readings of works-in-progress, and the public was used to enjoying public performance of various kinds (for example, theatrical shows or poetry contests at religious festivals). Wiseman has suggested that the public reading of *The Gallic War* was something of a hybrid of these activities: the reading performance of a literary work, moved from the privacy of a villa to the public square.[38] This theory opens up fascinating new interpretive possibilities for *The Gallic War*, since various elements of the text would have been received quite differently by a reading audience (who could pause or re-read at their convenience, compare Caesar's text with other documents, and who might be expected to have a working knowledge of Greek and Roman literature) and a listening audience (who did not have the benefit of the text before them and whose familiarity with literature, mythology, and other cultural references may have varied).

The Gallic War undeniably served political purposes for Caesar, but it is worthwhile to recall that Caesar was a prolific writer in many genres and that he eagerly participated in the literary conversations of his day, even while he was on campaign in Gaul.[39] It is not unreasonable to believe that Caesar viewed *The Gallic War* as a literary accomplishment in its own right and not merely an artefact of political propaganda. Thus, in addition to the political interpretation of various elements discussed here (and below), we might also keep in mind that Caesar may also have composed his narrative with an eye toward situating himself among other 'literary' authors. For example, Books 5 and 6 feature a number of references to other texts and traditions which may be read through both a political lens *and* a literary one. Allusion and references were

36 T. P. Wiseman, 'The Publication of *De Bello Gallico*' in K. Welch and A. Powell (eds), *Julius Caesar as Artful Reporter: The War Commentaries as Political Instruments*, 1–9 (London: Duckworth, 1998) and *The Roman Audience*; J. Gerrish, 'Heroic Resonances in Caesar's *Bellum Gallicum* 5', *Classical World* 111 (2018) 351–70.

37 See, e.g., F. Dupont, '*Recitatio* and the Reorganization of the Space of Public Discourse' transl. T. Habinek and A. Lardinois, in T. Habinek and A. Schiesaro (eds), *The Roman Cultural Revolution*, 44–59 (Cambridge: Cambridge University Press, 1997).

38 Wiseman, 'The Publication of *De Bello Gallicum*' 6 and *The Roman Audience*, 101–2.

39 For example, Cicero's correspondence with his brother Quintus, who was with Caesar in Gaul, indicates that Caesar made time even on campaign to read and comment on drafts of Cicero's poetry (*Q. Fr.* 2.16(15).5).

frequently employed by authors of historiography and other types of literature, like epic poetry. Caesar's allusions could serve his political agenda; for example, his references to the epic tradition serve to elevate his conquests to a heroic or mythological level in a way that may have appealed to a popular audience.[40] However, Caesar's references also put his work in dialogue with other texts in such a way as to demonstrate his keen awareness of literary traditions. For example, Grillo has argued that Caesar's allusions to Polybius in the Sabinus and Cotta episode liken the disaster at Atuatuca to the Roman catastrophe at Cannae in the Second Punic War, reminding Caesar's audience that "losing a battle does not mean losing a war."[41] Furthermore, Caesar's Polybian allusions demonstrate his command of historiographical tradition and technique and thus place him among the proper 'historians'. Not only did Caesar have a fine command of older literature, he was eager to show his awareness of the most recent publications, as well; this is suggested by his references to *De Rerum Natura*, a philosophical poem by his contemporary Lucretius that was probably published while Caesar was in Gaul.[42] Like any work of literature, *The Gallic War* thus offers a constellation of interpretive possibilities that should be seen as complementary rather than mutually exclusive.

III. *The Gallic War* Books V and VI

The War in Gaul, 54–53 BCE

Caesar opened the year 54 BCE with at least one goal in mind: a second, more glorious expedition to Britain. In 55, Caesar had made an expedition to Britain, the first Roman general to do so, but Caesar's fleet had been damaged by storms and he only received a fraction of the hostages he had demanded. Caesar surely hoped the second campaign would be more glorious, especially since, back in Rome, the construction of Pompey's theatre had greatly increased his triumviral colleague's popularity. However, Caesar's preparations for departure were interrupted by an internal dispute among the Treveri, a Gallic people who had been resistant to Caesar's

40 Gerrish, 'Heroic Resonances'; see also Comm. 5.25.1 and 5.34.4.

41 L. Grillo, 'Caesarian Intertextualities: Sabinus and Cotta in *BG* 5.26–37', *Classical Journal* 111 (2016) 257–79, 270; see also Comm. 5.28.2.

42 C. Krebs, 'Caesar, Lucretius, and the Dates of *De Rerum Natura* and the *Commentarii*', *Classical Quarterly* 63 (2013) 772–79; see also Comm. 5.14.6.

influence (5.1–2). Two nobles, Indutiomarus and Cingetorix, were rivals for power among the Treveri. Both appealed to Caesar, who offered his support to Cingetorix (5.3–4). Fearing further unrest in his absence, Caesar arranged for many Gallic leaders to 'accompany' him on his British voyage (that is, to serve as hostages); after suppressing a potential rebellion by Dumnorix, a leader of the Aedui, Caesar departed for Britain (5.5–8).

The British campaign was not the overwhelming victory Caesar had hoped for. The Romans struggled initially against the guerrilla tactics of the Britons (5.9–21). While Caesar's men finally gained the advantage and the British forces under the king Cassivellaunus were forced to capitulate, Caesar did not manage to extract much from them; he took hostages and imposed tribute, but did not leave a permanent settlement. This had to suffice; it was late in the season, and Caesar remained anxious about unrest on the mainland (5.22–4).

Caesar's anxieties were well-founded. The rest of the year was consumed by an explosive rebellion led by Ambiorix, a leader of the Eburones. Ambiorix won the support of many Gallic states and prominent individuals, including Indutiomarus of the Treveri, who was still enraged at Caesar's elevation of Cingetorix. Through a clever and deadly plan, Ambiorix gained the advantage over Caesar and caused the greatest Roman disaster of Caesar's campaigns. Feigning friendly concern, he approached Quintus Titurius Sabinus and Lucius Aurunculeius Cotta, who were in charge of the winter camp among the Eburones, and advised them to break camp and escape before a planned attack by the Gauls and Germans; he would offer them safe passage through his territory. Cotta advised that they should await Caesar's command; Sabinus, panicked, argued that the Gauls would not be so bold unless Caesar was on his way to Italy and too far away to help. After some debate, Sabinus won out and the Romans broke camp. They were soon ambushed by Ambiorix. Nearly the entire legion was slaughtered, and those who survived the attack committed suicide; only a few escaped to tell the tale (5.26–37).

Ambiorix next targeted the camp of Quintus Cicero (brother of the politician and author), who was stationed among the Nervii. When Quintus did not fall for the same ruse that had ensnared Sabinus and Coatta, Ambiorix and the Nervii besieged his camp (5.40–42). The fighting was fierce; Quintus barely survived the siege and his troops were nearly annihilated before Caesar arrived to relieve them (5.43–

52). Meanwhile, Labienus was among the Treveri, where Indutiomarus continued to foment rebellion. Indutiomarus was eventually slain, but the situation in Gaul remained unstable, as the groups already chafing under the Roman bit saw an opportunity to exploit Caesar's divided attention.

The revolt of 54 left Caesar with less time than usual for his typical winter routine (holding assizes in northern Italy) in 54/3 BCE. He decided to take swift action to pursue Ambiorix and seek revenge against the Gallic people who had joined the rebellion and who continued to defy his authority. Caesar was supported in this endeavor by a backup legion sent by Pompey (6.1). He turned first against the Nervii, and then on to the Senones and Carnutes, who had expelled their pro-Roman kings and refused Caesar's request to come to a meeting (6.2–4). Caesar then divided his forces; he focused on the Menapii, while Labienus was again sent against the Treveri (6.5–8). When he rejoined Labienus, Caesar decided to lead his forces across the Rhine, seeking revenge for the Germans' aid to Ambiorix and fearing that Ambiorix would find safe harbor there (6.9). Aided by the Ubii, the Romans confronted the Suebi, a German people whom Caesar had previously punished for harassing the Ubii. However, the Suebi made a tactical retreat and awaited the Roman advance on the edge of the Bacenis forest (6.10). Upon learning the location of the Suebi, Caesar was forced to abandon his attempt to push beyond the Rhine; he cited concerns about the food supply as his reason for returning to Gaul (6.29). Caesar then turned his attention once again to the pursuit of Ambiorix. He once again divided his forces, with Labienus advancing on the Menapii and Gaius Trebonius on the Atuatuci; Caesar himself headed for the Scaldis (Scheldt) river region, where he heard Ambiorix was taking cover among the Eburones (6.33). Caesar wasted the Eburones' territory with fury and vengeance (6.34–43) and executed Acco, the leader of the Senones, on whom he laid blame for the rebellion of the Senones and Carnutes earlier in the year. Ambiorix, however, escaped (6.44).

Some scholars who have argued for the serial, annual composition of *The Gallic War* allow that Caesar may not have written Book 5 during the winter of 54/3 BCE, but that Books 5 and 6 were composed together in the winter of 53/2. Ambiorix' revolt occupied the Romans until late in 54 and Caesar, eager to pursue Ambiorix and punish the states who supported him, assembled his legions earlier than usual, before the end of winter (6.3). Wiseman has posited that the chaotic winter of 54/3

forced Caesar to delay his write-up of 54 and that he worked on Books 5 and 6 together when he was able to return to his usual winter quarters at the end of 53.[43] In the absence of clear evidence for the composition and publication of *The Gallic War,* we can only speculate on the timing of Books 5 and 6, but there are some narrative and thematic continuities within these two books. Some of these continuities are shared to varying extent with other books of *The Gallic War*, but the third theme identified here ('reframing setbacks') is particularly conspicuous in Books 5 and 6.

Themes of Books V–VI

Justification of Caesar's Command

As was discussed above, constant antagonism from Cato and the *optimates* required Caesar to repeatedly justify his continuing command in Gaul. This point was particularly urgent in the winter of 53/2, since Caesar had spent so much of 54 and 53 dealing with the fallout of internal disputes among the Gallic states and *not* attaining the type of glorious victories that would easily make his case back in Rome. In order to argue for the necessity of his presence in Gaul, in Books 5 and 6 Caesar highlights the factional nature of the Gauls and the threat posed to the province by their internal instability. The Gallic/German digression in Book 6 opens with a proclamation about the Gauls' factionalism: "In Gaul there are factions not only in every state and every district and region, but practically in every individual household" (6.11.2). This generalization is borne out by the narrative of Books 5 and 6, in which Caesar seizes opportunities to emphasize the Gauls' inability to maintain domestic peace without his intervention; for example, in the opening chapters of Book 5, we see the Treveri turn to Caesar for help in resolving the dispute over their kingship (5.3–4). Later on, Ambiorix' revolt gains momentum from the conflict among the Treveri, since Ambiorix capitalized on Indutiomarus' anger at being passed over by Caesar. Book 5 also contains two more episodes in which Gallic states overthrow the king imposed by Caesar (the Carnutes at 5.25 and Senones at 5.54). After the execution or expulsion of these kings by revolutionary factions, the new regimes of both the Carnutes and Senones lead their states in open rebellion against Caesar (6.2–4). Caesar scapegoats and executes a certain Acco for leading the uprising, and order is restored (6.44); this story arc makes clear that the rejection

43 Wiseman, *The Roman Audience*, 102.

of Caesar's will leads to discord among the Gauls and eventually their punishment (rather than their freedom).

The case of Dumnorix demonstrates that even the friendlier Gallic states cannot be trusted in a revolution against Roman rule; the crisis is only averted by Caesar's order to eliminate Dumnorix (5.6–7). If even those states that had been treated generously by Caesar could potentially be induced against Rome by a rebellious faction,[44] it was clear that a forceful and continuous Roman presence was necessary, preferably under the leadership of the commander with the greatest knowledge of and experience confronting the Gauls' treacherous ways.

From a modern perspective, of course, we might view Caesar's case in Books 5-6 quite differently. What Caesar tried to justify as Rome's (or, rather, *his*) necessary, stabilizing, and civilizing presence might strike us today as an example of gross colonial overreach and circular logic (the imposition of Roman rule leads to factionalism within the Gallic states, which can only be suppressed by Roman intervention). However, within the Caesarian worldview, the internal logic of these books is consistent (however dubious): the Gauls pose a danger if left to their own devices, and, with his years of experience and gifts of leadership, Caesar possesses the unique ability to resolve disputes, restore peace to the Gauls, and protect Rome's interests. Caesar surely would have preferred to justify his command with new provinces and abundant plunder each year, but this was not possible for 54 and 53; however, by exploiting the Romans' fear of 'barbarians at the gates', so to speak, he still finds a way to demonstrate the necessity of his command.

Allegiance to the *Populus Romanus*

By the time he wrote Books 5 and 6, Caesar had been away from Rome for several years. As was discussed above, maintaining his status among the people was a perennial concern, but it may have felt particularly urgent by the winter of 53/2. The previous two years had seen the dissolution of the triumviral experiment. When Julia died in 54, Pompey had declined Caesar's offer to forge another marriage between their families; the death of Crassus in 53 brought an abrupt end to the arrangement, and Caesar could no longer rely on these colleagues to promote his interests in the city. Furthermore, as the triumvirs' interests had been gradually diverging

44 The Aedui did, in fact, eventually revolt, joining the uprising of Vercingetorix in 52 BCE.

over the previous years, Pompey had been paying increased attention to his own public profile. As prefect of the grain supply, he stabilized Rome's resources enough to provide abundantly for the city,[45] and the completion of his theatre complex in 55 had been widely celebrated.[46] Pompey's popularity was thus trending high; his third and most magnificent triumph, in 61 BCE, had perhaps faded from memory, but his public largesse seems to have renewed his favor among the Roman people. Thus, in 53/2 Caesar may have felt a strong impulse to shore up his popular base in whatever ways he could from a distance. Perhaps attempting to nudge his way past Pompey into the city landscape, in 54 he commissioned the Saepta Julia, a grand, marble, colonnaded plaza in the Campus Martius meant to replace an old voting place. While this was not completed until after Caesar's death, his plans were publicly known (Cic. *Att.* 4.16.8).

In addition to promising this lavish gift to the Roman people, Caesar also used Books 5 and 6 of *The Gallic War* to keep himself present in their minds and hearts. Forms of the phrase *populus Romanus* appear eleven times across these two books, with 9 instances concentrated in Book 5. As Ramage has noted, Caesar often employs the name of the Roman people in ways that connect the people with Rome's power and remind them that Caesar's conquests are in their name.[47] This holds true in Books 5 and 6, as Caesar emphasizes what the *populus Romanus* stands to gain or lose depending on his command. For example, the revolts of Indutiomarus and Ambiorix are framed as not just attacks against Caesar, but affronts to the Roman people (5.3.3, 27.4, 28.1, 29.4). Caesar also shows how the people will profit from his campaigns; the British expedition is a great victory, because it has caused the Britons to pay tribute to the *populus Romanus* (5.22.4). Caesar further appeals to the people by making flattering references to their history of dignified and disciplined customs and practices, often underscored by comparison with the 'uncivilized' enemy (5.41.7, 6.1.4, 6.7.8).

Moreover, these books feature several displays of conspicuous bravery by Caesar's rank-and-file legionaries and centurions. The soldiers' bravery in the face of fear is emphasized in Caesar's account of the ambush by Ambiorix, and their courage is underscored by comparison with the

---

45 App. *B Civ* 2.18.

46 Plut. *Pomp.* 53.1.

47 Ramage, 'The *populus Romanus, imperium,* and Caesar's Presence'.

legate Sabinus; Caesar notes that they still resisted bravely even though both Sabinus and fortune had 'abandoned' them (*nostri tametsi ab duce et a fortuna deserebantur,* 5.34). Chief centurions Titus Balventius and Quintus Lucanius are singled out by name and praised for 'bravery' (*viro forti*, 5.35.6, *fortissime pugnans*, 5.35.7) as they were wounded or killed in the fighting. Also lauded for bravery (*fortissime pugnans*, 5.37.5) in this episode is Lucius Petrosidius, a standard-bearer, who saves the standard at the expense of his own life. Perhaps the most memorable example of soldierly courage in Book 5 is the 'centurions' contest' (5.44), in which two of Caesar's soldiers, very brave men (*fortissimi viri*, 5.44.1) and long-time rivals Vorenus and Pullo, 'compete' with each other to show who is the more excellent soldier. First Vorenus saves Pullo from trouble, and then Pullo rescues Vorenus. In the end, their heroics are judged equally praiseworthy (5.44.14).[48] The elevation of these otherwise unknown soldiers creates the impression that Caesar is sharing credit for his victories with the common people. While it seems likely that this tactic was considered by Caesar's senatorial audience to be mere pandering, it may have been perceived as generous by others, particularly those who could imagine themselves or a loved one in the role of Vorenus or Pullo.

Reframing Setbacks

The years 54 and 53 presented Caesar with a unique challenge: they had not been very successful for the Romans. The second voyage to Britain could be considered an accomplishment, but it was not the spectacular victory Caesar had surely envisioned. Ambiorix' revolt was nothing short of catastrophic, causing the loss of the full legion under Sabinus and Cotta and the majority of the forces under Quintus Cicero; furthermore, Ambiorix was never caught. Adding to the ignominy were the embarrassing retreat from Germany and the costly siege of Atuatuca. In order to support Caesar's efforts to justify his command and maintain his popularity with the people, these setbacks had to be downplayed or reframed in a more positive light; if that was not possible, someone besides Caesar had to be held responsible for the setback. This required Caesar to thread the narrative needle carefully, lest he appear to be making excuses for himself or unfairly scapegoating subordinates.

48 This scene caught the attention of the creators of the HBO/BBC television series *Rome,* who developed the otherwise unknown Vorenus and Pullo as the series' main protagonists.

In some cases, Caesar easily found targets onto which he could deflect blame for his setbacks. For example, the conclusion of Caesar's British expedition in 54 was something of a letdown; he ordered the Britons to pay annual tribute to the Roman people but left behind no settlement nor occupying force. The Romans' hasty return to the mainland is justified as Caesar's pro-active response to concerns about uprisings among the Gauls (5.22.4). This explanation has the added benefit of reminding Caesar's audience of the need for his continued assignment to Gaul to control factionalism within the province (as was discussed above). The legate Sabinus provides another easy target of blame and is held fully responsible for the legion lost in the ambush by Ambiorix. Caesar is generally diplomatic in his criticism of his officers; although missteps are noted, Caesar's criticism is tactful and sometimes tempered by sharing the blame with 'luck' or 'chance', as is discussed below.[49] However, Sabinus receives particularly harsh condemnation for his role in the massacre of his legion. The entire episode was a catastrophe and Caesar's audience, regardless of individual status or opinion of Caesar, would no doubt be universally horrified. Despite Caesar's general hesitance to condemn his lieutenants (and despite his past praise for Sabinus, 3.17–19), Sabinus is made the primary scapegoat. He is described as treacherous, stupid, and cowardly, a wholly damning characterization unparalleled elsewhere in *The Gallic War*. Without another contemporary source it is impossible to know whether Caesar's treatment of Sabinus here is fair, but as Welch notes, "Caesar had no other choice if he was not to share in the blame."[50]

When there is no obvious target to blame for a failure or setback, Caesar occasionally suggests that fortune was to blame, suggesting that no human intervention (even by Caesar) could have changed the outcome. 'Fortune' was an ambivalent concept in Greek and Roman thought; the Latin *fortuna* and Greek τύχη did not necessarily denote *good* fortune, and sometimes meant just the opposite. Accordingly, *fortuna* is often best interpreted as 'luck' or 'chance', suggesting a force impervious to the efforts of men. Caesar uses *fortuna* in this way several times in Books 5 and 6 to deflect blame for his various setbacks and imply their inevitability. The doomed legion under Sabinus and Cotta is described as having been deserted by both Sabinus and fortune (5.34.2); in this

49 Welch, 'Caesar and His Officers', 96.
50 Welch, 'Caesar and His Officers', 96.

example, responsibility is split between human failure and fate (but, in any case, not attributable to Caesar). Likewise, Caesar cites the role of fortune in his failure to capture Ambiorix. Unlike Sabinus, Basilus (the officer who missed the opportunity to capture Ambiorix) is largely exonerated by Caesar, who invokes *fortuna* twice in his description of Ambiorix' escape (6.30.2 and 4). *Fortuna* also has a significant part in Caesar's account of the siege of Atuatuca by the Sugambri. Caesar introduces the episode by reminding us that fortune plays a great and disruptive role in warfare (6.35.2). After the Sugambri have been repelled, Caesar reflects on the costly siege. The Romans had made only one mistake, he judges, but that single miscalculation created the opportunity for the intervention of *fortuna* (6.42.2). In these episodes, Caesar thus uses the notion of capricious chance to deflect responsibility for his setbacks in 54 and 53 by attributing them to a force beyond the reach of his (or any mortal's) influence.

Narrative Features of Books V–VI

As is clear from the foregoing discussion, there was a lot at stake for Caesar in Books 5 and 6. Scholars have also observed that this is also the point in *The Gallic War* at which Caesar begins to use literary and historiographical devices like speeches and digressions more freely and elaborately.[51] As Wiseman points out, this increased attention to literary elements may reflect the difficult rhetorical tasks Caesar needed these books to perform.[52] The following sections discuss several narrative features of Books 5 and 6 and how Caesar used them to address the themes and goals of Books 5 and 6 discussed in the previous section.

Geography and Ethnography

The descriptions of Britain, Gaul, and Germany and their inhabitants are some of the most striking and memorable passages of Books 5–6. Geographical and ethnographical digressions were a regular feature of historical writing; the tradition had begun with the Greeks and seems to have been taken up by the early Roman historians.[53] Although *The*

51 See, e.g., Wiseman, *The Roman Audience*, 102 and T. Creer, 'Ethnography in Caesar's *Gallic War* and its Implications for Composition', *Classical Quarterly* 69 (2019) 246–63.

52 Wiseman, *The Roman Audience*, 102.

53 Most of the histories written by Romans before Caesar's day survive only in fragments,

Gallic War was not called a 'history' by Caesar's contemporaries, as was discussed above, Caesar freely employs this feature of historiography. Earlier books had featured brief descriptions of people and places (e.g., the earlier, less elaborate description of the Germans at 4.1–4) but the digressions of Books 5 and 6 are as elaborate and detailed as those written by 'real' historians.[54] In Book 5, Caesar marks his arrival in Britain with a brief excursus describing the geography of the island (5.12–13) and some of the Britons' cultural practices (5.14). The excursus on the Gauls and Germans in Book 6 is perhaps inappropriately called a 'digression', for it comprises nearly half of the book. Caesar devotes ten chapters to an overview of Gallic cultural and political practices (6.11–20), followed by a description of and comparison with the Germans, who are depicted as wild and uncivilized (6.21–24). The digression is crowned with an account of the wondrous creatures (including a unicorn) that inhabit the Hercynian Forest (6.25–28).

These geographical and ethnographic passages perform several functions. Broadly speaking, Caesar's descriptions of the groups he encountered on his campaigns reflect the colonialist nature of the Roman presence in Gaul. It is taken for granted by the author (and presumably by his audience) that the Gauls, Britons, and Germans are fundamentally inferior to the Romans. Like most ancient ethnography, these passages highlight those customs which seem most different from Roman practice (e.g., British polyandry) in order to emphasize the 'otherness' of these peoples and reaffirm the Romans' right to conquer them.[55] However, beyond reflecting Caesar's generally colonialist view of the peoples of Gaul, the geographies and ethnographies play more specific rhetorical and political roles when read individually in their literary and historical contexts. As has been discussed, in composing Books 5 and 6 Caesar

---

so it is difficult to say for certain how regular the practice was in early Latin historiography. The evidence suggests the early Roman historians followed Greek tradition here; for example, Cato's *Origines*, written in the second century BCE, included an ethnography of the Gauls. See additional discussion in Commentary on 5.12.1.

54 See Creer (2019) for the development of the ethnographies as evidence of serial composition.

55 For basic overviews of geography and ethnography in the Greek and Roman historical tradition, see E. Dench 'Ethnography and History' (1013–33) and J. Engles 'Geography and History' (1108–130) in J. Marincola (ed.), *A Companion to Greek and Roman Historiography* (Malden, MA: Wiley-Blackwell, 2011).

may have felt pressure to justify his modest success in Britain and his failure to conquer Germany. Allen-Hornblower and others have observed that the Gallic/German digression is positioned at the point where Caesar must decide whether to pursue the Suebi across the Rhine and into Germany.[56] In light of his description of Germany and its inhabitants as dangerous and unfamiliar, Caesar's decision not to pursue the Suebi seems eminently reasonable, based on a realistic risk assessment rather than cowardice or poor planning. The reader can hardly blame Caesar for standing down rather than pursuing wild, violent, and unpredictable men into a forest inhabited by mysterious and frightening beasts!

These digressions also encourage us to revisit the question of Caesar's literary ambitions. Caesar the author clearly intended his work to be something other than a bare record of fact and perhaps something more than 'mere' propaganda, particularly by the later books. By incorporating the digressions, a characteristic element of histories, he aligned himself with the historiographic tradition and showed literary craft equal to his predecessors. These passages also helped Caesar to establish his authority as a narrator.[57] He had seen many of these foreign and fascinating things for himself (though his description of the Hercynian creatures leaves much room for doubt that he had seen *everything* he describes). Caesar also implies that he performed diligent research to expand upon what he had observed by autopsy, though he generally leaves his sources unnamed or vague (e.g., *nonulli scripserunt*, "some people have written", 5.13.3).[58] Furthermore, the entertainment value of these passages should not be overlooked, particularly if we assume a popular audience as well as a senatorial one.

Speeches

Like geographical and ethnographic digressions, speeches were a regular feature of ancient historiography (and perhaps *commentarii*, as well).[59]

---

56 E. Allen-Hornblower, 'Beasts and Barbarians in Caesar's *Bellum Gallicum* 6.21–8', *Classical Quarterly* 64 (2014) 682–93.

57 J. Marincola, *Authority and Tradition in Ancient Historiography* (Cambridge: Cambridge University Press, 1997) 79.

58 A notable exception in these books is the mention by name of the 3rd century BCE Greek polymath Eratosthenes (and "some other Greeks") as a source for the Hercynian Forest (6.24.2).

59 For an overview of and bibliography on speeches in ancient historiography (and

Speeches could appear as direct quotations (*oratio recta*) or as an indirect report (*oratio obliqua*). *Oratio recta* is less common and, in many cases, seems to be reserved for passages of programmatic import; the switch to direct speech catches the reader's attention, which the author then can direct to a particular theme, argument, or characterization. The authenticity of speeches in historiography varies widely. Some historians report speeches they might have heard themselves, while others recount events from the distant past. Some speeches might be reproduced nearly verbatim, while others may be invented in full; most probably fall somewhere on the spectrum in between.[60]

Caesar often employs indirect speech to narrate a variety of ideas (e.g., his own thought process, the content of negotiations), while he uses direct speech more sparingly. The use of *oratio recta* increases with each book of *The Gallic War*, peaking with seven direct utterances in Book 7; some scholars have taken this development as evidence for serial composition and Caesar's literary evolution over time.[61] Books 5 and 6 of *The Gallic War* feature several examples of both *oratio obliqua* and *oratio recta.*[62] The instances of speech in these two books (both direct and indirect) often occur in the context of a detailed vignette that stands out from the less embellished surrounding narrative. Given that Caesar was not present for any of the four examples of direct speech in Books 5 and 6, we can assume some degree of authorial invention. The first instance of *oratio recta* occurs in the disastrous episode of Sabinus and Cotta. During their debate over whether to follow Ambiorix' advice, the legates each make their case in indirect speech (5.28–29); as the men deliberate, Sabinus rebukes Cotta in direct speech loudly enough for everyone to hear (5.30). The direct

particularly in Caesar) see L. Grillo, 'Speeches in the *Commentarii'*, in L. Grillo and C. Krebs (eds), *Cambridge Companion to the Writings of Julius Caesar* 131–43 (Cambridge: Cambridge University Press, 2018).

60 Thucydides, writing about contemporary events, claims that some of the speeches he records he heard himself, some he heard about from others, and in other cases he has done his best to approximate what "would have been appropriate" (τὰ δέοντα, 1.22) for the speaker to have said. At the other extreme is a historian like Livy, who recorded Rome's earliest history and thus had less expectation of precision (Pref. 6). Tacitus' treatment of Claudius' speech on Gallic citizenship (*Ann.* 11.23–4) offers a unique opportunity to see the historian's hand at work, since the text of the original is preserved on the Lyon Tablet (*CIL* XIII, 1668).

61 See Grillo, 'Speeches in the *Commentarii'* 132–34 for an overview of the arguments.

62 Grillo reckons 29 examples of *oratio obliqua* and 4 examples of *oratio recta* in Books 5–6 ('Speeches in the *Commentarii'*, 133).

quotation signals to the reader that Sabinus' words are fateful, and indeed they persuade the legion and cause Cotta to give in, to the ruin of all. The second speech occurs in the 'centurions' duel' (5.44). Pullo challenges Vorenus in direct speech to enter the battle with him, announcing that their rivalry will be settled that very day. This taunt provokes Vorenus to follow Pullo into the fray, where they both display exemplary bravery. In Book 6, Labienus is granted a short comment in direct speech, in which he urges his soldiers to fight as if Caesar were there himself, "watching your exploits with his own eyes" (6.8.3). Labienus gets the speech, but Caesar is still the star, as the brief *oratio recta* serves to manifest him at an event for which he was not present. Finally, an anonymous hostage from the Eburones is quoted at 6.35 advising the Sugambri to attack the Romans at Atuatuca. This sets off the final confrontation and narrative climax of Book 6, in which the Sugambri are repelled and driven back beyond the Rhine. Each of these four instances of direct speech is thus brief but impactful; they add drama and characterization and allow Caesar to call attention to and amplify the themes of the passages.

IV. Notes on the Text

The Latin text and critical apparatus provided here are that of W. Hering's Teubner edition (2008). The textual tradition of most every work presents challenges. As texts were copied and re-copied over the centuries, changes and emendations were made and errors were introduced (or corrected, sometimes incorrectly); the process might be likened to a game of 'Telephone'. Thus, we do not possess a single manuscript with Caesar's original words verbatim. It is the work of textual editors to compare the existing manuscripts, and, by noting similarities and differences, create a 'family tree' (*stemma*). The *stemma* allows us to see how the surviving manuscripts may have evolved from the original text and thus to make the best possible guess at Caesar's original words. Significant differences among the manuscripts, omissions, and proposed corrections are noted in a critical apparatus at the bottom of each page of an edited text.

Fortunately, the history of *The Gallic War*'s transmission is far less vexed than that of many other works (including *The Civil War*). "A great many manuscripts of Caesar exist," remarked Holmes, "but only nine or ten of them are now considered good." Hering offers the following *stemma*:

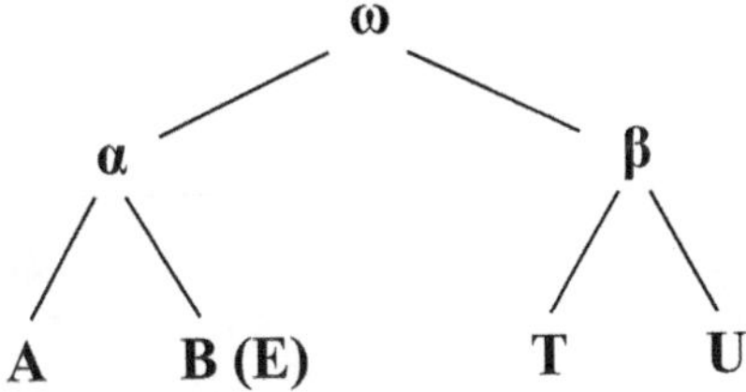

A = codex Amstelodamensis 73 (9th century)
B = codex Parisinus Latinus 5763 (9th century)
E = codex Parisinus Latinus 6842 B (9th century; excerpts from Books 1–5)
T = codex Parisinus Latinus 5764 (11th century)
U = codex Vaticanus Latinus 3324 (11th/12th century)

The extant manuscripts are divided into two groups denoted by α and β, each of which represents a posited or hypothetical common source for the later manuscripts in the branch. These two branches stem, in turn, from a posited common ancestor (denoted by ω, probably dating to the 4th or 5th century CE); Hering suggests that the two groups separated sometime before the Middle Ages. The manuscripts of the α-branch (**ABE**) contain only *The Gallic War*, while the β-branch manuscripts (**TU**) contain the full *corpus Caesarianum*. As Hering notes, there was keen interest in the history and customs of the Gauls among the monks of Fleury Abbey; this might explain the origin of the *Gallic War*-only tradition (and the development of **E,** a collection of excerpts focused on Gallic culture).

Hering's stemma indicates that **ABETU** should be considered the best surviving witnesses to the original text (that is, they have gone through fewer rounds of copying than the other extant manuscripts), and thus these are the manuscripts upon which Hering's text is primarily constructed. Hering also makes occasional reference to variant readings in some of the eliminated manuscripts: **M**, copied from **B**; **N** and **L**, copied from **B** (and sharing an error at 6.20.1 not present in **M**); **S**, derived from **B** via a lost intermediary; **R**, identical to **U** except at 5.24.7–8; and **Q** and **V**, which seem to be derived from the same source (either **A** or **T**). Fuller discussion of the textual tradition and critical apparatus may be found in the *Praefatio* of Hering's Teubner.

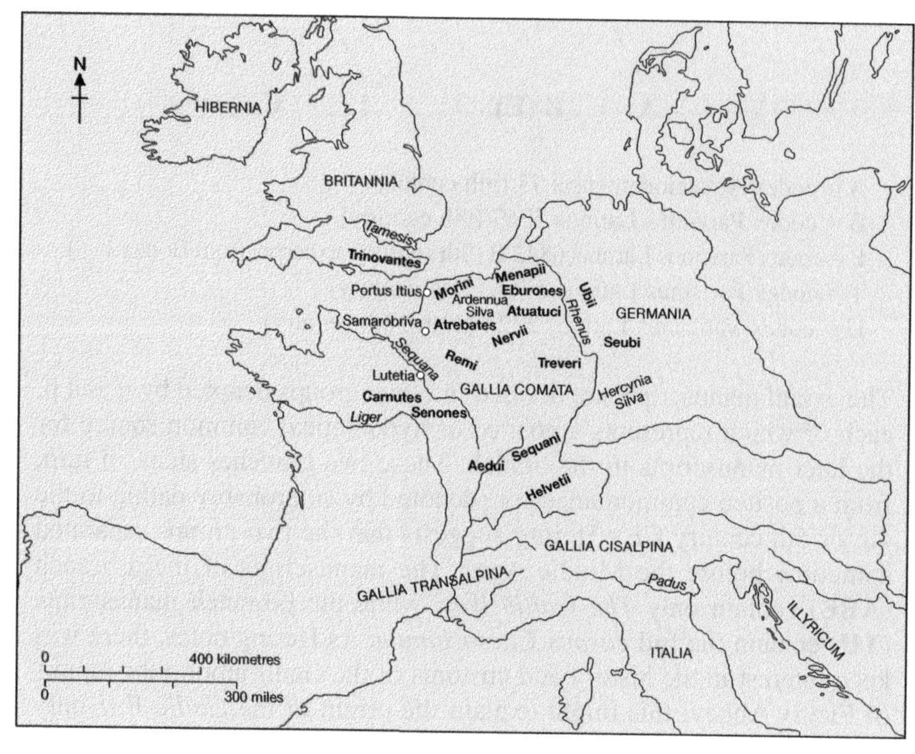

People and places in The Gallic War *Books 5–6*

BIBLIOGRAPHY

Adcock, F. E. 1956. *Caesar as Man of Letters*. Cambridge: Cambridge University Press.

Albrecht, M. von. 1997. *A History of Roman Literature. From Livius Andronicus to Boethius*. Leiden: Brill.

Albrecht, M. von. 1989. *Masters of Roman Prose from Cato to Apuleius*. Transl. Neil Adkins. Leeds: Francis Cairns.

Aldhouse-Green, Miranda. 2010. *Caesar's Druids: Story of an Ancient Priesthood*. New Haven, CT: Yale University Press.

Allen-Hornblower, Emily. 2014. 'Beasts and Barbarians in Caesar's *Bellum Gallicum* 6.21–8', *Classical Quarterly* 64: 682–93.

Barlow, Jonathan. 1998. 'Noble Gauls and their other in Caesar's Propaganda'. In *Julius Caesar as Artful Reporter: The War Commentaries as Political Instruments*, eds Kathryn Welch and Anton Powell. 139–70. London: Duckworth.

Batstone, William, and Damon, Cynthia. 2006. *Caesar's Civil War*. New York: Oxford University Press.

Blom, Henrietta van der. 2018. 'Caesar's Orations'. In *Cambridge Companion to the Writings of Julius Caesar*, eds Luca Grillo and Christopher Krebs, 193–205. Cambridge: Cambridge University Press.

Creer, Tyler. 'Ethnography in Caesar's *Gallic War* and its Implications for Composition', *Classical Quarterly* 69 (2019) 246–63.

Dench, Emma. 2011. 'Ethnography and History'. In *A Companion to Greek and Roman Historiography*, ed. John Marincola, 1013–33. Malden, MA: Wiley-Blackwell.

Dué, Casey and Ebbot, Mary. 2010. Iliad *10 and the Poetics of Ambush. A Multitext Edition with Essays and Commentary*. Hellenic Studies Series 39. Washington, DC: Center for Hellenic Studies.

Dupont, F. 1997. '*Recitatio* and the Reorganization of the Space of Public Discourse'. In *The Roman Cultural Revolution, eds* Habinek, T. and Schiesaro, A., transl. Habinek, T. and Lardinois, A. Cambridge: Cambridge University Press. 44–59.

Engles, Johannes. 2011. 'Geography and History'. In *A Companion to Greek and Roman Historiography*, ed. John Marincola, 1108–30. Malden, MA: Wiley-Blackwell.

Fowler, W. Warde. 1903. 'Caesar's Conception of *Fortuna', The Classical Review* 17: 153–56.

Freeman, Philip. 2001. *Ireland and the Classical World.* Austin: University of Texas Press.

Gaertner, Jan Felix and Hausburg, Bianca. 2013. *Caesar and the Bellum Alexandrinum: An Analysis of Style, Narrative Technique, and the Reception of Greek Historiography*. Göttingen: Vandenhoeck & Ruprecht.

Gelzer, M. 1968. *Caesar: Politician and Statesman.* Transl. P. Needham. Cambridge: Harvard University Press

Gerrish, Jennifer. 2018. 'Heroic Resonances in Caesar's *Bellum Gallicum* 5', *Classical World* 111: 351–70.

Grillo, Luca. 2018. 'Speeches in the *Commentarii'*. In *Cambridge Companion to the Writings of Julius Caesar*, eds Luca Grillo and Christopher Krebs, 131–43. Cambridge: Cambridge University Press.

Grillo, Luca. 2016. 'Caesarian Intertextualities: Sabinus and Cotta in *BG* 5.26–37', *Classical Journal* 111: 257–79.

Grünewald, Thomas. 2004. *Bandits in the Roman Empire: Myth and Reality*. Transl. John Drinkwater. London and New York: Routledge.

Hames, Raymond and Starkweather, Katherine E. 'A Survey of Non-Classical Polyandry', *Human Nature* 23: 149–72.

Holmes, T. Rice. 1914. *C. Iuli Casaris Commentarii Rerum in Gallia Gestarum VII.* Oxford: Clarendon Press.

Johnson, William A. 2012. *Readers and Reading Culture in the High Roman Empire: A Study of Elite Communities. Classical culture and society.* Oxford and New York: Oxford University Press.

Kelly, Gordon P. 2006. *A History of Exile in the Roman Republic*. Cambridge: Cambridge University Press.

King, Anthony. 1990. *Roman Gaul and Germany.* Berkeley: University of California Press.

Klotz, A. 1910. *Caesarstudien*. Leipzig: Teubner.

Krebs, Christopher. 2018a. 'The World's Measure: Caesar's Geographies of Gallia and Britannia in their Contexts and as Evidence of His World Map', *American Journal of Philology* 139: 93–122.

Krebs, Christopher. 2018b. 'More than Words: The *Commentarii* in their Propagandistic Context'. In *Cambridge Companion to the Writings of Julius Caesar*, eds Luca Grillo and Christopher Krebs, 29–42. Cambridge: Cambridge University Press.

Krebs, Christopher. 2018c. 'A Style of Choice'. In *Cambridge Companion*

to the *Writings of Julius Caesar*, eds Luca Grillo and Christopher Krebs, 110–30. Cambridge: Cambridge University Press.

Krebs, Christopher. 2013. 'Caesar, Lucretius, and the dates of *De Rerum Natura* and the *Commentarii'*, *Classical Quarterly* 63: 772–79.

Krebs, Christopher. 2006. ' "Imaginary Geography" in Caesar's *Bellum Gallicum'*, *American Journal of Philology* 127:111–36.

Kruschwitz, Peter. 2014. 'Gallic War Songs (II): Marcus Cicero, Quintus Cicero, and Caesar's Invasion of Britain', *Philologus* 158: 275–305.

Marincola, John. *Authority and Tradition in Ancient Historiography*. Cambridge: Cambridge University Press, 1997.

Moberly, Charles E. 1878. *The Commentaries of C. Julius Caesar*. Oxford: Clarendon Press.

Pezzini, Giuseppe. 2018. 'Caesar the Linguist: The Debate About the Latin Language'. In *Cambridge Companion to the Writings of Julius Caesar*, eds Luca Grillo and Christopher Krebs, 173–92. Cambridge: Cambridge University Press.

Ramage, E. S. 2002 'The *populus Romanus, imperium,* and Caesar's Presence in *De Bello Gallico'*, Athenaeum 90: 125–46.

Rambaud, Michel. 1966. *L'art de la deformation historique dans les Commentaires de César* (2nd edn). Paris: Les Belles Lettres.

Rasmussen, Detlef. 1963. *Caesars* Commentarii. *Stil und Stilwandel am Beispiel der direkten Rede*. Göttingen: Vandenhoeck & Ruprecht.

Rauh, Stanly H. 2015. 'The Tradition of Suicide in Rome's Foreign Wars', *Transactions and Proceedings of the American Philological Society* 145: 383–410.

Rey, Sarah. 2015. 'Roman Tears and their Impact: A Question of Gender?', *Clio: Women, Gender, History* 41: 246–64. Transl. Marian Rothstein.

Riggsby, Andrew. 2006. *Caesar in Gaul and Rome: War in Words*. Austin: University of Texas Press.

Shaw, Brent. 1984. 'Bandits in the Roman Empire', *Past and Present* 105: 3–52.

Skinner, Joseph E. 2012. *The Invention of Greek Ethnography: From Homer to Herodotus*. New York and Oxford: Oxford University Press.

Spence, Lewis. 1971 (2nd printing). *The History and Origins of Druidism*. New York: Samuel Weiser, Inc.

Spencer, J. A. 1848. *C. Julius Caesar's Commentaries on the Gallic War, with English Notes, Critical and Explanatory, a Lexicon, Indexes, Etc.* New York: D. Appleton and Company.

Welch, Kathryn. 1998. 'Caesar and His Officers in the Gallic War Commentaries'. In *Julius Caesar as Artful Reporter: The War Commentaries as Political Instruments*, eds Kathryn Welch and Anton Powell, 85–103. London: Duckworth.

Wiseman, T. P. 2015. *The Roman Audience: Classical Literature as Social History*. Oxford: Oxford University Press.

Wiseman, T. P. 1998. 'The Publication of *De Bello Gallico*'. In *Julius Caesar as Artful Reporter: The War Commentaries as Political Instruments*, eds Kathryn Welch and Anton Powell, 1–9. London: Duckworth.

JULIUS CAESAR

THE GALLIC WAR BOOK V

1 (1) Lucio Domitio Appio Claudio consulibus discedens ab hibernis Caesar in Italiam, ut quotannis facere consuerat, legatis imperat, quos legionibus praefecerat, uti, quam plurimas possent, hieme naves aedificandas veteresque reficiendas curarent. (2) earum modum formamque demonstrat. ad celeritatem onerandi subductionisque paulo facit humiliores, quam quibus in nostro mari uti consuevimus, atque id eo magis, quod propter crebras commutationes aestuum minus magnos ibi fluctus fieri cognoverat, ad onera ac multitudinem iumentorum transportandam paulo latiores, quam quibus in reliquis utimur maribus. (3) has omnes actuarias imperat fieri, quam ad rem multum humilitas adiuvat. (4) ea, quae sunt usui ad armandas naves, ex Hispania apportari iubet. (5) ipse conventibus Galliae citerioris peractis in Illyricum proficiscitur, quod a Pirustis finitimam partem provinciae incursionibus vastari audiebat. (6) eo cum venisset, civitatibus milites imperat certumque in locum convenire iubet. (7) qua re nuntiata Pirustae legatos ad eum mittunt, qui doceant nihil earum rerum publico factum consilio, seseque paratos esse demonstrant omnibus rationibus de inuriis satisfacere. (8) accepta oratione eorum Caesar obsides imperat eosque ad certam diem adduci iubet; nisi ita fecerint, sese bello civitatem persecuturum demonstrat. (9) iis ad diem adductis, ut imperaverat, arbitros inter civitates dat, qui litem aestiment poenamque constituant.

2 (1) His confectis rebus conventibusque peractis in citeriorem Galliam revertitur atque inde ad exercitum proficiscitur. (2) eo cum venisset, circumitis omnibus hibernis singulari militum studio in summa omnium rerum inopia circiter sescentas eius generis, cuius supra demonstravimus, naves et longas XXVIII invenit instructas neque multum abesse ab eo, quin paucis diebus deduci possint.

1 (1) In the consulship of Lucius Domitius and Appius Claudius, Caesar set out for Italy from his winter-quarters, as he was accustomed to do each year, and ordered the legates whom he had put in charge of the legions to build as many new ships as possible and to have the old ones refurbished that winter. He specified their style and form. (2) He made them a little lower than those we usually use in the Mediterranean Sea, for speedy loading and hauling ashore; this was especially important since he had learned that the waves were smaller in the Channel because of the frequent changes of the tide. He also made them a little bit wider than those we use in other seas, for transporting cargo and a large number of pack animals. (3) He instructed that all the ships should be equipped with oars; their low profile made this much easier. (4) He ordered that the materials for rigging the ships be brought in from Spain. (5) When the assizes in Nearer Gaul were finished he himself went to Illyricum, because he was hearing reports that the region bordering the province was being devastated in raids by the Pirustae. (6) He levied soldiers from the states when he arrived there and ordered them to meet at an appointed place. (7) When this was announced among the Pirustae, they sent legates to him to explain that none of these things had been done in an official capacity, and they indicated that they were ready to make the situation right in every way. (8) After he had heard their explanation, Caesar commanded that hostages be given and ordered that they should be brought on an appointed day; he warned that he would overwhelm their state with war if they did not do as he ordered. (9) They were brought to him on that day, just as he had ordered, and he assigned arbitrators between the states to assess the damage and decide the penalty.

2 (1) Once these affairs were settled and the assizes complete he returned to Nearer Gaul and from there went to meet his army. (2) When he had arrived there, he made his way around the entire camp. He discovered that his soldiers, with incredible dedication despite their total lack of necessities, had built about 600 ships of the type I described above as well as 28 long ships and that not

(3) conlaudatis militibus atque iis, qui negotio praefuerant, quid fieri velit, ostendit atque omnes ad portum Itium convenire iubet, quo ex portu commodissimum in Britanniam traiectum esse cognoverat, circiter milium passuum XXX transmissum a continenti. huic rei, quod satis esse visum est, militum relinquit. (4) ipse cum legionibus expeditis quattuor et equitibus DCCC in fines Treverorum proficiscitur, quod hi neque ad concilia veniebant neque imperio parebant Germanosque Transrhenanos sollicitare dicebantur.

3 (1) Haec civitas longe plurimum totius Galliae equitatu valet magnasque habet copias peditum Rhenumque, ut supra demonstravimus, tangit. (2) in ea civitate duo de principatu inter se contendebant, Indutiomarus et Cingetorix. (3) ex quibus alter, simulatque de Caesaris legionumque adventu cognitum est, ad eum venit, se suosque omnes in officio futuros neque ab amicitia p. R. defecturos confirmavit, quaeque in Treveris gererentur, ostendit. (4) at Indutiomarus equitatum peditatumque cogere iisque, qui per aetatem in armis esse non poterant, in silvam Arduennam abditis, quae ingenti magnitudine per medios fines Treverorum a flumine Rheno ad initium Remorum pertinet, bellum parare instituit. (5) sed posteaquam nonnulli principes ex ea civitate, et auctoritate Cingetorigis adducti et adventu nostri exercitus perterriti, ad Caesarem venerunt et de suis privatis rebus ab eo petere coeperunt, quoniam civitati consulere non posse<n>t, Indutiomarus veritus, ne ab omnibus desereretur, legatos ad Caesarem mittit: (6) sese idcirco ab suis discedere atque ad eum venire noluisse, quo facilius civitatem in officio contineret, ne omnis nobilitatis discessu plebs propter inprudentiam laberetur; (7) itaque civitatem

much work remained to be able to launch them in a few days. (3) Caesar praised the soldiers, explained to those who were in charge of the project what he wanted done, and ordered everyone to convene at Portus Itius; he had learned that the crossing to Britain was easiest from this port, a journey of about 30 miles from the mainland. He left behind as many troops as seemed sufficient for the task. (4) Caesar himself marched with four light-armed legions and eight hundred cavalry toward the border of the Treveri, because they had not come to his councils and were not obeying his authority; they were also said to be harassing the Germans beyond the Rhine.

3 (1) This state is by far the most powerful in all of Gaul in terms of cavalry and they have an abundance of infantry, as well; as I mentioned above, they border the Rhine. (2) In this state there were two men struggling for leadership, Indutiomarus and Cingetorix. (3) As soon as he learned that Caesar and his legion were approaching the latter went to meet him. He confirmed that he and all his supporters would continue to be in Caesar's obligation and that they would not break from their friendship with the Roman people, and he explained what was happening among the Treveri. (4) Indutiomarus, on the other hand, decided to prepare for war. He gathered cavalry and infantry and hid those who were unable to serve because of their age in the Ardennes forest, which stretches through the country of the Treveri with its great size, from the Rhine river to the border of the Remi. (5) But after a few leading men, both encouraged by the authority of Cingetorix and frightened at the arrival of our army, approached Caesar and began to plead with him about their own private situations (since they were not able to act on behalf of the state), Indutiomarus became afraid that he would be deserted by everyone and sent envoys to Caesar. (6) Through the envoys, Indutiomarus indicated that he had been unwilling to leave his people and go to meet Caesar. By staying where he was, he claimed, he could more easily keep his state in check, since the common people would not descend into disarray because of the absence of all the elites. (7) The state was

in sua potestate esse seque, si Caesar permitteret, ad eum in castra venturum et suas civitatisque fortunas eius fidei permissurum.

4 (1) Caesar etsi intellegebat, qua de causa ea dicerentur quaeque eum res ab instituto consilio deterreret, tamen, ne aestatem in Treveris consumere cogeretur omnibus rebus ad Britannicum bellum comparatis, Indutiomarum ad se cum ducentis obsidibus venire iussit. (2) his adductis, in iis filio propinquisque eius omnibus, quos nominatim evocaverat, consolatus Indutiomarum hortatusque est, uti in officio maneret; (3) nihilo tamen setius principibus Treverorum ad se convocatis hos singillatim Cingetorigi conciliavit, quod cum merito eius a se fieri intellegebat, tum magni interesse arbitrabatur eius auctoritatem inter suos quam plurimum valere, cuius tam egregiam in se voluntatem perspexisset. id factum graviter tulit Indutiomarus, suam gratiam inter suos minui, et qui iam ante inimico in nos animo fuisset, multo gravius hoc dolore exarsit.

5 (1) His rebus constitutis Caesar ad portum Itium cum legionibus pervenit. (2) ibi cognoscit LX naves, quae in Meldis factae erant, tempestate reiectas cursum tenere non potuisse atque eodem, unde erant profectae, revertisse. reliquas paratas ad navigandum atque omnibus rebus instructas invenit. (3) eodem equitatus totius Galliae convenit numero milium quattuor principesque ex omnibus civitatibus. (4) ex quibus perpaucos, quorum in se fidem perspexerat, relinquere in Gallia, reliquos obsidum loco secum ducere decreverat, quod, cum ipse abesset, motum Galliae verebatur.

thus under his control and, if Caesar would permit it, Indutiomarus would come meet him in camp and would entrust his own fortunes and those of the state to Caesar's good faith.

4 (1) Even though Caesar knew well why Indutiomarus said these things and what was keeping him from following through on his plan, he nevertheless ordered Indutiomarus to meet him with two hundred hostages, so that he would not be forced to waste the summer among the Treveri when all the preparations had been made for the British campaign. (2) When they were brought to him (among them Indutiomarus' son and other relatives, whom Caesar had summoned by name), Caesar reassured Indutiomarus and encouraged him to remain steadfast in his loyalty. (3) Nevertheless, he called the leaders of the Treveri to meet him and, one by one, reconciled them with Cingetorix. He did so in part because he believed he was acting in accordance with Cingetorix' merit but also because he judged that it was in his best interest that Cingetorix have the greatest possible authority among his own people, since he had demonstrated such noteworthy goodwill toward Caesar. (4) Indutiomarus was resentful that his own favor among his people was diminished; he had already been hostile toward us but he now burned more fiercely with resentment.

5 (1) When he had settled these matters Caesar proceeded to Portus Itius with his legions. (2) There he learned that sixty of the ships that had been built in the country of the Meldi had been driven back by a storm and were not able to hold course, nor were they able to return whence they had set out. However, he found that the remaining ships were prepared to sail and fitted them out with all the necessities. (3) A contingent of cavalry from all over Gaul numbering four thousand gathered in the same place, including leading men from all the states. (4) He decided to leave behind in Gaul a select few of them, whose loyalty to himself he knew well, and to take the rest of them with him as hostages, because he feared an uprising in Gaul in his absence.

6 (1) Erat una cum ceteris Dumnorix Haeduus, de quo a nobis antea dictum est. hunc secum habere in primis constituerat, quod eum cupidum rerum novarum, cupidum imperii, magni animi, magnae inter Gallos auctoritatis cognoverat. (2) accedebat huc, quod iam in concilio Haeduorum Dumnorix dixerat sibi a Caesare regnum civitatis deferri. quod dictum Haedui graviter ferebant neque recusandi aut deprecandi causa legatos ad Caesarem mittere audebant. (3) id factum ex suis hospitibus Caesar cognoverat. ille omnibus primo precibus petere contendit, ut in Gallia relinqueretur, partim quod insuetus navigandi mare timeret, partim quod religionibus impediri sese diceret. (4) posteaquam id obstinate sibi negari vidit, omni spe impetrandi adempta, principes Galliae sollicitare, sevocare singulos hortarique coepit, uti in continenti remanerent; (5) metu territare: non sine causa fieri, ut Gallia omni nobilitate spoliaretur; id esse consilium Caesaris, ut, quos in conspectu Galliae interficere vereretur, hos omnes in Britanniam traductos necaret; (6) fidem reliquis interponere, ius iurandum poscere, ut, quod esse ex usu Galliae intellexissent, communi consilio administrarent. haec a compluribus ad Caesarem deferebantur.

7 (1) Qua re cognita Caesar, quod tantum civitati Haeduae dignitatis tribuerat, coercendum atque deterrendum, quibuscumque rebus posset, Dumnorigem statuebat; (2) quod longius eius amentiam progredi videbat, prospiciendum, ne quid sibi ac rei publicae nocere posset. (3) itaque dies circiter XXV in eo loco commoratus, quod c[h]orus ventus navigationem impediebat, qui magnam partem omnis temporis in his locis flare consuevit, dabat operam, uti in officio Dumnorigem contineret, nihilo tamen setius omnia eius consilia cognosceret. (4) tandem indoneam nactus tempestatem milites equitesque conscendere naves iubet. (5) at omnium

6 (1) Among them was Dumnorix of the Aedui, whom I discussed earlier. Caesar decided that it was critical to keep Dumnorix with him, because he knew that he was eager for revolution, eager for power, and recognized for his great courage and great influence among the Gauls. (2) In addition, at a council of the Aedui Dumnorix had claimed that Caesar was handing over power of the state to him. The Aedui took this claim badly but did not dare to send Caesar envoys to either object or entreat him. (3) Caesar had learned about this from his supporters. At first Dumnorix tried using every excuse to plead with Caesar that he should be left behind in Gaul; first he claimed that he was afraid, since he was inexperienced at sea voyages, and then said that he was prevented by his religious scruples. (4) When he saw that Caesar firmly denied him and that all hope of his request being granted was lost, he began to rouse the leading men of Gaul, calling on them individually and urging them that they should remain on the mainland. (5) He tried frightening them: It was not without reason, he said, that Gaul was being stripped of its aristocracy. This was Caesar's plan: since he was afraid to kill them in the full sight of Gaul, he would lead them all over to Britain and slaughter them. (6) Dumnorix gave his word to the rest and sought an oath that they would govern with common purpose, doing what they judged to be in the best interest of Gaul. This was all reported to Caesar by many people.

7 (1) When Caesar learned about this, because he had given such authority to the Aeduan state he decided that Dumnorix was to be checked and deterred by whatever means possible. (2) Caesar saw that Dumnorix' unpredictability was dangerously out of control and decided that it was necessary to take precautions lest Dumnorix harm him or the republic. (3) Therefore, when he was delayed there for about twenty-five days because a northwest wind (which usually blows there for most of every season) prevented him from sailing, he made an effort to keep Dumnorix loyal (but also, at the same time, to learn all his plans). (4) When he at last had favorable weather, he ordered the soldiers and cavalry to embark on the ships. (5) However, while everyone was distracted, Dumnorix began to

inpeditis animis Dumnorix cum equitibus Haeduorum a castris insciente Caesare domum discedere coepit. (6) qua re nuntiata Caesar intermissa profectione atque omnibus rebus postpositis magnam partem equitatus ad eum insequendum mittit retrahique imperat; (7) si vim faciat neque pareat, interfici iubet, nihil eum se absente pro sano facturum arbitratus, qui praesentis imperium neglexisset. (8) ille autem revocatus resistere ac se manu defendere suorumque fidem implorare coepit, saepe clamitans liberum se liberaeque esse civitatis. (9) illi, ut erat imperatum, circumsistunt hominem atque interficiunt. at equites Haedui ad Caesarem omnes revertuntur.

8 (1) His rebus gestis, Labieno in continenti cum tribus legionibus et equitum milibus duobus relicto, ut portus tueretur et rei frumentariae provideret, quaeque in Gallia gererentur cognosceret, consiliumque pro tempore et pro re caperet, (2) ipse cum quinque legionibus et pari numero equitum, quem in continenti relinquebat, solis occasu naves solvit et leni Africo provectus, media circiter nocte vento intermisso, cursum non tenuit et longius delatus aestu orta luce sub sinistra Britanniam relictam conspexit. (3) tum rursus aestus commutationem secutus remis contendit, ut eam partem insulae caperet, qua optimum esse egressum superiore aestate cognoverat. (4) qua in re admodum fuit militum virtus laudanda, qui vectoriis gravibusque navigiis non intermisso remigandi labore longarum navium cursum adaequarunt. (5) accessum est ad Britanniam omnibus navibus meridiano fere tempore, neque in eo loco hostis est visus. (6) sed ut postea Caesar ex captivis cognovit, cum magnae manus eo convenissent, multitudine navium perterritae, quae cum annotinis privatisque, quas sui quisque commodi fecerat, amplius octingentae uno erant visae tempore, a litore discesserant ac se in superiora loca abdiderant.

make his way home, taking with him the Aeduan cavalry from the camps, all without Caesar's knowledge. (6) When this was reported to Caesar, he interrupted his plan to sail and postponed everything. He sent a large part of the cavalry in pursuit of Dumnorix and commanded that he be brought back. (7) He ordered that Dumnorix be killed if he resisted and did not obey; for, Caesar supposed, someone who had disobeyed his authority in his presence was certainly not going to act like a reasonable person in his absence. (8) However, when Dumnorix was recalled he began to resist and forcibly defend himself and to beg for the loyalty of his people, repeatedly shouting that he was a free man and a citizen of a free state. (9) As had been ordered, they surrounded the man and killed him, and all the Aeduan cavalry returned to Caesar.

8 (1) When this situation was resolved, Caesar left Labienus on the mainland with three legions and two thousand cavalry to guard the port and look after the food supply, to keep an eye on what was happening in Gaul, and to take counsel as was appropriate in a given moment or situation. (2) Caesar himself set sail at sunset with five legions and the same number of cavalry he had left behind on the mainland and was carried by a gentle southwest wind. However, when the wind died down in the middle of the night, he could not hold course and was carried too far by the tide; when the sun rose, he saw Britain behind him on the left. (3) Then, by rowing with the tide when it changed again, he tried to reach the part of the island where, as he had learned the previous summer, it would be easiest to disembark. (4) The spirit of the troops during this task was particularly commendable. Although their vessels were heavy transport ships, they equaled the speed of warships by never letting up the pace of their rowing. (5) Caesar reached Britain at nearly midday with all his ships, and there was no enemy visible there. (6) However, as Caesar later learned from some prisoners, large groups had in fact gathered there, but because they were frightened by the large number of ships (more than 800 of which appeared at one time, some retained from the previous year and some private ships individuals had chartered for their own convenience), they backed away from the shore and hid on higher ground.

9 (1) Caesar exposito exercitu in loco castris idoneo capto, ubi ex captivis cognovit, quo in loco hostium copiae consedissent, cohortibus decem ad mare relictis et equitibus trecentis, qui praesidio navibus essent. de tertia vigilia ad hostes contendit, eo minus veritus navibus, quod in litore molli atque aperto deligatas ad ancoras relinquebat et praesidio navibus Quintum Atrium praefecit. (2) ipse noctu progressus milia passuum circiter XII hostium copias conspicatus est. (3) illi equitatu atque essedis ad flumen progressi ex loco superiore nostros prohibere et proelium committere coeperunt. (4) repulsi ab equitatu se in silvas abdiderunt, locum nacti egregie et natura et opere munitum, quem domestici belli, ut videbatur, causa iam ante praeparaverant; (5) nam crebris arboribus succisis omnes introitus erant praeclusi. (6) ipsi ex silvis rari propugnabant nostrosque intra munitiones ingredi prohibebant. (7) at milites legionis septimae testudine facta et aggere ad munitiones adiecto locum ceperunt eosque ex silvis expulerunt paucis vulneribus acceptis. (8) sed eos fugientes longius Caesar prosequi vetuit, et quod loci naturam ignorabat, et quod magna parte diei consumpta munitioni castrorum tempus relinqui volebat.

10 (1) Postridie eius diei mane tripertito milites equitesque in expeditionem misit, ut eos, qui fugerant, persequerentur. (2) his aliquantum itineris progressis cum iam extremi essent in prospectu, equites a Quinto Atrio ad Caesarem venerunt, qui nuntiarent superiore nocte maxima coorta tempestate prope omnes naves adflictas atque in litus eiectas esse, quod neque ancorae funesque subsisterent neque nautae gubernatoresque vim tempestatis pati possent. (3) itaque ex eo concursu navium magnum esse incommodum acceptum.

9 (1) Caesar had disembarked with the army and chosen a suitable location for camp when he learned from some prisoners where the enemy troops were positioned. He left behind ten cohorts and three hundred cavalry on the shore to guard the ships. Around third watch he went to confront the enemy, worrying less about the ships because he was leaving them tied at anchor on a sandy, open shore and had appointed Quintus Atrius to guard the fleet. (2) Caesar had advanced about twelve miles that night when he spotted the enemy. (3) They had made their way to the river on horseback and in chariots and began to block our men from reaching higher ground and to try to provoke a battle. (4) Driven back by our cavalry, the enemy hid in the forest. They occupied a place that was well-fortified both by nature and also by human effort, which, as it seemed, they had built sometime earlier because of a civil war, (5) for all the entrances were blocked with numerous fallen trees. (6) They fought from the woods in scattered groups and prevented our men from making their way within the fortifications. (7) But the soldiers of the Seventh Legion seized control of the place by making a tortoise formation and throwing a rampart up against the fortification, and they drove the enemy out of the woods while receiving only a few wounds themselves. (8) However, Caesar stopped them from pursuing the fleeing enemy any further, both because he was unfamiliar with the nature of the area and because, with the great part of the day already spent, he wanted to leave time to fortify the camps.

10 (1) The next morning at daybreak, Caesar sent infantry and cavalry in three divisions on a mission to pursue those who had fled. (2) They had advanced a little ways, though the rear of the division was still in sight, when cavalry sent by Quintus Atrius came to Caesar to announce that during the previous night a powerful storm had blown in and nearly all the ships were damaged and cast upon the beach, since neither the anchors nor the ropes had held nor were the sailors or helmsmen able to weather the force of the storm. (3) As a result, a great deal of damage had been caused by the collision of the ships.

11 (1) His rebus cognitis Caesar legiones equitatumque revocari atque initinere resistere iubet, ipse ad naves revertitur. (2) eadem fere, quae ex nuntiis litterisque cognoverat, coram perspicit, sic ut amissis circiter XL navibus reliquae tamen refici posse magno negotio viderentur. (3) itaque ex legionibus fabros deligit et ex continenti alios arcessi iubet. (4) Labieno scribit, ut quam plurimas possit iis legionibus, quae sint apud eum, naves instituat. (5) ipse, etsi res erat multae operae ac laboris, tamen commodissimum esse statuit omnes naves subduci et cum castris una munitione coniungi. (6) in his rebus circiter dies X consumit, ne nocturnis quidem temporibus ad laborem militum intermissis. (7) subductis navibus castrisque egregie munitis easdem copias quas ante praesidio navibus relinquit, ipse eodem, unde redierat, proficiscitur. (8) eo cum venisset, maiores iam undique in eum locum copiae Britannorum convenerant summa imperii bellique administrandi communi consilio permissa Cassivellauno, cuius fines a maritimis civitatibus flumen dividit, quod appellatur Tamesis, a mari circiter milia passuum LXXX. (9) huic superiore tempore cum reliquis civitatibus continentia bella intercesserant. sed nostro adventu permoti Britanni hunc toti bello imperioque praefecerant.

12 (1) Britanniae pars interior ab iis incolitur, quos natos in insula ipsi memoria proditum dicunt, (2) maritima pars ab iis, qui praedae ac belli inferendi causa ex Belgio transierant – qui omnes fere iis nominibus civitatum appellantur, quibus orti ex civitatibus eo pervenerunt – et bello inlato ibi remanserunt atque agros colere coeperunt. (3) hominum est infinita multitudo creberrimaque aedificia fere Gallicis consimilia, pecorum numerus ingens. (4) utuntur aut aere aut nummo aureo aut taleis ferreis ad certum

11 (1) When Caesar learned about these things, he ordered the legions and cavalry to be called back and to abort their march and he himself returned to the ships. (2) He saw for himself essentially the same things that he had learned from the messengers and letters: namely, that about forty ships were destroyed, though the rest seemed like they could be repaired with a great effort. (3) Accordingly, he chose workmen out of the legions and ordered that others be summoned from the mainland. (4) He wrote to Labienus that he should build as many ships as possible with the legions under his command. (5) Although the task was difficult and laborious, Caesar decided that it would be most expedient to haul in all the ships and bring them together behind the same fortification as the camp. (6) He spent about ten days on this, and the soldiers did not take a break from their work even at night. (7) When the ships had been brought ashore and the camp fortified extremely well, he left behind the same forces as before to guard the ships, and Caesar himself set out for the same place from which he had turned back. (8) When he had arrived there, even greater forces from all over had come together in that same place, having entrusted the highest command and the direction of the war to Cassivellaunus by common consent. Cassivellaunus' territory was separated from that of the coastal states by the river called the Tamesis, about 80 miles from the sea. (9) In the past, there had been nonstop wars between him and the other states, but the Britons were disturbed by our arrival and placed him in charge of the entire war and its conduct.

12 (1) The interior part of Britain is inhabited by those who (they say, according to tradition) were born from the island itself. (2) The coastal part was settled by those who crossed over from Belgium seeking plunder or looking to start a war. Almost all of these are named for the cities from which they started out when they migrated to Britain. After waging war, they remained there and began to cultivate the land. (3) Their population is huge; their buildings are packed close together much like the Gauls', and there is an abundance of cattle. (4) They use either bronze or gold

pondus examinatis pro nummo. (5) nascitur ibi plumbum album in mediterraneis regionibus, in maritimis ferrum, sed eius exigua est copia. aere utuntur inportato. materia cuiusque generis ut in Gallia est praeter fagum atque abietem. (6) leporem et gallinam et anserem gustare fas non putant. haec tamen alunt animi voluptatisque causa. loca sunt temperatiora quam in Gallia remissioribus frigoribus.

13 (1) Insula natura triquetra, cuius unum latus est contra Galliam. huius lateris alter angulus, qui est ad Cantium, quo fere omnes ex Gallia naves adpelluntur, ad orientem solem, inferior ad meridiem spectat. hoc pertinet circiter milia passuum quingenta. (2) alterum vergit ad Hispaniam atque occidentem solem. qua ex parte est Hibernia insula, dimidio minor, ut existamatur, quam Britannia, sed pari spatio transmissus atque ex Gallia est in Britanniam. (3) in hoc medio cursu est insula, quae appellatur Mona. complures praeterea minores obiectae insulae existimantur. de quibus insulis nonnulli scripserunt dies continuos XXX sub bruma<m> esse noctem. (4) nos nihil de eo percontationibus rep[p]eriebamus, nisi certis ex aqua mensuris breviores esse quam in continenti noctes videbamus. huius est longitudo lateris, ut fert illorum opinio, septingentorum milium. (6) tertium est contra septentriones. cui parti nulla est obiecta terra, sed eius angulus lateris maxime ad Germaniam spectat. hoc milia passuum octingenta in longitudinem esse existimatur. (7) ita omnis insula est in circuitu vicies centum milium passuum.

14 (1) Ex iis omnibus longe sunt humanissimi, qui Cantium incolunt, quae regio est maritima omnis, neque multum a Gallica differunt consuetudine.(2) interiores plerique frumenta non serunt, sed lacte et carne vivunt pellibusque sunt vestiti. omnes vero se Britanni vitro inficiunt, quod caeruleum efficit colorem, atque hoc horribiliores sunt in pugna aspectu. (3) capilloque sunt promisso atque omni parte corporis rasa praeter caput et labrum superius.

coins or iron bars measured to a certain weight instead of coins. (5) Tin is produced in the inland regions and iron on the coast, but the supply of that is low. They use imported bronze. There is timber of every type, as in Gaul, except for beech and pine. (6) They consider it taboo to eat hares or hens or geese, but they do keep these as pets. The area is more temperate than in Gaul and the winters are moderate.

13 (1) The island is triangular in shape, and one of its sides faces Gaul. One of the corners of this side, which is in Kent, where nearly all the ships from Gaul land, faces the east, and the lower corner faces south. This side stretches about five hundred miles. (2) The other side slopes toward Spain and the west. The island Hibernia lies off this side, smaller by half, it is thought, than Britain, but the distance between them is the same as the distance between Britain and Gaul. (3) In the middle of this crossing is an island called Mona. Many other small islands are thought to lie nearby. Some people have written about these islands that, in the middle of the winter, night lasts for thirty straight days. (4) We were not able to learn anything about this through our inquiries, but we did observe (using precise water-clock measurements) that the nights are shorter than on the mainland. (5) The length of this side, according to the locals' claim, is seven hundred miles. (6) The third side faces north. There is no land off this side, but the angle of this side mainly faces Germany. This side is thought to be about eight hundred miles in length. (7) Thus, the whole island is two thousand miles in circumference.

14 (1) The people who live in Kent (a region which is all coastal) are by far the most civilized here, and they do not differ much from the Gauls in their customs. (2) Those who dwell inland do not plant crops but live on milk and meat and dress in pelts. All the Britons, though, stain themselves with woad, which gives them a blue color, and because of this they look more terrifying in battle. (3) Their hair is long and they shave every part of their bodies except the head and

(4) uxores habent deni duodenique inter se communes et maxime fratres cum fratribus parentesque cum liberis. (5) sed qui sunt ex iis nati, eorum habentur liberi, quo primum virgo quaeque deducta est.

15 (1) Equites hostium essedariique acriter proelio cum equitatu nostro in itinere conflixerunt, ita tamen ut nostri omnibus partibus superiores fuerint atque eos in silvas collesque compulerint. (2) sed compluribus interfectis cupidius insecuti nonnullos ex suis amiserunt. (3) at illi intermisso spatio, imprudentibus nostris atque occupatis in munitione castrorum, subito se ex silvis eiecerunt impetuque in eos facto, qui erant in statione pro castris collocati, acriter pugnaverunt, (4) duabusque missis subsidio cohortibus a Caesare, atque his primis legionum duarum, cum eae perexiguo intermisso loci spatio inter se constitissent, novo genere pugnae perterritis nostris per medios audacissime perruperunt seque inde incolumes receperunt. (5) eo die Quintus Laberius Durus tribunus militum interficitur. illi pluribus submissis cohortibus repelluntur.

16 (1) Toto hoc in genere pugnae cum sub oculis omnium ac pro castris dimicaretur, intellectum est nostros propter gravitatem armorum, quod neque insequi cedentes possent neque ab signis discedere auderent, minus aptos esse ad huius generis hostem, (2) equites autem magno cum periculo proelio dimicare, propterea quod illi etiam consulto plerumque cederent et, cum paulum ab legionibus nostros removissent, ex essedis desilirent et pedibus dispari proelio contenderent. (3) equestris autem proelii ratio et cedentibus et insequentibus par atque idem periculum inferebat. (4) accedebat huc, ut numquam conferti, sed rari magnisque intervallis proeliarentur stationesque dispositas haberent atque alios alii deinceps exciperent integrique et recentes defatigatis succederent.

upper lip. (4) They share ten or twelve wives in groups, especially brothers with brothers and fathers with their sons. (5) Any children born from these marriages are considered the offspring of the man to whom the mother was first married as a virgin.

15 (1) The enemy cavalry and chariots fought fiercely with our cavalry on the march, but our men still turned out to be superior in every respect and drove the enemy into the forest and the hills. (2) However, because they had killed many of the enemy, they pursued a little too eagerly and lost a few of their own. (3) After a short time, though, when our troops were distracted and occupied with fortifying the camp, the enemy burst out of the woods, attacked those who were stationed in front of the camp, and fought fiercely. (4) Although two cohorts had been sent by Caesar to support them – and these were the first cohorts of the two legions – and though they had taken up a position with a small space in between them, our men were terrified by this new type of fighting and the enemy burst through the middle with incredible daring and then retreated unharmed. (5) Quintus Laberius Durus, a military tribune, was killed on that day. When more cohorts were sent in, the enemy was driven back.

16 (1) The whole battle went like this. They fought in plain view of everyone and right in front of the camp; it was clear that our men were not well-suited to fighting this type of enemy because of the weight of our armor, since they were not able to pursue the enemy when they retreated, nor did they dare to abandon formation. (2) Moreover, it was clear that our cavalry engaged in this battle at great risk, particularly because the enemy often retreated intentionally and then, when they had drawn our men a ways off from the legions, they leaped down from their chariots and fought on foot in a mismatched battle. (3) This style of cavalry fighting thus brought equal and identical danger to both those retreating and those pursuing. (4) In addition, they never fought in close formation, but were scattered at great intervals, and they had reserves spaced out and each relieved the other in turn as fresh, rested fighters replaced the fatigued.

17 (1) Postero die procul a castris hostes in collibus constiterunt rarique se ostendere et lenius quam pridie nostros equites proelio lacessere coeperunt. (2) sed meridie cum Caesar pabulandi causa tres legiones atque omnem equitatum cum Gaio Trebonio legato misisset, repente ex omnibus partibus ad pabulatores advolaverunt, sic uti ab signis legionibusque non absisterent. (3) nostri acriter in eos impetu facto reppulerunt neque finem sequendi fecerunt, quo<a>d subsidio confisi equites, cum post se legiones viderent, (4) praecipites hostes egerunt magnoque eorum numero interfecto neque sui colligendi neque consistendi aut ex essedis desiliendi facultatem dederunt. (5) ex hac fuga protinus, quae undique convenerant, auxilia discesserunt, neque post id tempus umquam summis nobiscum copiis hostes contenderunt.

18 (1) Caesar cognito consilio eorum ad flumen Tamesim in fines Cassivellauni exercitum duxit. quod flumen uno omnino loco pedibus atque hoc aegre transiri potest. (2) eo cum venisset, animum advertit ad alteram fluminis ripam magnas esse copias hostium instructas. (3) ripa autem erat acutis sudibus praefixisque munita, eiusdemque generis sub aqua defixae sudes flumine tegebantur. (4) his rebus cognitis a captivis perfugisque Caesar praemisso equitatu confestim legiones subsequi iussit. (5) sed ea celeritate atque eo impetu milites ierunt, cum capite solo ex aqua extarent, ut hostes impetum legionum atque equitum sustinere non possent ripasque dimitterent ac se fugae mandarent.

19 (1) Cassivellaunus, ut supra demonstravimus, omni deposita spe contentionis, dimissis amplioribus copiis, milibus circiter quattuor essedariorum relictis itinera nostra servabat paulumque ex via

17 (1) The next day, the enemy stationed themselves on hills far off from camp and began to appear in scattered groups and to attack our cavalry less aggressively than the day before. (2) At midday, however, when Caesar had sent three legions and the whole cavalry with the legate Gaius Trebonius to search for food, the enemy suddenly flew at the foragers from all directions, in such a way that they could not break formation. (3) Our men made a fierce attack against the enemy and drove them back, and they did not stop chasing them until the cavalry, made confident by backup, since they saw the legions behind them, (4) drove the enemy headlong into flight. They killed a great number and gave the enemy no opportunity to rally or take a stand or jump down from their chariots. (5) Immediately after this retreat, the auxiliaries which had gathered from all over scattered, and after this point the enemy did not challenge us with all their forces again.

18 (1) When Caesar learned the enemy's plan he led the army into the territory of Cassivellaunus as far as the Tamesis River, which it is possible to cross by foot in just one place and even there only with difficulty. (2) Once he had arrived there, he noticed that large numbers of the enemy were marshalled on the other side of the river. (3) In addition, the bank was fortified with sharpened stakes that had been positioned along it, and stakes just like this had been positioned underwater and were concealed by the river. (4) When Caesar learned these things from hostages and deserters he sent the cavalry in the lead and ordered the legions to follow right behind them. (5) Even though only their heads stayed above water, our soldiers fought with such speed and force that the enemy were not able to endure the attack by our legions and cavalry, and they deserted the banks and took to flight.

19 (1) As I mentioned earlier, Cassivellaunus had given up all hope of a direct attack. The greater part of his forces had been dismissed, with about four thousand charioteers left behind. Cassivellaunus kept an eye on our march, staying back a bit from the road and

excedebat locisque impeditis ac silvestribus sese occultabat atque iis regionibus, quibus nos iter facturos cognoverat, pecora atque homines ex agris in silvas compellebat et, (2) cum equitatus noster liberius praedandi vastandique causa se in agros effunderet, omnes viis notis semitisque essedarios ex silvis emittebat et magno cum periculo nostrorum equitum cum his confligebat atque hoc metu latius vagari prohibebat. (3) relinquebatur ut neque longius ab agmine legionum discedi Caesar pateretur et tantum in agris vastandis incendiisque faciendis hostibus noceretur, quantum labore atque itinere legionarii milites efficere poterant.

20 (1) Interim Trinovantes, prope firmissima earum regionum civitas – ex qua Mandubracius adulescens Caesaris fidem secutus ad eum in continentem [Galliam] venerat, cuius pater [inianuvetitius] in ea civitate regnum obtinuerat interfectusque erat a Cassivellauno, ipse fuga mortem vitaverat –, (2) legatos ad Caesarem mittunt pollicenturque sese ei dedituros atque imperata facturos. (3) petunt ut Mandubracium ab iniuria Cassivellauni defendat atque in civitatem mittat, qui praesit imperiumque obtineat. (4) his Caesar imperat obsides XL frumentumque exercitui Mandubraciumque ad eos mittit. illi imperata celeriter fecerunt, obsides ad numerum frumentumque miserunt.

21 (1) Trinovantibus defensis atque ab omni militum iniuria prohibitis Cenimagni Segontiaci Ancalites Bibroci Cassi legationibus missis sese Caesari dedunt. (2) ab his cognoscit non longe ex eo loco oppidum Cassivellauni abesse silvis paludibusque munitum, quo satis magnus hominum pecorisque numerus convenerit. (3) oppidum autem Britanni vocant, cum silvas impeditas vallo atque fossa munierunt, quo incursionis hostium vitandae causa convenire consuerunt. (4) eo proficiscitur cum legionibus. locum reperit egregie natura atque opere munitum. tamen hunc duabus ex

hiding himself in dense and wooded places. In the areas where he had learned we would be marching, he drove all the livestock and people from the fields into the woods and, (2) when our cavalry wandered out too far in the fields to pillage and lay waste, he sent all the charioteers out of the forest along the familiar and well-worn ways and engaged them at great danger to our cavalry; by instilling this fear he prevented our men from traveling very far. (3) As a result, Caesar could not allow anyone to travel far from the main column of the legions; he ordered that, by wasting and burning the fields, the legionary soldiers cause as much damage as they could accomplish despite the difficulty of the march.

20 (1) The Trinovantes were arguably the most powerful state in the area. One of them, the young Mandubracius, had come to meet Caesar on the mainland to seek his protection; his father had held power in that state but was killed by Cassivellaunus, and Mandubracius had fled for his life. (2) These Trinovantes sent envoys to Caesar and promised that they would surrender to him and would do what he ordered. (3) They asked that Caesar defend Mandubracius against harm from Cassivellaunus and that he send Mandubracius to their state to take charge and hold command. (4) Caesar ordered forty hostages from them as well as food for his army and sent them Mandubracius. They completed his orders quickly and sent the requested number of hostages and food.

21 (1) The Trinovantes were thus safe and protected from any violence from the soldiers. The Cenimagni, Segontiaci, Ancalites, Bibroci, and Cassi then surrendered to Caesar through their own envoys. (2) Caesar learned from them that Cassivellaunus' stronghold was not that far away and that it was protected by forests and marshes, where a substantial number of men and cattle had been collected. (3) (The Britons call it a 'stronghold' when they fortify the dense woods with a rampart or a moat, which is what they usually do to avoid enemy attacks.) (4) Caesar went there with his legions. He discovered that the place was extremely well fortified by both

partibus oppugnare contendit. (5) hostes paulisper morati militum nostrorum impetum non tulerunt seseque alia ex parte oppida eiecerunt. (6) magnus ibi numerus pecoris repertus multique in fuga sunt conprehensi atque interfecti.

22 (1) Dum haec in his locis geruntur, Cassivellaunus ad Cantium, quod esse ad mare supra demonstravimus, quibus regionibus quattuor reges praeerant, Cingetorix Carvilius Taximagulus Segovax, nuntios mittit atque his imperat, uti coactis omnibus copiis castra navalia de inproviso adoriantur atque oppugnent. (2) ii cum ad castra venissent, nostri eruptione facta multis eorum interfectis, capto etiam nobili duce Lugotorige suos incolumes reduxerunt. (3) Cassivellaunus hoc proelio nuntiato, tot detrimentis acceptis, vastatis finibus, maxime etiam permotus defectione civitatum, legatos per Atrebatem Commium de deditione ad Caesarem mittit. (4) Caesar, cum constituisset hiemare in continenti propter repentinos Galliae motus, neque multum aestatis superesset atque id facile extrahi posse intellegeret, obsides imperat, et quid in annos singulos vectigalis p.R. Britannia penderet constituit. (5) interdicit atque imperat Cassivellauno, ne Mandubracio neu Trinovantibus noceat.

23 (1) Obsidibus acceptis exercitum reducit ad mare, naves invenit refectas. (2) his deductis, quod et captivorum magnum numerum habebat et nonnullae tempestate deperierant naves, duobus commeatibus exercitum reportare instituit. (3) ac sic accidit, uti ex tanto navium numero tot navigationibus neque hoc neque superiore anno ulla omnino navis, quae milites portaret, desideraretur, (4) at ex iis, quae inanes ex continenti ad eum remitterentur – [et] prioris commeatus expositis militibus et quas postea Labienus faciendas curaverat numero LX –, perpaucae locum caperent, reliquae

nature and human effort. Still, he decided to attack it from two directions. (5) The enemy stayed for only a short time; they were not able to withstand our attack and withdrew to another part of the stronghold. (6) A great number of cattle were found there and many of the enemy were apprehended and killed in flight.

22 (1) While that was happening there, Cassivellaunus sent messengers to Kent (which I noted above is on the coast) where four kings reign – Cingetorix, Carvilius, Taximagulus, and Segovax. Cassivellaunus ordered them to gather all their troops and attack the camp by the shore and take it by surprise. (2) When they arrived at the camp, our men rushed forth; they killed many of the enemy and even captured a high-ranking leader named Lugotorix, and then led our own men back safely. (3) When the battle was reported to him Cassivellaunus was distressed by how many losses he had suffered, how his territory had been ravaged, and especially by the defection of some states. He sent envoys to Caesar to negotiate surrender through Commius of the Atrebates. (4) Caesar had decided to winter on the mainland because of the risk of sudden uprisings in Gaul; furthermore, not much of the season remained and he realized that this conflict could easily drag on. Therefore, he demanded hostages and decided what amount of tribute Britain would pay each year to the Roman people. (5) He strictly forbade Cassivellaunus from harming Mandubracius or the Trinovantes.

23 (1) When he had received the hostages, Caesar led the army back to the sea and found that the ships had been repaired. (2) After launching these, he decided to transport the army in two trips, because he now had a number of hostages and a few of the ships had been lost in the storm. (3) It turned out that no ship that had carried soldiers this year or the year before was lost. (4) But of those ships that had been sent empty to him from the mainland (since the soldiers from the prior trip had disembarked) and of those sixty that Labienus had been in charge of building, few of

fere omnes reicerentur. (5) quas cum aliquamdiu Caesar frustra ex<s>pectasset, ne anni tempore a navigatione excluderetur, quod aequinoctium suberat, necessario angustius milites conlocavit ac summa tranquillitate consecuta cum solvisset vigilia, prima luce terram attigit omnesque incolumes naves perduxit.

24 (1) Subductis navibus concilioque Gallorum Samarobrivae peracto, quod eo anno frumentum in Gallia propter siccitates angustius provenerat, coactus est aliter ac superioribus annis exercitum in hibernis conlocare legionesque in plures civitates distribuere. (2) ex quibus unam in Morinos ducendam Gaio Fabio legato dedit, alteram in Nervios Quinto Ciceroni, tertiam in Essu<vi>os Lucio Roscio; quartam in Remis cum Tito Labieno in confinio Treverorum hiemare iussit. (3) tres in Belgis conlocavit; his M. Crassum quaestorem et Lucium Munatium Plancum et Gaium Trebonium legatos praefecit. (4) unam legionem, quam proxime trans Padum conscripserat, et cohortes V in Eburones, quorum pars maxima est inter Mosam ac Rhenum, qui sub imperio Ambiorigis et Catu<v>olci erant, misit. (5) his militibus Quintum Titurium Sabinum et Lucium Aurunculeium Cottam legatos praeesse iussit. (6) ad hunc modum distributis legionibus facillime inopiae frumentariae sese mederi posse existimavit. (7) atque harum tamen omnium legionum hiberna praeter eam, quam Lucio Roscio in pacatissimam et quietissimam partem ducendam dederat, milibus passuum centum continebantur. (8) ipse interea, quoad legiones conlocatas munitaque hiberna congnovisset, in Gallia morari constituit.

them reached their destination and almost all the rest were driven back. (5) Caesar waited for them for a while in vain, (6) hoping that the timing would not prevent him from sailing (because it was almost the equinox). He was forced to crowd the soldiers in quite tightly. When a great calm settled in at the beginning of the second watch he weighed anchor; at dawn he reached land and brought in all the ships unharmed.

24 (1) The ships were docked and a council of Gauls was held at Samarobriva. Because of a drought the harvest in Gaul that year was quite meager, and so Caesar was forced to assign his army to winter quarters according to a different plan than in previous years and to distribute the legions among more states. (2) One of these legions he assigned to the legate Gaius Fabius, to lead into the territory of the Morini; another to Quintus Cicero, to lead to the Nervii; a third to Lucius Roscius, to lead to the Essuvi; and a fourth he ordered to winter with Titus Labienus among the Remi near their border with the Treveri. (3) He located three legions among the Belgae and put the quaestor Marcus Crassus and the legates Lucius Munatius Plancus and Gaius Trebonius in charge of them. (4) He sent one legion (the one which he had raised most recently on the other side of the Po) and five cohorts among the Eburones, most of whose territory is between the Meuse and the Rhine and who were under the command of Ambiorix and Catuvolcus. (5) He put the legates Quintus Titurius Sabinus and Lucius Aurunculeius Cotta in charge of these troops. (6) Caesar thought that by distributing the legions in this way he would easily be able to mitigate the food shortage. (7) The winter quarters of all the legions except one, which he had assigned Lucius Roscius to lead to the most peaceful and stable area, were still contained within 100 miles. (8) Meanwhile, Caesar himself decided to remain in Gaul until the legions were settled and the winter camps were fortified.

25 (1) Erat in Carnutibus summo loco natus Tasgetius, cuius maiores in sua civitate regnum obtinuerant. (2) huic Caesar pro eius virtute atque in se benevolentia, quod in omnibus bellis singulari eius opera fuerat usus, maiorum locum restituerat. (3) tertium iam hunc annum regnantem inimicis iam multis palam ex civitate <. . .> et iis auctoribus eum interfecerunt. (4) defertur ea res ad Caesarem. ille veritus, quod ad plures pertinebat, ne civitas eorum inpulsu deficeret, Lucium Plancum cum legione ex Belgio celeriter in Carnutes proficisci iubet ibique hiemare, quorumque opera cognoverit Tasgetium interfectum, hos comprehensos ad se mittere. (5) interim ab omnibus legatis quaestoribusque, quibus legiones tradiderat, certior factus est in hiberna perventum locumque hibernis esse munitum.

26 (1) Diebus circiter quindecim, quibus in hiberna ventum est, initium repentini tumultus ac defectionis ortum est ab Ambiorige et Catuvolco. (2) qui cum ad fines regni sui Sabino Cottaeque praesto fuissent frumentumque in hiberna comportavissent, Indutiomari Treveri nuntiis inpulsi suos concitaverunt subitoque oppressis lignatoribus magna manu ad castra oppugnanda venerunt. (3) cum celeriter nostri arma cepissent vallumque ascendissent atque una ex parte Hispanis equitibus emissis equestri proelio superiores fuissent, desperata re hostes suos ab oppugnatione reduxerunt. (4) tum suo more conclamaverunt, uti aliqui ex nostris ad conloquium prodiret: habere sese, quae de re communi dicere vellent, quibus rebus controversias minui posse sperarent.

25 (1) Among the Carnutes there was a well-born man named Tasgetius, whose ancestors had won the kingship in their state. (2) Because of Tasgetius' courage and his own goodwill toward him (since he had benefitted from his exceptional help in all the wars) Caesar had restored Tasgetius to the rank of his ancestors. (3) He was in his third year as ruler when his enemies killed him, with many of his fellow citizens openly complicit. (4) This event was reported to Caesar. Because so many people were involved he was afraid the whole state would defect. Caesar ordered Lucius Plancus to make his way quickly from Belgium to the Carnutes with his legion and to winter there; he also ordered Plancus to apprehend and send to him anyone who had known about the plan to kill Tasgetius. (5) Meanwhile, Caesar was informed by all the legates and quaestors to whom he had entrusted the legions that they had arrived at winter quarters and had fortified the place as a winter camp.

26 (1) About fifteen days after they arrived in the winter camp, the beginning of a sudden revolt and defection was instigated by Ambiorix and Catuvolcus. (2) Although they had met in person with Sabinus and Cotta at the borders of their kingdom and had brought food into their winter camp, they were spurred on by messages from Indutiomarus the Treveran and incited their own people to action. They attacked some men who were gathering wood and then in a large group went on to attack the camp. (3) Our men quickly took up arms and ascended the rampart and, when the Spanish cavalry were sent in from one direction, they were victorious in a cavalry battle. Having lost their opportunity, the enemy retreated from the attack. (4) Then, according to their custom, they shouted that one of our men should come forth for a discussion. There was something, they said, that they wished to discuss in our common interest, by which they hoped that our disputes could be resolved.

27 (1) Mittitur ad eos conloquendi causa Gaius Arpinius eques Romanus, familiaris Quinti Titurii, et Quintus Iunius ex Hispania quidam, qui iam ante missu Caesaris ad Ambigorem ventitare consuerat. apud quos Ambiorix ad hunc modum locutus est: (2) sese pro Caesaris in se beneficiis plurimum ei confiteri debere, quod eius opera stipendio liberatus esset, quod Atuatucis finitimis suis pendere consuesset, quodque ei et filius et fratris filius a Caesare remissi essent, quos Atuatuci obsidum numero missos apud se in servitute et catenis tenuissent. (3) neque id, quod fecerit de oppugnatione castrorum, aut iudicio aut voluntate sua fecisse, sed coactu civitatis, suaque esse eiusmodi imperia, ut non minus haberet iuris in se multitudo, quam ipse in multitudinem. (4) civitati porro hanc fuisse belli causam, quod repentinae Gallorum coniurationi resistere non potuerit. id se facile ex humilitate sua probare posse, quod non adeo sit imperitus rerum, ut suis copiis populum Romanum superari posse confidat. (5) sed esse Galliae commune consilium: omnibus hibernis Caesaris oppugnandis hunc esse dictum diem, ne qua legio alterae legioni subsidio venire posset. (6) non facile Gallos Gallis negare potuisse, praesertim cum de recuperanda communi libertate consilium initum videretur. (7) quibus quoniam pro p[r]ietate satisfecerit, habere nunc se rationem officii pro beneficiis Caesaris; monere, orare Titurium pro hospitio, ut suae ac militum saluti consulat. (8) magnam manum Germanorum conductam Rhenum transisse; hanc adfore biduo. (9) ipsorum esse consilium, velintne prius, quam finitimi sentiant, eductos ex hibernis milites aut ad Ciceronam aut ad Labienum deducere, quorum alter milia passuum circiter quinquaginta, alter paulo amplius ab iis absit. (10) illud se polliceri et iure iurando confirmare, tutum se iter per suos fines daturum. (11) quod cum

27 (1) Gaius Arpinius, a Roman knight and friend of Sabinus, and one Quintus Iunius from Spain, who had frequently gone to meet with Ambiorix in the past at Caesar's request, were sent to speak with Ambiorix and Catuvolcus. Ambiorix addressed them along these lines: (2) he admitted that he was in great debt to Caesar because of the favors he had shown him – that thanks to his help he had been freed from a tribute he used to pay to his neighbors, the Atuatuci, and that his son and brother's son, whom the Atuatuci had kept for themselves in servitude and chains when they were sent among a number of hostages, had been sent back to him by Caesar. (3) The action he took in attacking the camp he had not taken according to his own judgment or by his own free will, but under compulsion from the state. His rule was such that the masses had no less authority over him than he had over them. (4) The state, on the other hand, had gone to war because they could not withstand a sudden conspiracy of the Gauls. He could easily prove this by his own weakness, since he was not so ignorant of the situation as to believe that he could conquer the Roman people with his own forces. (5) But, Ambiorix continued, this was the plan that had been agreed upon throughout Gaul: a day had been appointed to attack all of Caesar's winter camps so that no legion would be able to come to the aid of another. (6) It was not easy for Gauls to say no to other Gauls, especially since the plan seemed to have been undertaken for the sake of recovering their shared freedom. (7) Because he had met his obligation to the state, he now took into consideration the duty that he owed for Caesar's favors. Due to their history of hospitality, Ambiorix said, he warned and even prayed that Sabinus would take this into consideration for his soldiers' safety and his own. (8) A large band of Germans had been hired and had crossed the Rhine; they would be there in two days. (9) It was their decision whether they wanted to lead their soldiers out of winter camps and draw them off to Cicero or Labienus' camps (one of which was about fifty miles away, the other a little farther) before the neighboring peoples noticed. (10) Ambiorix promised and confirmed it with an oath that he would give them safe passage through his territory. (11) By doing these things, he was both looking out for the interests

faciat, et civitati sese consulere, quod hibernis levetur, et Caesari pro eius meritis gratiam referre. hac oratione habita discedit Ambiorix.

28 (1) Arpinius et Iunius, quae audierant, ad legatos deferunt. illi repentina re perturbati, etsi ab hoste ea dicebantur, tamen non neglegenda existimabant maximeque hac re permovebantur, quod civitatem ignobilem atque humilem Eburonum sua sponte p.R. bellum facere ausam vix erat credendum. (2) itaque ad consilium rem deferunt magnaque inter eos existit controversia. (3) Lucius Aurunculeius compluresque tribuni militum et primorum ordinum centuriones nihil temere agendum neque ex hibernis iniussu Caesaris discedendum existimabant; (4) quantasvis <Gallorum>, magnas etiam copias Germanorum sustineri posse munitis hibernis docebant; rem esse testimonio, quod primum hostium impetum multis ultro vulneribus inlatis fortissime sustinuerint; (5) re frumentaria non premi; interea et ex proximis hibernis et a Caesare conventura subsidia; (6) postremo quid esse levius aut turpius quam auctore hoste de summis rebus capere consilium?

29 (1) Contra ea Titurius sero facturos clamitabat, cum maiores manus hostium adiunctis Germanis convenissent, aut cum aliquid calamitatis in proximis hibernis esset acceptum. brevem consulendi esse occasionem. (2) Caesarem arbitrari profectum in Italiam; neque aliter Carnutes interficiendi Tasgetii consilium fuisse capturos, neque Eburones, si ille adesset, tanta contemptione nostri ad castra venturos esse; (3) non hostem auctorem, sed rem spectare; subesse Rhenum; magno esse Germanis dolori Ariovisti mortem et superiores nostras victorias; (4) ardere Galliam tot

of his state, because he was relieving them of the Romans' winter quarters, and also returning a favor owed to Caesar. When he had finished his speech Ambiorix departed.

28 (1) When Arpinius and Iunius heard this, they reported it to the legates. They were alarmed by the sudden development; even though it had been reported by the enemy they thought his words should not be ignored. They were particularly troubled by the fact that the obscure and humble state of the Eburones dared, of their own free will, to wage war against the Roman people; it seemed scarcely believable. (2) And so they brought the matter to a council, and a fierce quarrel arose between them. (3) Cotta and several of the military tribunes and centurions of the first rank argued that nothing should be done rashly, nor should they depart from winter camp without an order from Caesar. (4) They pointed out that they could withstand any number of Gauls, even great forces of Germans, in their fortified winter camps; the proof was that they had withstood the initial enemy attack very bravely and on top of that they had even inflicted many wounds. (5) Furthermore, they were not short on food. Meanwhile, help would come from the nearby camps and from Caesar himself. (6) Finally, what would be more thoughtless or shameful than to make plans about the most important matters according to the advice of the enemy?

29 (1) Sabinus shouted back that by the time a larger band of enemies had been assembled with the neighboring Germans joining in or some other disaster had befallen the winter camps, it would be too late to act. There was little time for debate. (2) He reckoned that Caesar was on his way to Italy; otherwise the Carnutes would not have made their plan to assassinate Tasgetius, nor would the Eburones have come to our camp so arrogantly if Caesar had been nearby. (3) He was not heeding the enemy's advice, but the situation itself. The Rhine was nearby; the death of Ariovistus and our recent victories were sources of resentment among the Germans; (4) Gaul was fuming at the many insults they had

contumeliis acceptis sub populi Romani imperium redactam superiore gloria rei militaris ex<s>tincta. (5) postremo quis hoc sibi persuaderet sine certa spe Ambiorigem ad eius modi consilium descendisse? (6) suam sententiam in utramque partem esse tutam; si nihil esset durius, nullo cum periculo ad proximam legionem perventuros; si Gallia omnis cum Germanis consentiret, unam esse in celeritate positam salutem. (7) Cottae quidem atque eorum, qui dissentirent, consilium quem haberet exitum? in quo si praesens periculum non, at certe longinqua obsidione fames esset timenda.

30 (1) Hac in utramque partem disputatione habita, cum a Cotta primisque ordinibus acriter resisteretur, "vincite" inquit "si ita vultis" Sabinus et id clariore voce, ut magna pars militum exaudiret; (2) "neque is sum" inquit "qui gravissime ex vobis mortis periculo terrear: hi sapient: si gravius quid acciderit, abs te rationem repsocent; (3) qui, si per te liceat, perendino die cum proximis hibernis coniuncti communem cum reliquis belli casum sustineant, non reiecti et relegati longe a ceteris aut ferro aut fame intereant."

31 (1) Consurgitur ex consilio; comprehendunt utrumque et orant, ne sua dissensione et pertinacia rem in summum periculum deducant; (2) facilem esse rem, seu maneant seu proficiscantur, si modo unum omnes sentiant ac probent; contra in dissensione nullam se salutem perspicere. (3) res disputatione ad mediam noctem perducitur. tandem dat Cotta permotus manus, superat sententia Sabini. pronuntiatur prima luce ituros. (4) consumitur vigiliis reliqua pars noctis, cum sua quisque miles circumspiceret, quid

suffered, being reduced under the rule of the Roman people and seeing their former military glory extinguished. (5) Finally, he asked, who could convince himself that Ambiorix had stooped to a plan like this without full confidence? (6) His own plan, Sabinus said, was safe either way. If nothing very troubling happened, they would make their way without danger to the closest legion. If all of Gaul conspired with the Germans, their only hope of safety was speed. (7) Anyhow, what would be the result of Cotta's plan (and those who agreed with him)? Even if there was no danger at present, the hunger brought about by a long siege was certainly to be feared.

30 (1) Arguments were made on both sides, but when there was fierce resistance from Cotta and the centurions, Sabinus said in a loud voice so that most of the soldiers could hear him: "You all win, if that's how you want it. (2) But I am not the one among you," he continued, "who fears the risk of death the most gravely. These men will know it. If anything very serious happens, they will seek an explanation from you, Cotta. (3) They are men who would, if you would permit it, join with the nearest camp the day after tomorrow and endure the misfortunes of war with the others rather than die in battle or by famine, exiled and isolated far away from the rest."

31 (1) They got up to leave the meeting. Their supporters stopped them both and begged that they not create the greatest danger through their own conflict and stubbornness. The situation was an easy one whether they stayed or went, provided that they all felt the same and came to an agreement. On the other hand, the men said, they could see no hope of safety in the current conflict. (3) The matter was drawn out by this dispute until the middle of the night. At last Cotta yielded, though greatly distressed, and Sabinus' plan prevailed. It was announced that they would set out at dawn. (4) The rest of the night was consumed by wakefulness, as each soldier evaluated his possessions and debated what he

secum portare posset, quid ex instrumento hibernorum relinquere cogeretur. (5) omnia excogitantur, quare nec sine periculo maneatur et languore militum et vigiliis periculum augeatur. (6) prima luce sic ex castris proficiscuntur ut quibus esset persuasum non ab hoste, sed ab homine amicissimo Ambiorige consilium datum, longissimo agmine maximisque impedimentis.

32 (1) At hostes, posteaquam ex nocturno fremitu vigiliisque de profectione eorum senserunt, conlocatis insidiis bipertito in silvis opportuno atque occulto loco a milibus passuum circiter duobus Romanorum adventum ex<s>pectabant, (2) et cum se maior pars agminis in magnam convallem demisisset, ex utraque parte eius vallis subito se ostenderunt novissimosque premere et primos prohibere ascensu atque inquissimo nostris loco proelium committere coeperunt.

33 (1) Tum demum Titurius, ut qui nihil ante providisset, trepidare et concursare cohortesque disponere, haec tamen ipsa timide atque ut eum omnia deficere viderentur; quod plerumque iis accidere consuevit, qui in ipso negotio consilium capere coguntur. (2) at Cotta, qui cogitasset haec posse in itinere accidere atque ob eam causam profectionis auctor non fuisset, nulla in re communi saluti deerat, et in appellandis cohortandisque militibus imperatoris et in pugna militis officia praestabat. (3) cum propter longitudinem agminis minus facile omnia per se obire et quid quoque loco faciendum esset providere possent, iusserunt pronuntiari, ut impedimenta relinquerent atque in orbem consisterent. (4) quod consilium etsi in eiusmodi casu reprehendendum non est, tamen incommode accidit. (5) nam et nostris militibus spem minuit et

would be able to bring with him and what tools from the winter camp he would have to leave behind. (5) They came up with every justification for why they could not remain there without danger and why that danger would be increased by the soldiers' exhaustion and the watches. (6) And so at dawn they set out from the camp like men who were fully convinced they were following advice given by Ambiorix not as an enemy but as a devoted friend. The column was extremely long, and the baggage was heavy.

32 (1) When they perceived that our men were going to depart, thanks to the soldiers' wakefulness and the commotion in the night, the enemy set up an ambush in two places in the woods in a convenient and well-hidden spot about two miles away and awaited the Romans' approach. (2) And when most of the column had made its way into a large ravine, the enemy suddenly appeared on either side of the valley. They began trying to hold back our rearguard, to keep our advance guard from climbing out, and to force them to fight in a place that was most unfavorable to them.

33 (1) Only then was Sabinus afraid, since he had not anticipated anything. He scrambled and arranged the cohorts but did it so fearfully that it seemed like all his faculties were failing him; this is what tends to happen to those who are forced to create a plan in the heat of the moment. (2) But Cotta, who *had* anticipated that this could happen on the march and for precisely this reason had not advocated for it, had neglected nothing in the interest of their common safety. He played the roles of both commander and soldier by encouraging and calling on the soldiers by name and by taking part in the fighting himself. (3) When, because of the length of the column, it became difficult to attend to everything themselves and to provide for whatever that needed to be done at every point, they gave orders to pass the word that they were to abandon the baggage and form a circle. (4) This was not a blameworthy plan in such a dire situation, but it turned out badly anyhow. (5) For it robbed our men of hope and made the enemy

hostes ad pugnam alacriores effecit, quod non sine summo timore et desperatione id factum videbatur. (6) praeterea accidit – quod fieri necesse erat –, ut vulgo milites ab signis discederent, quaeque quisque eorum carissima haberet, ab impedimentis petere atque arripere properaret, clamore et fletu omnia complerentur.

34 (1) At barbaris consilium non defuit. nam duces eorum tota acie pronuntiari iusserunt, nequis ab loco discederet; illorum esse praedam atque illis reservari, quaecumque Romani reliquissent; proinde omnia in victoria posita existimarent. (2) erant et numero et virtute pugnandi pares. nostri tametsi ab duce et a fortuna deserebantur, tamen omnem spem salutis in virtute ponebant, et quotiens quaeque cohors procurrerat, ab ea parte magnus numerus hostium cadebat. (3) qua re animadversa Ambiorix pronuntiari iubet, ut procul tela coniciant neu propius accedant, et quam in partem Romani impetum fecerint, cedant; (4) levitate armorum et cotidiana exercitatione nihil his noceri posse; rursus se ad signa recipientes insequantur.

35 (1) Quo praecepto ab iis diligentissime observato, cum quaepiam cohors ex orbe excesserat atque impetum fecerat, hostes velocissime refugiebant. (2) interim eam partem nudari necesse erat et ab latere aperto tela recipere. (3) rursus cum in eum locum, unde erant egressi, reverti coeperant, et ab iis, qui cesserant, et ab iis, qui proximi steterant, circumveniebantur. (4) sin autem locum tenere vellent, nec virtuti locus relinquebatur neque ab tanta multitudine coniecta tela conferti vitare poterant. (5) tamen tot incommodis conflictati multis vulneribus acceptis resistebant et magna parte diei consumpta, cum a prima luce ad horam octavam

all the more eager to fight, because it was clear that they would not have done this except in the greatest fear and desperation. (6) Moreover, the inevitable happened when the soldiers openly broke ranks and each man hurried to find and snatch out of the baggage whatever was most important to him. There was commotion and weeping all around.

34 (1) The barbarians, on the other hand, did not lack a plan. Their leaders ordered it to be announced all down the battle line that no one should leave his post. The plunder was theirs, and whatever the Romans left behind was reserved for them; they should keep in mind, then, that all hope lay in their victory. (2) The armies were well-matched both in number and in their bravery during battle. Although our men had been deserted both by their leader and by fortune, they still entrusted all hope of safety to their courage, and every time a cohort advanced, there a great number of the enemy fell. (3) When Ambiorix noticed this, he ordered that word be passed on that they should throw their weapons from a distance and not advance any farther; wherever the Romans made an attack, they should fall back. No harm would be able to come to them thanks to the lightness of their arms and their daily training. When the Romans retreated to their standards, they should pursue.

35 (1) The enemy obeyed this command most diligently, and when any of the cohorts broke out of the circle and made an attack, they fell back with great speed. (2) Meanwhile, this necessarily exposed part of our formation and the missile attack was received on their open flank. (3) When they started to return to the position they had left they were surrounded by both those who had fallen back and those who were posted nearby. (4) But if, on the other hand, they tried to stand their ground, there was no room for courage, nor were they able to avoid being hit by the weapons thrown by the throng of enemies. (5) Despite being hindered by so many setbacks and receiving many wounds, our men fought back; although the great part of the day was spent fighting (since it raged from dawn until

pugnaretur, nihil, quod ipsis esset indignum, committebant. (6) tum Tito Balventio, qui superiore anno primum pilum duxerat, viro forti et magnae auctoritatis, utrumque femur tragula traicitur; (7) Quintus Lucanius eiusdem ordinis, fortissime pugnans, dum circumvento filio subvenit, interficitur. (8) Lucius Cotta legatus omnes cohortes ordinesque adhortans in adversum os funda vulneratur.

36 (1) His rebus permotus Quintus Titurius cum procul Ambiorigem suos cohortantem conspexisset, interpretem suum Gnaeum Pompeium ad eum mittit rogatum, ut sibi militibusque parcat. (2) ille appellatus respondet: si velit secum conloqui, licere; sperare a multitudine impetrari posse, quod ad militum salutem pertineat; ipsi vero nihil nocitum iri inque eam rem se suam fidem interponere. (3) ille cum Cotta saucio communicat, si videatur, pugna ut excedant et cum Ambiorige una conloquantur; sperare se ab eo de sua ac militum salute impetrari posse. Cotta se ad armatum hostem iturum negat atque in eo perseverat.

37 (1) Sabinus, quos in praesentia tribunos militum circum se habebat, et primorum ordinum centuriones se sequi iubet, et cum propius Ambiorigem accessisset, iussus arma abicere imperatum facit suisque, ut idem faciant, imperat. (2) interim dum de condicionibus inter se agunt longiorque consulto ab Ambiorige instituitur sermo, paulatim circumventus interficitur. (3) tum vero suo more victoriam conclamant atque ululatum tollunt impetuque in nostro facto ordines perturbant. (4) ibi Lucius Cotta pugnans interficitur cum maxima parte militum. reliqui se in castra recipiunt, unde erant egressi. (5) ex quibus Lucius Petrosidius

the eighth hour), they did nothing unworthy of themselves. (6) Then Titus Balventius, who had become chief centurion the year before, a brave man who showed great leadership, was pierced through both thighs by a javelin. (7) Quintus Lucanius, who held the same rank, was killed while he was fighting bravely and trying to aid his son, who had been surrounded. (8) The legate Cotta was encouraging all the cohorts and ranks when he was struck right in the face with a sling bullet.

36 (1) Sabinus was greatly distressed by these events, and when he saw Ambiorix off in the distance urging on his men, he sent his interpreter Gnaeus Pompey to ask that Ambiorix spare Sabinus himself and his soldiers. (2) When he was addressed, Ambiorix replied that if Sabinus wanted to speak with him, he was welcome to. He hoped that he would be able to persuade his group to obey as it pertained to the safety of Sabinus' soldiers. No harm would come to Sabinus, at least; he gave his word about that. (3) Sabinus proposed to the wounded Cotta that, if it seemed right to him also, they should leave battle and speak with Ambiorix together; he hoped that their safety and that of the soldiers could be assured by Ambiorix. Cotta said that he would not go to meet an armed enemy and remained resolute in the matter.

37 (1) Sabinus ordered the military tribunes who were with him at the moment and the centurions to follow. When he drew closer to Ambiorix, he was ordered to throw down his weapons; he did as he was told and commanded his own men to do the same. (2) Meanwhile, while they were discussing the terms of surrender, Ambiorix intentionally dragged out the conversation; Sabinus was gradually surrounded and then killed. (3) Then the enemy proclaimed victory in their accustomed way: they let out a howl and attacked our ranks, scattering them. (4) There Cotta fell while fighting, along with most of our soldiers. The rest retreated into the camp from where they had set out. (5) One of our men, the standard-bearer Lucius Petrosidius, was pursued by a large

aquilifer, cum magna multitudine hostium premeretur, aquilam intra vallum proiecit, ipse pro castris fortissime pugnans occiditur. (6) illi aegre ad noctem oppugnationem sustinent. noctu ad unum omnes desperata salute se ipsi interficiunt. (7) pauci ex proelio elapsi incertis itineribus per silvas ad Titum Labienum legatum in hiberna perveniunt atque eum de rebus gestis certiorem faciunt.

38 (1) Hac victoria sublatus Ambiorix statim cum equitatu in Atuatucos, qui erant eius regno finitimi, proficiscitur. neque noctem neque diem <iter> intermittit peditatumque se subsequi iubet. (2) re demonstrata Atuatucisque concitatis postero die in Nervios pervenit hortaturque, ne sui in perpetuum liberandi atque ulciscendi Romanos pro iis, quas acceperint, iniuriis occasionem dimittant. (3) interfectos esse legatos duos magnamque partem exercitus interisse demonstrat; (4) nihil esse negotii subito oppressam legionem, quae cum Cicerone hiemet, interfici. se ad eam rem profitetur adiutorem. facile hac oratione Nerviis persuadet.

39 (1) Itaque confestim dimissis nuntiis ad Ceutrones, Grudios, Levacos, Pleumoxios, Geidumnos, qui omnes sub eorum imperio sunt, quam maximas possunt manus cogunt et de inproviso ad Ciceronis hiberna advolant, nondum ad eum fama de Titurii morte perlata. (2) h[u]ic quoque accidit – quod fuit necesse –, ut nonnulli milites, qui lignationis munitionisque causa in silvas discessissent, repentino equitum adventu interciperentur. (3) his circumventis magna manu Eburones, Nervii, Atuatuci atque horum omnium socii clientesque legionem oppugnare incipiunt. nostri celeriter ad arma concurrunt, vallum conscendunt. (4) aegre is dies sustentatur, quod omnem spem hostes in celeritate ponebant atque hanc adepti victoriam in perpetuum se fore victores confidebant.

group of the enemy; he cast the eagle inside the rampart and died fighting most bravely in front of the camp. (6) Our men barely withstood the attack until nightfall. That night, with no hope of safety remaining, every single one of them committed suicide. (7) A few men escaped from the battle and, though the paths were unfamiliar, made their way through the woods to Titus Labienus at his winter camp and informed him what had happened.

38 (1) Elated at this victory, Ambiorix immediately made his way with his cavalry to the Atuatuci, who neighbor his kingdom. He marched without stopping for a night and a day and ordered his infantry to follow him. (2) He explained the situation, and the Atuatuci were emboldened. The next day, he went to the Nervii and urged them not to pass up on the opportunity to free themselves forever and to take revenge on the Romans for the injuries they had suffered. (3) Ambiorix told them that two legates had been killed and that a great part of their army had also perished. (4) It would be no challenge to launch a sudden attack against the legion wintering with Cicero and slaughter them, and he promised that he himself would assist. Ambiorix easily persuaded the Nervii with this speech.

39 (1) And so messengers were sent right away to the Ceutrones, the Grudii, Levaci, Plaumoxii, and Geidumni, who were all under the rule of the Nervii. They raised the largest force they could and unexpectedly swooped in on the winter camp of Cicero, where the news of Sabinus' death had not yet arrived. (2) The inevitable happened again; a few of the soldiers who had gone into the woods to cut wood and build fortifications were intercepted by the sudden approach of the enemy cavalry. (3) They were surrounded by a huge group as the Eburones, Nervii, Atuatuci, and all their allies and dependents began to attack the legion. Our men rushed quickly to arms and mounted the rampart. (4) They barely withstood the attack for a day, since the enemy had placed all their hope in their speed and believed that if they won this particular victory, they would remain victorious for good.

40 (1) Mittuntur ad Caesarem confestim a Cicerone litterae, magnis propositis praemiis, si pertulissent; obsessis omnibus viis missi intercipiuntur. (2) noctu ex materia, quam munitionis causa comportaverant, turres admodum centum XX excitantur incredibili celeritate. quae deesse operi videbantur, perficiuntur. (3) hostes postero die multo maioribus coactis copiis castra oppugnant, fossam complent. (4) a nostris eadem ratione qua pridie resistitur. (5) hoc idem reliquis deinceps fit diebus. nulla pars nocturni temporis ad laborem intermittitur. non aegris, non vulneratis facultas quietis datur. (6) quaecumque ad proximi diei oppugnationem opus sunt, noctu comparantur. multae praeustae sudes, magnus muralium pilorum numerus instituitur. turres contabulantur, pinnae loricaeque ex cratibus attexuntur. (7) ipse Cicero, cum tenuissima valetudine esset, ne nocturnum quidem sibi tempus ad quietem relinquebat, ut ultro militum concursu ac vocibus sibi parcere cogeretur.

41 (1) Tum duces principesque Nerviorum, qui aliquem sermonis aditum causamque amicitiae cum Cicerone habebant, conloqui sese velle dicunt. (2) facta potestate eadem, quae Ambiorix cum Titurio egerat, commemorant: (3) omnem esse in armis Galliam; Germanos Rhenum transisse; Caesaris reliquorumque hiberna oppugnari. (4) addunt etiam de Sabini morte; Ambiorigem ostentant fidei faciendae causa. (5) errare eos dicunt, si quicquam ab iis praesidii sperent, qui suis rebus diffidant; sese tamen hoc esse in Ciceronem populumque Romanum animo, ut nihil nisi hiberna recusent atque hanc inveterascere consuetudinem nolint; (6) licere illis per se incolumibus ex hibernis discedere et, quascumque in partes velint, sine metu proficisci. (7) Cicero ad haec unum modo respondit: non esse consuetudinem p.R. ullam accipere ab hoste

40 (1) Dispatches were immediately sent from Cicero to Caesar, with great rewards being promised if messengers could successfully deliver them. All the roads were occupied, though, and those who had been sent out were intercepted. (2) During the night about 120 towers were built unbelievably quickly out of the material which the men had collected for their construction. They repaired any part of the defenses that seemed insufficient. (3) The next day the enemy attacked the camp with an even greater force they had gathered and filled in the trench. (4) Our men fought back in the same way as the day before. (5) The same thing happened every day. No part of the night was free from work, and there was no chance of rest for the sick or wounded. (6) Whatever was needed for the next day's attack was prepared overnight. Many fire-sharpened stakes and a great number of mural javelins were prepared. The towers were fitted with floors, and battlements and breastworks were woven on with wicker. (7) Although he was in very poor health, Cicero himself did not even allow himself the night for rest, with the result that he was compelled by the pleas of the soldiers, who crowded around him, to spare himself.

41 (1) Then some of the leaders and chieftains of the Nervii, who had the pretext of friendship as an excuse to address Cicero, said that they wanted to speak with him. (2) When this was granted, they said the same things that Ambiorix had used on Sabinus: (3) all of Gaul was in arms; the Germans had crossed the Rhine; the winter camps of Caesar and the others were under siege. (4) They added, furthermore, the death of Sabinus, and produced Ambiorix to verify it. (5) It was a mistake, they said, for those who could not rely on themselves to expect help from anyone else. Nevertheless, regarding Cicero and the Roman people, the Nervii were of the opinion that they would refuse them nothing except for accommodating their winter quarters, which they did not want to become a habitual practice. (6) They would permit the Romans to depart from the camp unharmed and to travel without fear wherever they wanted. (7) Cicero replied only this: it was not the habit of the Roman people to accept terms from an armed

armato condicionem; (8) si ab armis discedere velint, se adiutore utantur legatosque ad Caesarem mittant; sperare se pro eius iustitia, quae petierint, impetraturos.

42 (1) Ab hac spe repulsi Nervii vallo pedum X et fossa pedum XV hiberna cingunt. (2) haec et superiorum annorum consuetudine a nostris cognoverant et quosdam de exercitu nacti captivos ab his docebantur. (3) sed nulla ferramentorum copia, quae sunt ad hunc usum idonea, gladiis caespites circumcidere, manibus sagulisque terram exhaurire cogebantur. (4) qua quidem ex re hominum multitudo cognosci potuit. nam minus horis tribus milium pedum XV in circitu munitionem perfecerunt (5) reliquisque diebus turres ad altitudinem valli, falces testudinesque, quas idem captivi docuerant, parare ac facere coeperunt.

43 (1) Septimo oppugnationis die maximo coorto vento ferventes fusili ex argilla glandes fundis et iacula fervefacta in casas, quae more Gallico stramentis erant tectae, iacere coeperunt. (2) hae celeriter ignem comprehenderunt et venti magnitudine in omnem castrorum locum distulerunt. (3) hostes maximo clamore, sicuti parta iam atque explorata victoria, turres testudinesque agere et scalis vallum ascendere coeperunt. (4) ac tanta militum virtus atque ea praesentia animi fuit, ut, cum undique flamma torrerentur maximaque telorum multitudine premerentur suaque omnia impedimenta atque omnes fortunas conflagrare intellegerent, non modo dimigrandi causa de vallo decederet nemo, sed paene ne respiceret quidem quisquam ac tum omnes acerrime fortissimeque pugnarent. (5) hic dies nostris

enemy. If they were willing to lay down arms, they might employ his services as an advocate and send envoys to Caesar; in light of Caesar's reputation for justice, he said, he expected they would obtain that which they sought.

42 (1) Disappointed in their hope of deceiving Cicero, the Nervii surrounded the camp with a rampart 10 feet high and a trench 15 feet wide. (2) They had learned these methods from us through the experience of previous years, and, having taken a few hostages from our army, also learned from them. (3) But they did not have the abundance of tools necessary for this purpose, and so they were compelled to hack at the earth with their swords and to dig up dirt with their hands and carry it in their cloaks. (4) In this process it was possible to estimate the number of their forces, for in less than three hours they completed a fortification three miles in circumference. (5) In the following days they planned and built towers in the right proportion to the rampart and made grappling hooks and protective covers, all as the hostages had taught them to do.

43 (1) On the seventh day of the siege a great wind kicked up and the enemy began to hurl red-hot bullets made of softened clay with slings and heated javelins into the soldiers' huts, which had been covered with thatched roofs in the Gallic style. (2) They caught fire immediately and because of the strong wind it spread throughout the camp. (3) The enemy let out a great shout, as if their victory were already won and secured, and began to move their towers and covers and to scale the walls on ladders. (4) But the courage and presence of mind of our soldiers were so outstanding that, even though on all sides they were scorched by the flames and attacked by an onslaught of weapons, and at the same time they knew that all their baggage and property was going up in flames, not only did no one climb down the rampart to flee, not a single one even looked back and they all fought as fiercely and bravely as possible. (5) This day was by far the worst for our men. However, that day

longe gravissimus fuit. sed tamen hunc habuit eventum, ut eo die maximus numerus hostium vulneraretur atque interficeretur, ut se sub ipso vallo constipaverant recessumque primis ultimi non dabant. (6) paulum quidem intermissa flamma et quodam loco turri adacta et contingente vallum, tertiae cohortis centuriones ex eo, quo stabant, loco recesserunt suosque omnes removerunt, nutu vocibusque hostes, si introire vellent, vocare coeperunt. quorum progredi ausus est nemo. (7) tum ex omni parte lapidibus coniectis deturbati turrisque succensa est.

44 (1) Erant in ea legione fortissimi viri centuriones, qui primis ordinibus adpropinquarent, Titus Pullo et Lucius Vorenus. (2) hi perpetuas inter se controversias habebant, uter alteri anteferretur, omnibusque annis de loco summis simultatibus contendebant. (3) ex his Pullo, cum acerrime ad munitiones pugnaretur, "quid dubitas," inquit, "Vorene? aut quem locum probandae virtutis tuae ex<s>pectas? hic dies de nostris controversiis iudicabit." (4) haec cum dixisset, procedit extra munitiones, quaeque hostium pars confertissima est visa, eam inrumpit. (5) ne Vorenus quidem tum sese vallo continet, sed omnium veritus existimationem subsequitur. (6) tum mediocri spatio relicto Pullo pilum in hostes inmittit atque unum ex multitudine procurrentem traicit. quo percusso exanimatoque hunc scutis protegunt hostes, in illum universi tela coniciunt neque dant regrediendi facultatem. (7) transfigitur scutum Pulloni et verutum in balteo defigitur. (8) avertit hic casus vaginam et gladium educere conanti dextram moratur manum impeditumque hostes circumsistunt. (9) succurrit inimicus illi Vorenus et laboranti subvenit. (10) ad hunc se confestim a Pullone omnis multitudo convertit. (11) illum veruto transfixum arbitrantur. (12) gladio comminus rem gerit Vorenus atque uno interfecto reliquos paulum propellit. (13) dum cupidius instat, in locum deiectus inferiorem concidit. huic rursus circumvento subsidium fert Pullo, atque ambo

also saw a great number of the enemy wounded and even killed, since they got stuck under the rampart and the men in the rear did not leave room for the first group to fall back. (6) When the fire had died down a little, in one place an enemy tower was moved up to touch the rampart. The centurions of the third cohort fell back from where they were stationed and moved all their men out. They then began to call out the enemy with gestures and shouts, asking whether they wanted to come in. None of them dared to advance. (7) Then they were struck by stones thrown from every direction and the tower was set on fire.

44 (1) In this legion were Titus Pullo and Lucius Vorenus, extremely brave men, centurions who were nearing the first rank. (2) They were constantly debating which of them should outrank the other, and every year they competed for rank with fierce rivalry. (3) Pullo, when the fighting at the fortifications was at its most intense, said, "Why do you hesitate, Vorenus? What opportunity to prove your courage are you waiting for? This day will decide our rivalry!" (4) As soon as he said this, he advanced beyond the fortification and broke into the fighting where the enemy ranks seemed the densest. (5) Nor, indeed, did Vorenus stay within the rampart, but fearing the judgment of everyone else he followed close behind. (6) Fighting at close range, Pullo hurled his spear at the enemy and hit one of the mob as he was running. Since he was shaken and dazed, the enemy protected him with shields; they all hurled their weapons at Pullo and gave him no chance to retreat. (7) Pullo's shield was pierced and a dart stuck in his sword-belt. (8) This setback knocked his scabbard aside and obstructed his hand when he was trying to draw his sword, and the enemy surrounded him while he was hampered. (9) His rival Vorenus rushed to his aid and helped him as he was struggling. (10) Immediately the whole host turned upon him and away from Pullo. (11) He, they supposed, had been killed by the dart. (12) Vorenus fought up close with his sword; when he had killed one man he drove the rest back a bit. (13) However, when he pursued too eagerly, he tripped and fell into a hollow. Now Vorenus was the one surrounded, and

incolumes compluribus interfectis summa cum laude sese intra munitiones recipiunt. (14) sic fortuna in contentione et certamine utrumque versavit, ut alter alteri inimicus auxilio salutique esset neque diiudicari posset, uter utri virtute anteferendus videretur.

45 (1) Quanto erat in dies gravior atque asperior oppugnatio et maxime, quod magna parte militum confecta vulneribus res ad paucitatem defensorum pervenerat, tanto crebriores litterae nuntiique ad Caesarem mittebantur. quorum pars deprehensa in conspectu nostrorum militum cum cruciatu necabatur. (2) erat unus intus Nervius nomine Vertico, loco natus honesto, qui a prima obsidione ad Ciceronem perfugerat suamque ei fidem praestiterat. (3) hic servo spe libertatis magnisque persuadet praemiis, ut litteras ad Caesarem deferat. (4) has ille iaculo inligatas effert et Gallus inter Gallos sine ulla suspicione versatus ad Caesarem pervenit. (5) ab eo de periculis Ciceronis legionisque cognoscitur.

46 (1) Caesar acceptis litteris hora circiter unadecima diei statim nuntium in Bellovacos ad Marcum Crassum quaestorem mittit, cuius hiberna aberant ab eo milia passuum XXV. (2) iubet media nocte legionem proficisci celeriterque ad se venire. (3) exit cum nuntio Crassus. alterum ad Gaium Fabium legatum mittit, ut in Atrebatium fines legionem adducat, qua sibi iter faciendum sciebat. (4) scribit Labieno, si reip. commodo facere possit, cum legione ad fines Nerviorum veniat. reliquam partem exercitus, quod paulo aberat longius, non putat ex<s>pectandam. equites circiter quadringentos ex proximis hibernis colligit.

Pullo came to his aid. They killed several of the enemy and, both unharmed, retreated within the fortifications to great praise. (14) And so Fortune gave them each a turn in their rivalry and contest, such that despite their antagonism each one helped and even saved the other; it was impossible to judge which one seemed superior to the other in courage.

45 (1) The more difficult and violent the fighting grew each day (especially because a great number of our forces were wounded and the task had fallen to a small number of defenders), the more frequently reports and messengers were sent to Caesar. Some of them were captured and, in full view of our men, tortured and killed. (2) Within the camp there was a certain Nervian named Vertico, a well-born man who had fled to Cicero at the beginning of the siege and had proven his loyalty to him. (3) By holding out hope of freedom and great rewards he convinced a slave to bring a letter to Caesar. (4) The slave carried the letter by tying it fast to a javelin and, fitting in as if he were just another Gaul among Gauls, delivered it to Caesar without rousing suspicion. (5) This is how Caesar learned about the dangers to Cicero and the legions.

46 (1) Caesar received this letter around the eleventh hour and immediately sent a messenger to the quaestor Marcus Crassus, who was in the territory of the Bellovaci and whose winter camp was about twenty-five miles away from him. (2) He ordered the legion to set out at midnight and come to him at once. (3) Crassus set out as soon as he received the message. Caesar sent another dispatch to the legate Gaius Fabius ordering that he lead his legion to the borders of the Atrebates, where Caesar knew he himself would have to march. (4) He wrote to Labienus that he should come to the borders of the Nervii if he were able to do so without risking their common safety. Caesar did not think he should wait for the rest of the army, which was a little further away; he gathered about four hundred cavalry from the nearby winter camp.

47 (1) Hora circiter tertia ab antecursoribus de Crassi adventu certior factus eo die milia passuum XX progreditur. (2) Crassum Samarobrivae praeficit legionemque ei attribuit, quod ibi impedimenta exercitus, obsides civitatum, litteras publicas frumentumque omne, quod eo tolerandae hiemis causa devexerat, relinquebat. (3) Fabius, ut imperatum erat, non ita multum moratus in itinere cum legione occurrit. (4) Labienus interitu Sabini et caede cohortium cognita, cum omnes ad eum Treverorum copiae venissent, veritus ne, si ex hibernis fugae similem profectionem fecisset, hostium impetum sustinere non posset, praesertim quos recenti victoria efferri sciret, litteras Caesari remittit, quanto cum periculo legionem ex hibernis educturus esset, rem gestam in Eburonibus perscribit, docet omnes equitatus peditatusque copias Treverorum tria milia passuum longe ab suis castris consedisse.

48 (1) Caesar consilio eius probato, etsi opinione trium legionum deiectus ad duas redierat, tamen unum communis salutis auxilium in celeritate ponebat. (2) venit magnis itineribus in Nerviorum fines. ibi ex captivis cognoscit, quae apud Ciceronem gerantur quantoque in periculo res sit. (3) tum cuidam ex equitibus Gallis magnis praemiis persuadet, uti ad Ciceronem epistulam deferat. (4) hanc Graecis conscriptam litteris mittit, ne intercepta epistula nostra ab hostibus consilia cognoscantur. (5) si adire non possit, monet, ut tragulam cum epistula ad ammentum deligata intra munitiones castrorum abiciat. (6) in litteris scribit se cum legionibus profectum celeriter adfore; hortatur, ut pristinam virtutem retineat. (7) Gallus periculum veritus, ut erat praeceptum, tragulam mittit. (8) haec casu ad turrim adhaesit neque a nostris biduo animadversa tertio die a quodam milite conspicitur, dempta ad Ciceronem defertur. (9) ille perlectam in conventu militum recitat maximaque omnes

47 (1) After he learned of Crassus' arrival from his advance party around the third hour, he marched ahead twenty miles that day. (2) He placed Crassus in charge at Samarobriva and assigned him a legion, because he was leaving behind there the baggage of the army, some hostages of the states, public documents, and all the grain which he had brought for surviving the winter. (3) As he had been ordered, Fabius and his legion met Caesar on his march after a short delay. (4) When Labienus heard about the slaughter of Sabinus and the cohorts, since all the forces of the Treveri had come upon him, he was afraid that if he ordered a departure from his winter camp it would appear to be a retreat and that he would not be able to survive an attack by the enemy, especially since he knew their spirits would be high thanks to their recent victory. He sent a letter to Caesar indicating how much danger he would risk by leading his legion out of winter camp. He wrote, in addition, about what had happened among the Eburones, and told Caesar that all the cavalry and infantry of the Treveri had taken up position three miles from his own camp.

48 (1) Caesar approved of this plan. Although he was disappointed in his expectation he would have three legions and was reduced to only two, he nevertheless placed all hope for their common safety in his speed. (2) By long marches he came to the borders of the Nervii. There he learned from hostages what was happening at Cicero's camp and how much danger he was in. (3) He offered a large reward to convince one of the Gallic cavalry to take a letter to Cicero. (4) He wrote the letter he sent in Greek so that if it were intercepted the enemy would not learn our plans. (5) If the courier could not reach Cicero, Caesar advised, he should hurl a javelin within the fortifications of the camp with the letter bound to the thong. (6) Caesar wrote in the letter that he would come quickly with his legions and urged that Cicero maintain his long-standing courage. (7) The Gaul became afraid of the danger and, as he had been instructed, threw over the javelin. (8) By chance, the javelin got stuck in the rampart and went unnoticed by our men for two days; on the third day it was spotted by a certain soldier, who took it down and brought it to Cicero. (9) Once he had read it himself,

laetitia adficit. (10) tum fumi incendiorum procul videbantur, quae res omnem dubitationem adventus legionum expulit.

49 (1) Galli re cognita per exploratores obsidionem relinquunt, ad Caesarem omnibus copiis contendunt. (2) haec erant armata[e] circiter milia LX. Cicero data facultate Gallum ab eodem Verticone, quem supra demonstravimus, repetit, qui litteras ad Caesarem deferat. hunc admonet, iter caute diligenterque faciat. (3) perscribit in litteris hostes ab se discessisse omnemque ad eum multitudinem convertisse. (4) quibus litteris circiter media nocte Caesar adlatis suos facit certiores eosque ad dimicandum animo confirmat. (5) postera die luce prima movet castra et circiter milia passuum quattuor progressus trans vallem magnam et rivum multitudinem hostium conspicatur. (6) erat magni periculi res tantulis copiis iniquo loco dimicare. tum, quoniam obsidione liberatum Ciceronem sciebat, aequo animo remittendum de celeritate existimabat. (7) consedit et, quam aequissimo loco potest, castra communit atque haec, etsi erant exigua per se, vix hominum milium septem, praesertim nullis cum impedimentis, tamen angustiis viarum, quam maxime potest, contrahit, eo consilio, ut in summam contemptionem hostibus veniat. (8) interim speculatoribus in omnes partes dimissis explorat, quo commodissime itinere valles transire possit.

50 (1) Eo die parvulis equestribus proeliis ad aquam factis utrique sese suo loco continent: (2) Galli, quod ampliores copias, quae nondum convenerant, ex<s>pectabant, (3) Caesar, si forte timoris simulatione hostes in suum locum elicere posset, ut citra vallem pro castris proelio contenderet; si id efficere non posset, ut exploratis

Cicero read out the letter before the assembled soldiers and they were filled with the greatest joy. (10) Then the smoke of the fires was spotted far off, which dispelled any doubt about the arrival of the legions.

49 (1) When the Gauls learned of this development through their scouts, they abandoned the siege and marched toward Caesar with all their forces. (2) These numbered around sixty thousand. Cicero, now that he had the opportunity, asked that same Vertico I mentioned above to find him a Gaul to carry messages back to Caesar. Cicero advised him to make the journey cautiously and deliberately. (3) In these messages he wrote that the enemy had departed from his camp and that the whole multitude was headed for Caesar. (4) When Caesar received these letters in the middle of the night he apprised his troops of their content and inspired them with courage for fighting. (5) The next day at dawn he moved the camp and had advanced about four miles when he spied the enemy across a broad valley and river. (6) It was most dangerous to fight with such a small force on unfavorable terrain. For the time being, since he knew that Cicero had been freed from the siege, he thought he could ease up on his speed without worry. (7) He stopped there and set up camp in the most favorable place possible. Even though the camp was already small in itself, since there were barely seven thousand men (and even these without baggage), he compressed it further by narrowing the passageways as much as possible with the idea that this would inspire the greatest disdain in the enemy. (8) Meanwhile, he sent scouts in every direction to investigate the easiest path by which to cross the valley.

50 (1) That day there were minor cavalry skirmishes by the water but each side kept to its own position. (2) The Gauls did so because they were awaiting additional forces that had not yet arrived, (3) while Caesar wanted to see if he could draw the enemy toward him by feigning fear, so that he could engage them in front of his own camp on this side of the valley. If he were not able to do

itineribus minore cum periculo vallem rivumque transiret. (4) prima luce hostium equitatus ad castra accedit proeliumque cum nostris equitibus committit. (5) Caesar consulto equites cedere seque in castra recipere iubet, simul ex omnibus partibus castra altiore vallo muniri portasque obstrui atque in his administrandis rebus quam maxime concursari et cum simulatione agi timoris iubet.

51 (1) Quibus omnibus rebus hostes invitati copias traducunt aciemque iniquo loco constituunt, (2) nostris vero etiam de vallo deductis propius accedunt et tela intra munitionem ex omnibus partibus coniciunt (3) praeconibusque circummissis pronuntiari iubent, seu quis Gallus seu Romanus velit ante horam tertiam ad se transire, sine periculo licere. post id tempus non fore potestatem. (4) ac sic nostros contempserunt, ut obstructis in speciem portis singulis ordinibus caespitum, quod ea non posse introrumpere videbantur, alii vallum manu scindere, alii fossas complere inciperent. (5) tum Caesar omnibus portis eruptione facta equitatuque emisso celeriter hostes in fugam dat, sic uti omnino pugnandi causa resisteret nemo, magnumque ex iis numerum occidit atque omnes armis exuit.

52 (1) Longius prosequi veritus, quod silvae paludesque intercedebant – neque enim parvulo detrimento illorum locum relinqui videbat – , omnibus suis incolumibus eodem die ad Ciceronem pervenit. (2) institutas turres, testudines munitionesque hostium admiratur. legione producta cognoscit non decimum quemque esse reliquum militem sine vulnere; (3) ex his omnibus iudicat rebus, quanto

so, he could still cross the valley and river with minimal danger since he had scouted out the paths. (4) At dawn, the enemy cavalry approached the camp and engaged our cavalry in battle. (5) Caesar ordered the cavalry to give way intentionally and to retreat within the camp, and at the same time he ordered that the camp be fortified with a higher rampart on all sides and that the gates be closed; furthermore, he instructed that in doing these things the men should rush about as frantically as possible and create the appearance of fear.

51 (1) Drawn in by all these efforts, the enemy led their forces over and drew up their battle line in an unfavorable position. (2) Since our men had been led down from the rampart they approached nearer and hurled their weapons from all sides within the fortification. (3) They sent around heralds and ordered it to be announced that any man, Gaul or Roman, who wished to come over to them before the third hour would be allowed to without danger. After that point it would not be permitted. (4) The gates had been blocked with a just single layer of turf for show, and, since it seemed like they would be unable to break through the gates, the enemy had such disdain for our men that some began to pull down the rampart by hand and others began to fill in the trenches. (5) Then Caesar ordered his men to burst forth in attack from every gate and sent out the cavalry. He put the enemy to flight, and not a single one of them stood his ground to fight back. Caesar killed a great number of them and stripped them all of their arms.

52 (1) Caesar was afraid to pursue them too far, because there were woody and marshy areas in between, and he saw that the enemy had retreated at no small loss to their forces. He made his way that same day to the camp of Cicero with all his forces intact. (2) He marveled at the towers that had been built and the protective covers and other fortifications of the enemy. When the legion was brought out to meet him he saw that not even a tenth of the soldiers were left unwounded. (3) From all these signs he understood

cum periculo et quanta cum virtute res sint administratae. (4) Ciceronem pro eius merito legionemque conlaudat. centuriones singillatim tribunosque militum appellat, quorum egregiam fuisse virtutem testimonio Ciceronis cognoverat. de casu Sabini et Cottae certius ex captivis cognoscit. (5) postero die contione habita rem gestam proponit, milites consolatur et confirmat: (6) quod detrimentum culpa et temeritate legati sit acceptum, hoc aequiore animo ferendum docet, quod beneficio deorum immortalium et virtute eorum expiato incommodo neque hostibus diutina laetitia neque ipsis longior dolor relinquatur.

53 (1) Interim ad Labienum per Remos incredibili celeritate de victoria Caesaris fama perfertur, ut cum ab hibernis Ciceronis milia passuum abesset circiter LX eoque post horam nonam diei Caesar pervenisset, ante mediam noctem ad portas castrorum clamor oriretur, quo clamore significatio victoriae gratulatioque ab Remis Labieno fieret. (2) hac fama ad Treveros perlata Indutiomarus, qui postero die castra Labieni oppugnare decreverat, noctu profugit copiasque omnes in Treveros reducit. (3) Caesar Fabium cum legione in sua remittit hiberna, ipse cum tribus legionibus circum Samarobrivam trinis hibernis hiemare constituit, et quod tanti motus Galliae ex<s>titerant, totam hiemem ipse ad exercitum manere decrevit. (4) nam illo incommodo de Sabini morte perlato omnes fere Galliae civitates de bello consultabant, nuntios legationesque in omnes partes dimittebant, et quid reliqui consilii caperent atque unde initium belli fieret, explorabant nocturnaque in locis desertis concilia habebant. (5) neque ullum fere totius hiemis tempus sine sollicitudine Caesaris intercessit, quin aliquem de consiliis ac motu Gallorum nuntium acciperet. (6) in his ab Lucio Roscio quaestore, quem legioni tertiae decimae praefecerat,

how much danger they had been in and with what courage they had conducted themselves. (4) He praised Cicero and the legion for their service. He also recognized individually the centurions and military tribunes whose courage had been outstanding, as he learned from Cicero's account. He learned from some hostages about the disaster that befell Sabinus and Cotta. (5) The next day he held an assembly and informed the camp of what had happened; he offered consolation to the soldiers and raised their spirits. (6) The defeat had occurred because of the misconduct and rashness of a legate. It should be endured with a calm spirit, he said, because thanks to the immortal gods and their own courage the disaster had been avenged; no lasting joy was granted to the enemy, nor would their own grief be long-lived.

53 (1) Meanwhile, news of Caesar's victory was brought to Labienus by the Remi so quickly that, even though Labienus was about sixty miles away from Cicero's camp and Caesar had not reached it until after the ninth hour, before midnight there was a commotion at the gates of Labienus' camp signaling the victory and the Remi's congratulations for Labienus. (2) When the same news reached the Treveri, Indutiomarus, who had decided the day before to besiege Labienus' camp, fled under cover of night and led all his forces back to the territory of the Treveri. (3) Caesar sent Fabius and his legion back to their winter camp, and Caesar himself decided to remain for the winter with three legions in three camps around Samarobriva; because there were such disruptive events taking place in Gaul, he decided that he should remain there with the army. (4) For when news of Sabinus' disaster spread nearly all the Gallic states had started making plans for war and sent messengers and envoys to every region and tried to find out what plan the other states had and where the war would begin; they held meetings at night in out-of-the-way places. (5) Hardly a moment passed for Caesar that winter without anxiety or without him receiving news of some plot or uprising among the Gauls. (6) Among this correspondence he learned from the quaestor Lucius Roscius, whom he had left in charge of the thirteenth legion,

certior factus est magnas Gallorum copias earum civitatum, quae Ar<e>moricae appellantur, oppugnandi sui causa convenisse neque longius milibus passuum octo ab hibernis suis afuisse, (7) sed nuntio allato de victoria Caesaris discessisse, adeo ut fugae similis discessus videretur.

54 (1) At Caesar principibus cuiusque civitatis ad se evocatis alias territando, cum se scire, quae fierent, denuntiaret, alias cohortando magnam partem Galliae in officio tenuit. (2) tamen Senones, quae est civitas in primis firma et magnae inter Gallos auctoritatis, Cavarinum, quem Caesar apud eos regem constituerat, cuius frater Moritasgus adventu in Galliam Caesaris cuiusque maiores regnum obtinuerant, interficere publico consili conati, cum ille praesensisset ac profugisset, usque ad fines insecuti regno domoque expulerunt (3) et missis ad Caesarem satisfaciendi causa legatis, cum is omnem ad se senatum venire iussisset, dicto audientes non fuerunt. (4) tantum apud homines barbaros valuit esse aliquos repertos principes belli inferendi tantamque omnibus voluntatis commutationem attulit, ut praeter Haeduos et Remos – quos praecipuo semper honore Caesar habuit, alteros pro vetere ac perpetua erga p. R. fide, alteros pro recentibus Gallici belli officiis – nulla fere civitas fuerit non suspecta nobis. (5) idque adeo haud scio mirandumne sit cum conpluribus aliis de causis, tum maxime, quod, qui virtute belli omnibus gentibus praeferebantur, tantum se eius opinionis deperdidisse, ut a p.R. imperia perferrent, gravissime dolebant.

55 (1) Treveri vero atque Indutiomarus totius hiemis nullum tempus intermiserunt, quin trans Rhenum legatos mitterent, civitates sollicitarent, pecunias pollicerentur, magna parte exercitus nostri interfecta multo minorem superesse dicerent partem. (2) neque tamen ulli civitati Germanorum persuaderi potuit, ut

that large forces from the Gallic states called the Armoricae had gathered to besiege Roscius and were not more than eight miles from his camp. (7) However, when Caesar's victory was reported they retreated so hastily it seemed like they had been put to flight.

54 (1) Caesar summoned the leading men of each city. Some of those whom he summoned he terrified by informing them that he knew what they were doing; he kept a large part of Gaul in his allegiance by encouraging others. (2) Nevertheless, the Senones, a state of great power and authority among the Gauls, decided by popular decision to kill Cavarinus, whom Caesar had installed as their king; Cavarinus' brother Moritasgus had been king at the time of Caesar's arrival in Gaul and his ancestors had held the office before him. When Cavarinus anticipated their plan and fled, the Senones chased him all the way to their borders and expelled him from both his throne and his home. (3) They sent envoys to Caesar to apologize, but when he ordered that their entire senate present themselves to him, they did not obey. (4) The fact that they had found willing instigators of war swayed the barbarians and brought about such a change of heart that besides the Aedui and Remi – whom Caesar had always held in particular esteem, the former because of their long-standing and enduring loyalty to the Roman people, the latter because of their recent service during the Gallic War – there was scarcely a state we did not distrust. (5) For a number of reasons, I am not sure why anyone would be surprised by this, particularly since the Gauls used to surpass all other nations in their courage in war, and so they found it deeply painful to have lowered their reputation to the point that they must obey the commands of the Roman people.

55 (1) The Treveri and Indutiomarus did not let a day go by that winter without sending envoys across the Rhine, stirring up the states, promising rewards, and claiming that it would be easy to overcome what was left of our army now that they had killed the greater part. (2) Nevertheless, they were unable to persuade any

Rhenum transiret, cum se bis expertos dicerent, Ariovisti bello et Tenctherorum transitu, non esse amplius fortunam temptaturos. (3) hac spe lapsus Indutiomarus nihilo minus copias cogere, exercere, a finitimis equos parare, exsules damnatosque tota Gallia magnis praemiis ad se adlicere coepit. (4) ac tantam sibi iam his rebus in Gallia auctoritatem comparaverat, ut undique ad eum legationes concurrerent, gratiam atque amicitiam publice privatimque peterent.

56 (1) Ubi intellexit ultro ad se venire, altera ex parte Senones Carnutesque conscientia facinoris instigari, altera Nervios Atuatucosque bellum Romanis parare, neque sibi voluntariorum copias defore, si ex finibus suis progredi coepisset, armatum concilium indicit. (2) hoc more Gallorum est initium belli. quo lege communi omnes puberes et armati convenire coguntur. qui ex iis novissimus venit, in conspectu multitudinis omnibus cruciatibus adfectus necatur. (3) in eo concilio Cingetorigem, alterius principem factionis, generum suum, quem supra demonstravimus Caesaris secutum fidem ab eo non discessisse, hostem iudicat bonaque eius publiccat. (4) his rebus confectis in concilio pronuntiat arcessitum se a Senonibus et Carnutibus aliisque compluribus Galliae civitatibus. (5) huc iter facturum per fines Remorum eorumque agros populaturum ac, priusquam id faciat, castra Labieni oppugnaturum. quae fieri velit, praecipit.

57 (1) Labienus, cum et loci natura et manu munitissimis castris sese teneret, de suo ac legionis periculo nihil timebat, ne quam occasionem rei bene gerendae dimitteret, cogitabat. (2) itaque a

of the German states to cross the Rhine, since, as they said, they had tried that twice, in the war of Ariovistus and the migration of the Tenctheri, and that they would not tempt fate any more. (3) Although disappointed in this hope, Indutiomarus still began to gather and train troops, to request cavalry from neighboring peoples, and to invite exiles and convicts from all over Gaul to his cause with great rewards. (4) He had already gained such a reputation for himself throughout Gaul by these measures that envoys approached him from all over and sought his favor and friendship both publicly and privately.

56 (1) When he perceived that they were coming to him voluntarily – that, on the one hand, the Senones and the Carnutes were motivated by guilt for their crime and, on the other hand, the Nervii and Atuatuci were preparing a war against the Romans – and that he would not lack forces of volunteers if he began to advance beyond his own borders, Indutiomarus called an armed council. (2) This is the customary way for Gauls to declare war. According to a common law, all the young men are armed and called to assemble; whoever arrives last is tortured by all methods in full sight of the group and then killed. (3) At that assembly, Indutiomarus declared Cingetorix, the leader of the other faction and his own son-in-law (whom I mentioned earlier as having made a promise to Caesar not to betray him), a public enemy and confiscated his property. (4) When these things were done, he announced to the assembly that he had been called upon by the Senones and Carnutes and many other of the Gallic states. (5) He intended to march through the territory of the Remi and ravage their fields and, before he did that, besiege the camp of Labienus. He explained to the assembly what he wanted to be done.

57 (1) Labienus did not fear any danger to himself or his legion, since he was stationed in a camp that was well-fortified both by the nature of the place itself and by his efforts. He intended not to let any opportunity of success pass him by. (2) When he learned

Cingetorige atque eius propinquis oratione Indutiomari cognita, quam in concilio habuerat, circummittit ad finitimas civitates equitesque undique evocat. (3) his certum diem conveniendi dicit. interim prope cotidie cum omni equitatu Indutiomarus sub castris eius vagabatur, alias ut situm castrorum cognosceret, alias conloquendi aut territandi causa. equites plerumque omnes tela intra vallum coniciebant. (4) Labienus suos intra munitiones continebat timorisque opinionem, quibuscumque poterat rebus, augebat.

58 (1) Cum maiore in dies contemptione Indutiomarus ad castra accederet, nocte una intromissis equitibus omnium finitimarum civitatum, quos arcessendos curaverat, tanta diligentia omnes suos custodiis intra castra continuit, ut nulla ratione ea res enuntiari aut ad Treveros perferri posset. (2) interim ex consuetudine cotidiana Indutiomarus ad castra accedit atque ibi magnam partem diei consumit. equites tela coniciunt et magna cum contumelia verborum nostros ad pugnam evocant. (3) nullo ab nostris dato responso, ubi visum est, sub vesperum dispersi ac dissipati discedunt. (4) subito Labienus duabus portis omnem equitatum emittit. praecipit atque interdicit, perterritis hostibus atque in fugam coniectis – quod fore, sicut accidit, videbat – unum omnes petant Indutiomarum, neu quis quem alium prius vulneret, quam illum interfectum viderit, quod mora reliquorum spatium nactum illum effugere nolebat. (5) magna proponit iis, qui occiderint, praemia. summittit cohortes equitibus subsidio. (6) comprobat hominis consilium Fortuna, et cum unum omnes peterent, in ipso fluminis vado deprehensus Indutiomarus interficitur caputque eius refertur in castra. redeuntes equites, quos possunt, consectantur atque occidunt. (7) hac re cognita omnes Eburonum et Nerviorum, quae convenerant, copiae discedunt, pauloque habuit post id factum Caesar Galliam quietiorem.

from Cingetorix and his relatives about the speech Indutiomarus delivered in the assembly, he sent messengers around to the neighboring states and recalled cavalry from all over. (3) He set a specific day for them to convene. Meanwhile, nearly every day Indutiomarus would roam near his camp with his whole cavalry, sometimes scoping out the site of the camp, other times trying to parley or frighten the Romans. The cavalry would usually hurl weapons within the rampart. (4) Labienus held his men back within the fortifications and tried by every means possible to increase the enemy's belief that he was afraid.

58 (1) Each day Indutiomarus approached the camp with greater boldness. Within one night, all the cavalry which Labienus had taken the initiative to summon from neighboring states arrived, and he confined his own men inside the camp with guards so carefully that it could not be announced or reported to the Treveri by any means. (2) Meanwhile, Indutiomarus approached the camp, as was his daily routine, and spent the greater part of the day there. The cavalry threw weapons and called out our men to battle with great insults. (3) They received no response from our men, and when it seemed like the right time they departed and scattered. (4) Suddenly Labienus sent the entire cavalry forth through the two gates. He commanded that, when the enemy became terrified and fled – he knew this would happen, and it did – they should all pursue Indutiomarus himself. No one should wound any other man before they confirmed that Indutiomarus had been killed, because Labienus refused to let him escape by taking advantage of the delay if they pursued the others. (5) He promised great rewards to whoever killed Indutiomarus. (6) Fortune approved of his plan. They all pursued Indutiomarus alone; he was captured and killed at the very ford of the river, and his head was brought back to the camp. On their return, the cavalry chased and killed everyone they could. (7) When they learned all this, all the forces of the Eburones and Nervii that had assembled departed. For a short time after this, Caesar governed a quieter Gaul.

JULIUS CAESAR

THE GALLIC WAR BOOK VI

1 (1) Multis de causis Caesar maiorem Galliae motum ex<s>pectans per Marcum Silanum, Gaium Antistium Reginum, Titum Sextium legatos dilectum habere instituit. (2) simul ab Gnaeo Pompeio proconsule petit, quoniam ipse ad urbem cum imperio rei p. causa remaneret, quos ex Cisalpina Gallia consul[is] sacramento rogavisset, ad signa convenire et ad se proficisci iuberet, (3) magni interesse etiam in reliquum tempus ad opinionem Galliae existimans tantas videri Italiae facultates, ut, si quid esset in bello detrimenti acceptum, non modo id brevi tempore sarciri, sed etiam maioribus augeri copiis posset. (4) quod cum Pompeius et rei p. et amicitiae tribuisset, celeriter confecto per suos dilectu tribus ante exactam hiemem et constitutis et adductis legionibus duplicatoque earum cohortium numero, quas cum Quinto Titurio amiserat, et celeritate et copiis docuit, quid p.R. disciplina atque opes possent.

2 (1) Interfecto Indutiomaro, ut docuimus, ad eius propinquos a Treveris imperium defertur. illi finitimos Germanos sollicitare et pecuniam polliceri non desistunt. (2) cum a proximis impetrare non possent, ulteriores temptant. inventis nonnullis civitatibus iure iurando inter se confirmant obsidibusque de pecunia cavent. Ambigorem sibi societate et foedere adiungunt. (3) quibus rebus cognitis Caesar cum undique bellum parari videret, Nervios, Atuatucos ac Menapios adiunctis Cisrhenanis omnibus Germanis esse in armis, Senones ad imperatum non venire et cum Carnutibus finitimisque civitatibus consilia communicare, a Treveris Germanos crebris legationibus sollicitari, maturius sibi de bello cogitandum putavit.

1 (1) Caesar had many reasons to expect a more serious uprising in Gaul, and decided to hold a levy overseen by his legates Marcus Silanus, Gaius Antistius Reginus, and Titus Sextius. (2) At the same time, he asked the proconsul Gnaeus Pompey (since Pompey was staying near the city while maintaining his military command for the sake of the republic) that he order the troops he had levied from Cisalpine Gaul as consul to be convened and set out to meet Caesar. (3) Caesar thought it was of great importance for the future regarding public opinion in Gaul that the resources of Italy should appear so great that, if any loss should be sustained in war, not only could it be remedied quickly, but in fact be compensated for with even greater forces. (4) When Pompey had granted this (for the good of the republic and also their friendship), Caesar quickly completed the levy through his legates and three legions were formed and led to him before the end of the winter, and the number of cohorts which had been lost with Sabinus was doubled. Caesar thus demonstrated with both his speed and his forces what the discipline and power of the Roman people could accomplish.

2 (1) When Indutiomarus was killed, as I have described, his power was transferred by the Treveri to his relatives. They did not back down from agitating the neighboring Germans and promising them money. (2) Since they were not able to obtain anything from those nearest to them, they tried some who lived further away. They found some states who were interested and made an agreement with a mutual oath and took hostages as surety for the money. They also allied Ambiorix with themselves through an alliance and a treaty. (3) When Caesar learned of these things he saw that war was being prepared on all sides: the Nervii, Atuatuci, and Menapii were in arms, supported by all the Germans on this side of the Rhine; the Senones did not come when ordered and were discussing plans with the Carnutes and neighboring states, and the Germans were being recruited by the Treveri with frequent embassies. He decided that he should make plans for war sooner than he had expected.

3 (1) Itaque nondum hieme confecta proximis quattuor coactis legionibus de inproviso in fines Nerviorum contendit et, (2) priusquam illi aut convenire aut profugere possent, magno pecoris atque hominum numero capto atque ea praeda militibus concessa vastatisque agris in deditionem venire atque obsides sibi dare coegit. (3) eo celeriter confecto negotio rursus in hiberna legiones reduxit. (4) concilio Galliae primo vere, uti instituerat, indicto, cum reliqui praeter Senones, Carnutes Treverosque venissent, initium belli ac defectionis hoc esse arbitratus, ut omnia postponere videretur, concilium Luteciam Parisiorum transfert. (5) confines erant hi Senonibus civitatemque patrum memoria coniunxerant, sed ab hoc consilio afuisse existamabantur. (6) hac re pro suggestu pronuntiata eodem die cum legionibus in Senones proficiscitur magnisque itineribus eo pervenit.

4 (1) Cognito eius adventu Acco, qui princeps eius consilii fuerat, iubet in oppida multitudinem convenire. conantibus, priusquam id effici posset, adesse Romanos nuntiatur. (2) necessario sententia desistunt legatosque deprecandi causa ad Caesarem mittunt. adeunt per Haeduos, quorum antiquitus erat in fide civitas. (3) libenter Caesar petentibus Haeduis dat veniam excusationemque accipit, quod aestivum tempus instantis belli, non quaestionis esse arbitrabatur. (4) obsidibus imperatis centum hos Haeduis custodiendos tradit. (5) eodem Carnutes legatos obsidesque mittunt usi deprecatoribus Remis, quorum erant in clientela. eadem ferunt responsa. (6) peragit concilium Caesar equitesque imperat civitatibus.

3 (1) And so before the winter had even ended, Caesar consolidated the four closest legions and marched without warning into the territory of the Nervii. (2) Before they were able to either organize or flee, after capturing a large number of cattle and people and offering them as loot to his soldiers and wasting the fields, he compelled them to surrender and give him hostages. (3) That task was swiftly accomplished and Caesar led his legions back to their winter camps. (4) He summoned a council of Gaul at the beginning of the spring, as was his established practice. When the remainder besides the Senones, Carnutes, and Treveri came, he decided that this was the beginning of war and revolt and transferred the council to Lutetia in the land of the Parisii so that it would seem like he was setting everything else aside. (5) The Parisii bordered the Senones and had allied with their state in the previous generation but were believed to be uninvolved in this uprising. (6) Caesar announced this from the tribunal and, on that same day, set out against the Senones with his legions and arrived in their territory by long marches.

4 (1) When he learned of Caesar's approach, Acco, the leader of the plot, ordered the people to gather in the towns. They tried to do so but the arrival of the Romans was announced to them before they could. (2) There was no choice but to abandon their plan, and they sent envoys to Caesar to ask forgiveness. They approached him through the Aedui, whose state had been loyal to Caesar for a long time. (3) When the Aedui asked, he freely granted pardon and accepted their explanation since he thought the summer was the time for an impending war, not for an investigation. (4) Caesar demanded one hundred hostages and handed them over to be guarded by the Aedui. (5) At the same time, the Carnutes sent envoys and hostages; they used the Remi as mediators, since the Carnutes were their dependents. (6) Caesar concluded the council and ordered the states to contribute cavalry.

5 (1) Hac parte Galliae pacata totus et mente et animo in bellum Treverorum et Ambiorigis insistit. (2) Cavarinum cum equitatu Senonum secum proficisci iubet, ne quis aut ex huius iracundia aut ex eo, quod meruerat, odio civitatis motus existat. (3) his rebus constitutis, quod pro explorato habebat Ambiorigem proelio non esse contenturum, reliqua eius consilia animo circumspiciebat. (4) erant Menapii propinqui Eburonum finibus, perpetuis paludibus silvisque muniti, qui uni ex Gallia de pace ad Caesarem legatos numquam miserant. cum his esse hospitium Ambiorigi sciebat. (5) item per Treveros venisse Germanis in amicitiam cognoverat. haec prius illi detrahenda auxilia existimabat, quam ipsum bello lacesseret, ne desperata salute aut se in Menapios abderet, aut cum Transrhenanis congredi cogeretur. (6) hoc inito consilio totius exercitus impedimenta ad Labienum in Treveros mittit duasque ad eum legiones proficisci iubet. (7) ipse cum legionibus expeditis quinque in Menapios proficiscitur. illi nulla coacta manu loci praesidio freti in silvas paludesque confugiunt suaque eodem conferunt.

6 (1) Caesar partitis copiis cum Gaio Fabio legato et M. Crasso quaestore celeriterque effectis pontibus adit tripertito, aedificia vicosque incendit, magno pecoris atque hominum numero potitur. (2) quibus rebus coacti Menapii legatos ad eum pacis petendae causa mittunt. (3) ille obsidibus acceptis hostium se habiturum numero confirmat, si aut Ambiorigem aut eius legatos finibus suis recepissent. (4) his confirmatis rebus Commium Atrebatem cum equitatu custodis loco in Menapiis relinquit. ipse in Treveros proficiscitur.

5 (1) Since this part of Gaul was now quiet, Caesar dedicated his whole mind and spirit to the war with the Treveri and Ambiorix. (2) He ordered Cavarinus to accompany him along with the cavalry of the Senones, lest any uprising break out because of Cavarinus' hot temper or the hatred he had incurred in that state. (3) When these things had been arranged, since he considered it certain that Ambiorix was not going to rush into battle, Caesar started thinking over his other plans. (4) The Menapii were neighbors of the Eburones and were protected by endless marshes and forests; they alone of the Gauls had never sent envoys to Caesar to make peace. Caesar knew that they had a relationship of hospitality with Ambiorix. (5) He also learned that, through the Treveri, they had made friends of the Germans. Caesar decided that he needed to deprive Ambiorix of this support before provoking him to war, lest in despair for his safety he either hide among the Menapii or be driven to join with the peoples beyond the Rhine. (6) Once Caesar had decided upon this plan he sent the baggage of the whole army to Labienus, who was in the territory of the Treveri, and ordered the legions to proceed to meet him. (7) Caesar himself set out with five light-armed legions against the Menapii. The Menapii placed their trust in the natural fortification of their location and did not assemble a regular army; they fled into the woods and swamps and brought all their possessions there.

6 (1) Caesar divided his forces with the legate Gaius Fabius and the quaestor Marcus Crassus. Bridges were built quickly and Caesar led his three divisions in attack. They burned the houses and the villages and captured a large number of cattle and men. (2) Boxed in by Caesar's assault, the Menapii sent envoys to him to seek peace. (3) Caesar accepted hostages from them and made it clear that he would count them among his enemies if they received either Ambiorix or his envoys within their borders. (4) Once these things were settled he left Commius of the Atrebates with some cavalry as a guard over the Menapii. Caesar himself proceeded against the Treveri.

7 (1) Dum haec a Caesare geruntur, Treveri magnis coactis peditatus equitatusque copiis Labienum cum una legione, quae in eorum finibus hiemabat, adoriri parabant. (2) iamque ab eo non longius bidui via aberant, cum duas venisse legiones missu Caesaris cognoscunt. (3) positis castris a milibus passuum quindecim auxilia Germanorum ex<s>pectare constituunt. (4) Labienus hostium cognito consilio sperans temeritate eorum fore aliquam dimicandi facultatem, praesidio quinque cohortium impedimentis relicto cum XXV cohortibus magnoque equitatu contra hostem proficiscitur et mille passuum intermisso spatio castra communit. (5) erat inter Labienum atque hostem difficili transitu flumen ripisque praeruptis. hoc neque ipse transire habebat in animo neque hostes transituros existimabat. (6) augebatur auxiliorum cotidie spes. loquitur in consilio palam, quoniam Germani adpropinquare dicantur, sese suas exercitusque fortunas in dubium non devocaturum et postero die prima luce castra moturum. (7) celeriter haec ad hostes deferuntur, ut ex magno Gallorum equitum numero nonnullos Gallicis rebus favere natura cogebat. (8) Labienus noctu tribunis militum primisque ordinibus convocatis, quid sui sit consilii, proponit et, quo facilius hostibus timoris det suspicionem, maiore strepitu et tumultu quam p. R. fert consuetudo castra moveri iubet. his rebus fugae similem profectionem efficit. (9) haec quoque per exploratores ante lucem in tanta propinquitate castrorum ad hostes deferuntur.

8 (1) Vix agmen novissimum extra munitiones processerat, cum Galli cohortati inter se ne speratam praedam ex manibus dimitterent – longum esse perterritis Romanis Germanorum auxilium ex<s>pectare, neque suam pati dignitatem, ut tantis copiis tam exiguam manum, praesertim fugientem atque impeditam, adoriri non audeant – flumen transire et iniquo loco committere

7 (1) While Caesar was thus occupied, the Treveri organized large forces of infantry and cavalry prepared to attack Labienus and the legion which was wintering within their borders. (2) They were already within two days' march when they learned that two legions were approaching, sent by Caesar. (3) They set up camp fifteen miles away and decided to wait for backup from the Germans. (4) Labienus understood the enemy's plan and hoped that their rashness would give him an opportunity to attack. He left five cohorts to guard the baggage and advanced against the enemy with twenty-five cohorts and a large number of cavalry; he set up his own camp about a mile away. (5) Between Labienus and the enemy was a river that was difficult to cross and had steep banks. Labienus did not plan to try crossing it, nor did he think the enemy would attempt to do so. (6) The enemy's hope of reinforcements increased each day. Labienus announced publicly to a council that, since the Germans were said to be approaching, he would not risk his own fortunes and those of his army any further and the next day he would move his camp at dawn. (7) This was swiftly relayed to the enemy, since some of the Gallic cavalry were naturally disposed to favor Gallic interests. (8) That night, Labienus called together the military tribunes and the centurions of the first rank and explained to them what his plan was. He ordered them to strike camp more loudly and frantically than was typical for the Romans in order to more readily create the appearance of fear before the enemy; with this scheme he made their departure look like a retreat. (9) Because the camps were so close, these things were also reported to the enemy by their scouts before dawn.

8 (1) The rear of the division had scarcely advanced beyond the fortifications when the Gauls started urging each other not to let the rewards they hoped for slip through their hands. It was a waste of time, they said, to wait for reinforcement from the Germans when the Romans were terrified. Moreover, their pride would not allow them not to be bold and attack such a small band, particularly one that was hindered and in retreat, given their own substantial forces. They should cross the river and provoke battle

proelium non dubitant. (2) quae fore suspicatus Labienus, ut omnes citra flumen eliceret, eadem usus simulatione itineris placide progrediebatur. (3) tum praemissis paulum impedimentis atque in tumulo quodam collocatis "habetis" inquit "milites, quam petistis facultatem; (4) hostem impedito atque iniquo loco tenetis: praestate eandem nobis ducibus virtutem, quam saepenumero imperatori praestitistis, atque illum adesse et haec coram cernere existimate." (5) simul signa ad hostem converti aciemque derigi iubet et paucis turmis praesidio ad impedimenta dimissis reliquos equites ad latera disponit. (6) celeriter nostri clamore sublato pila in hostes inmittunt. illi, ubi praeter spem, quos fugere credebant, infestis signis ad se ire viderunt, impetum modo ferre non potuerunt ac primo concursu in fugam coniecti proximas silvas petierunt. (7) quos Labienus equitatu consectatus magno numero interfecto compluribus captis paucis post diebus civitatem recepit. nam Germani, qui auxilio veniebant, percepta Treverorum fuga sese domum contulerunt. (8) cum his propinqui Indutiomari, qui defectionis auctores fuerant, comitati eos ex civitate excesserunt. (9) Cingetorigi, quem ab initio permansisse in officio demonstravimus, principatus atque imperium est traditum.

9 (1) Caesar, postquam ex Menapiis in Treveros venit, duabus de causis Rhenum transire constituit. (2) quarum una erat, quod auxilia contra se Treveris miserant, altera, ne ad eos Ambiorix receptum haberet. (3) his constitutis rebus paulo supra eum locum, quo ante exercitum traduxerat, facere pontem instituit. (4) nota atque instituta ratione magno militum studio paucis diebus opus efficitur. (5) firmo in Treveris ad pontem praesidio relicto, ne

without hesitation, despite the unfavorable location. (2) Labienus had anticipated this and, continuing his plan to deceive them, was advancing calmly in hopes of drawing them beyond the river. (3) He sent the baggage a little bit ahead and had it gathered on a certain hill. Labienus then spoke: "You have the opportunity you were seeking, men. (4) You have the enemy tied up in an unfavorable location: show the same courage to your leaders that you have so many times showed to your general, and imagine that he is here with you, watching your exploits with his own eyes." (5) Labienus ordered his men to assemble in formation facing the enemy and to deploy the battle line at once. A few troops were left behind to guard the baggage and he positioned the rest of the cavalry on the flanks. (6) Our men quickly let out a battle cry and hurled their weapons at the enemy. When the enemy realized that, contrary to their expectations, the army that they had believed was in retreat was in fact attacking them, they were not even able to endure this first wave; at the first onslaught they were put to flight and made for the closest woods. (7) Labienus pursued with the cavalry. A large number of the enemy were killed and many more taken captive. After a few days, he took back control of the state, because the Germans, who had been coming to provide aid, turned back for home when they learned of the retreat of the Treveri. (8) The relatives of Indutiomarus, who had started the rebellion, followed them and withdrew from the state. (9) Supreme power and command were transferred to Cingetorix, who had remained loyal since the beginning, as I have said.

9 (1) After Caesar made his way from the Menapii to the Treveri, he decided to cross the Rhine for two reasons. (2) For one thing, the Germans had sent help to the Treveri against him; secondly, he wanted to prevent Ambiorix from having a refuge there. (3) Once he had settled upon this plan Caesar decided to build a bridge a little ways above the place where he had crossed with his army before. (4) Since the strategy was familiar and well-established, the task was accomplished in just a few days thanks to the great energy of the soldiers. (5) Caesar left a substantial guard at the

quis ab his subito motus oriretur, reliquas copias equitatumque traducit. (6) Ubii, qui ante obsides dederant atque in deditionem venerant, purgandi sui causa ad eum legatos mittunt, qui doceant neque ex sua civitate auxilia in Treveros missa neque ab se fidem laesam. (7) petunt atque orant, ut sibi parcat, ne communi odio Germanorum innocentes pro nocentibus poenas pendant; si amplius obsidum velit, dari pollicentur. (8) cognita Caesar causa re[p]perit ab Suebis auxilia missa esse, Ubi[h]orum satisfactionem accipit, aditus viasque in Suebos perquirit.

10 (1) Interim paucis post diebus fit ab Ubiis certior Suebos omnes in unum locum copias cogere atque iis nationibus, quae sub eorum sunt imperio, denuntiare, uti auxilia peditatus equitatusque mittant. (2) his cognitis rebus rem frumentarium providet, castris idoneum locum deligit. Ubiis imperat, ut pecora deducant suaque omnia ex agris in oppida conferant, sperans barbaros atque imperitos homines inopia cibariorum adductos ad iniquam pugnandi condicionem posse deduci; (3) mandat, ut crebros exploratores in Suebos mittant quaeque apud eos gerantur cognoscant. (4) illi imperata faciunt et paucis diebus intermissis referunt: Suebos omnes, posteaquam certiores nuntii de exercitu Romanorum venerint, cum omnibus suis sociorumque copiis, quas coegissent, penitus ad extremos fines se recepisse; (5) silvam esse ibi infinita magnitudine, quae appellatur Bacenis; hanc longe introrsus pertinere et pro nativo muro obiectam Cheruscos ab Sueborum Suebosque ab Cheruscorum iniuriis incursionibusque prohibere. ad eius silvae initium Suebos adventum Romanorum ex<s>pectare constituisse.

bridge on the side of the Treveri so that they would not rebel unexpectedly, and led across the rest of his troops and cavalry. (6) The Ubii, who had previously given hostages and surrendered to Caesar, sent legates to him to defend themselves; they explained that their state had sent no aid to the Treveri and that they had not betrayed Caesar's loyalty. (7) They asked and begged that he spare them and that they not pay the penalty for his general hatred of the Germans, being treated as guilty even though they were innocent. If Caesar wanted more hostages, they promised they would give them. (8) Caesar investigated their claim and learned that the aid had been sent by the Suebi; he accepted the solution proposed by the Ubii and researched the approaches and routes to the territory of the Suebi.

10 (1) A few days later, while he was working on that, Caesar learned from the Ubii that the Suebi had gathered all their forces in one place and that they were demanding that the states under their authority send auxiliary forces, both infantry and cavalry. (2) When Caesar learned about this he made provisions for the grain supply and chose a suitable location for camp. He ordered the Ubii to contribute livestock and to bring all their possessions from the fields into the towns, hoping that the Suebi, being ignorant barbarians, could be compelled by the lack of food to fight despite the unfavorable circumstances. Caesar instructed the Ubii to send scouts at frequent intervals and to find out what was afoot among them. (4) The Ubii did as instructed and a few days later reported back: once fairly reliable reports about the presence of the Roman army had reached them, all the Suebi had retreated to the far reaches of their territory with their own forces and those they had demanded from their allies. (5) There was an enormous forest there called the Bacenis; it stretched deep into their territory and functioned like a natural wall preventing the Cherusci from the attacks and incursions of the Suebi, and vice-versa. The Suebi had decided to wait for the Romans' arrival at the edge of this forest.

11 (1) Quoniam ad hunc locum perventum est, non alienum esse videtur de Galliae Germaniaeque moribus et, quo differant hae nationes inter sese, proponere. (2) in Gallia non solum in omnibus civitatibus atque in omnibus pagis partibusque, sed p<a>ene etiam in singulis domibus factiones sunt earumque factionum sunt principes, (3) qui summam auctoritatem eorum iudicio habere existimantur, quorum ad arbitrium iudiciumque summa omnium rerum consiliorumque redeat. (4) idque eius rei causa antiquitus institutum videtur, ne quis ex plebe contra potentiorem auxilii egeret. suos enim quisque opprimi et circumveniri non patitur neque, aliter si faciat, ullam inter suos habet auctoritatem. (5) haec eadem ratio est in summa totius Galliae; namque omnes civitates in partes divisae sunt duas.

12 (1) Cum Caesar in Galliam venit, alterius factionis principes erant Haedui, alterius Sequani. (2) hi cum per se minus valerent, quod summa auctoritas antiquitus erat in Haeduis magnaeque eorum erant clientelae, Germanos atque Ariovistum sibi adiunxerant eosque ad se magnis iacturis pollicitationibusque perduxerant. (3) proeliis vero conpluribus factis secundis atque omni nobilitate Haeduorum interfecta tantum potentia antecesserant, (4) ut magnam partem clientium ab Haeduis ad se traducerent obsidesque ab his principum filios acciperent et publice iurare cogerent nihil se contra Sequanos consilii inituros, et partem finitimi agri per vim occupatam possiderent Galliaeque totius principatum obtinerent. (5) qua necessitate adductus Diviciacus auxilii petendi causa Romam ad senatum profectus infecta re redierat. (6) adventu Caesaris facta commutatione rerum, obsidibus Haeduis redditis, veteribus clientelis restitutis, novis per Caesarem comparatis, quod ii, qui se ad eorum amicitiam adgregaverant, meliore condicione

11 (1) Since we have arrived at this point, it seems like a good time to explain the customs of Gaul and Germany and how these nations are different from each other. (2) In Gaul there are factions not only in every state and every district and region, but practically in every individual household. (3) The leaders of these factions are those who are thought to have the most authority according to the judgment of their countrymen, and so the final decision in all matters and plans is referred to their mediation and judgment. (4) This system seems to have been established long ago so that no one among common people lacks assistance against the more powerful; each man refuses to allow his people to be oppressed or constrained since otherwise he would have no authority among his own associates. This same principle applies in Gaul as a whole, for all the states can be divided into two factions.

12 (1) When Caesar arrived in Gaul, the Aedui were the leaders of one faction and the Sequani the other. (2) The latter were not particularly strong on their own, since the greatest authority had traditionally belonged to the Aedui (and the Aedui had many clients); accordingly, the Sequani had allied with the Germans and Ariovistus and secured their loyalty with abundant gifts and promises. (3) But after numerous victories in battle and, furthermore, the slaughter of the entire nobility of the Aedui, the Sequani then surpassed them in power so much (4) that they induced most of the clients of the Aedui to join them instead and received the children of their leaders as hostages and compelled them to swear publicly that they would not take any action against the Sequani. Furthermore, the Sequani occupied part of the neighboring territory, which they had gained by force, and secured the leadership of all Gaul. (5) It was because of this situation that Diviciacus went to Rome to seek aid, but had returned to Gaul without success. (6) When Caesar arrived in Gaul the situation changed. The hostages were returned to the Aedui; their old clients were restored and new ones were added through Caesar's influence, because those who flocked to their friendship saw that they enjoyed better conditions and fairer rule. Since the

atque aequiore imperio se uti videbant, reliquis rebus eorum gratia dignitateque amplificata Sequani principatum dimiserant. (7) in eorum locum Remi successerant. quos quod adaequare apud Caesarem gratia intellegebatur, ii, qui propter veteres inimicitias nullo modo cum Haeduis coniungi poterant, se Remis in clientelam dicabant. (8) hos illi diligenter tuebantur. ita et novam et repente collectam auctoritatem tenebant. (9) eo tum statu res erat, ut longe principes haberentur Haedui, secundum locum dignitatis Remi obtinerent.

13 (1) In omni Gallia eorum hominum, qui aliquo sunt numero atque honore, genera sunt duo. nam plebes paene servorum habetur loco, quae nihil audet per se, nullo adhibetur consilio. (2) plerique cum aut aere alieno aut magnitudine tributorum aut iniuria potentiorum premuntur, sese in servitutem dicant. (3) nobilibus in hos eadem omnia sunt iura, quae dominis in servos. sed de his duobus generibus alterum est druidum, alterum equitum. (4) illi rebus divinis intersunt, sacrificia publica ac privata procurant, religiones interpretantur. ad hos magnus adulescentium numerus disciplinae causa concurrit magnoque hi sunt apud eos honore. (5) nam fere de omnibus controversiis publicis privatisque constituunt, et si quod est admissum facinus, si caedes facta, si de hereditate, de finibus controversia est, idem decernunt, praemia poenasque constituunt. (6) si qui aut privatus aut populus eorum decreto non stetit, sacrificiis interdicunt. (7) haec poena apud eos est gravissima. quibus ita est interdictum, hi numero impiorum ac sceleratorum habentur, his omnes decedunt, aditum eorum sermonemque defugiunt, ne quid ex contagione in incommodi accipiant, neque his petentibus ius redditur neque honos ullus communicatur. (8) his autem omnibus druidibus praeest unus, qui summam inter eos habet auctoritatem. (9) hoc mortuo aut, si qui ex reliquis excellit dignitate, succedit aut, si sunt plures pares, suffragio druidum

favor and position of the Aedui were once again increased in all respects, the Sequani lost their pre-eminence. (7) The Remi succeeded in their place. Since it was clear that the Remi were equal to the Aedui in Caesar's favor, those who were not able to ally with the Aedui because of some long-standing hostility declared themselves clients of the Remi. (8) The Remi protected these peoples diligently, and in this way maintained their new and suddenly acquired authority. (9) The state of things at this time was such that the Aedui were considered the chief people by far and the Remi held second place in status.

13 (1) In all of Gaul there are two classes of men who are considered of any importance and honor. For the common people are basically slaves; they dare to do nothing on their own and are invited to no deliberations. (2) Since the majority of them are in debt or overwhelmed by the amount of tribute owed or by abuse at the hands of the powerful, they say that they are in servitude. (3) Indeed, the rights the nobility possess over them are the same as owners have over slaves. But, turning back to the two classes: one is the class of Druids, the other of knights. (4) The former are concerned with religious matters; they oversee public and private sacrifices and interpret questions of religion. A large number of young people flock to them for instruction, and the Druids hold great honor among the Gallic people. (5) For they adjudicate nearly all public and private disputes, and when any crime is confessed or someone is murdered, or if there is any dispute about inheritance or borders, they decide these cases and set the rewards or penalties. (6) If anyone does not abide by their decision, whether a private individual or a group of people, the Druids bar them from sacrifices. (7) This is their most severe punishment. Those who have been barred in this way are considered impious and criminal; everyone avoids them, and they receive no justice or honor when they seek it. (8) One of the Druids outranks all the rest and has the ultimate authority among them. (9) When he dies, if one of the surviving group excels the rest in worthiness he will succeed the deceased; if there are a number of equals the

adlegitur. nonnumquam etiam armis de principatu contendunt. (10) hi certo anni tempore in finibus Carnutum, quae regio totius Galliae media habetur, considunt in loco consecrato. huc omnes undique, qui controversias habent, conveniunt eorumque decretis iudiciisque parent. (11) disciplina in Britannia reperta atque inde in Galliam translata esse existimatur, (12) et nunc qui diligentius eam rem cognoscere volunt, plerumque illo discendi causa proficiscuntur.

14 (1) Druides a bello abesse consuerunt neque tributa una cum reliquis pendunt. militiae vacationem omniumque rerum habent inmunitatem. (2) tantis excitati praemiis et sua sponte multi in disciplinam conveniunt et a parentibus propinquisque mittuntur. (3) magnum ibi numerum versuum ediscere dicuntur. itaque annos nonnulli vicenos in disciplina permanent. neque fas esse existimant ea litteris mandare, cum in reliquis fere rebus, publicis privatisque rationibus, Graecis utantur litteris. (4) id mihi duabus de causis instituisse videntur, quod neque in vulgum disciplinam efferi velint neque eos, qui discunt, litteris confisos minus memoriae studere, quod fere plerisque accidit, ut praesidio litterarum diligentiam in perdiscendo ac memoriam remittant. (5) in primis hoc volunt persuadere, non interire animas, sed ab aliis post mortem transire ad alios, atque hoc maxime ad virtutem excitari putant metu mortis neglecto. (6) multa praeterea de sideribus atque eorum motu, de mundi ac terrarium magnitudine, de rerum natura, de deorum immortalium vi ac potestate disputant et iuventuti tradunt.

matter is referred to a vote among the Druids. On more than one occasion they have decided the leadership with arms. (10) The Druids meet at a set time of year in a consecrated place within the territory of the Carnutes, which is considered the center of Gaul. Everyone who has a dispute comes here from all over Gaul and they obey the decisions and judgments of the Druids. (11) This practice seems to have been discovered in Britain and translated from there into Gaul. (12) Even now, those who wish to study the subject thoroughly often travel to Britain to learn.

14 (1) The Druids customarily do not engage in warfare, nor do they pay tribute together with everyone else. They are exempt from all military service. (2) Motivated by such great rewards, many of them willingly come together to study or are sent by their parents and relatives. (3) It is said that they learn a large number of verses in their studies, and so some spend as many as twenty years studying. They believe that it is not right to put these things in writing, although in nearly all other contexts, both public and private, they use Greek. (4) I believe they do this for two reasons. First, because they do not want the knowledge to become common and second, because they do not want those who learn it to rely more on the written version than their memory, since it does frequently happen that they lose their ability to study diligently and remember through the crutch of writing. (5) Among their most important teachings is that souls do not perish, but rather after death they pass into someone else. They think that this is the greatest incentive to display virtue, and death is not considered fearful to them. (6) They also have many debates about the stars and their movements, the size of the world and the earth, the way the universe works, and the strength and power of the immortal gods, and they hand down this tradition to their youth.

15 (1) Alterum genus est equitum. hi, cum est usus atque aliquod bellum incidit – quod ante Caesaris adventum fere quotannis accidere solebat, uti aut ipsi iniurias inferrent aut inlatas propulsarent –, omnes in bello versantur, atque eorum ut quisque est genere copiisque amplissimus, (2) ita plurimos circum se ambactos clientesque habet. hanc unam gratiam potentiam noverunt.

16 (1) Natio est omnis Gallorum admodum dedita religionibus, atque ob eam causam, (2) qui sunt adfecti gravioribus morbis quique in proeliis periculisque versantur, aut pro victimis homines immolant aut se immolaturos vovent, administrisque ad ea sacrificia druidibus utuntur, (3) quod, pro vita hominis nisi hominis vita reddatur, non posse deorum inmortalium numen placari arbitrantur, publiceque eiusdem generis habent instituta sacrificia. (4) alii inmani magnitudine simulacra habent, quorum contexta viminibus membra vivis hominibus complent. quibus succensis circumventi flamma exanimantur homines. (5) supplicia eorum, qui in furto aut latrocinio aut aliqua noxia, sint comprehensi, gratiora dis immortalibus esse arbitrantur. sed cum eius generis copia deficit, etiam ad innocentium supplicia descendunt.

17 (1) Deum maxime Mercurium colunt. huius sunt plurima simulacra, hunc omnium inventorem artium ferunt, hunc viarum atque itinerum ducem, hunc ad quaestus pecuniae mercaturasque habere vim maximam arbitrantur. (2) post hunc Apollinem et Martem et Iovem et Minervam. de his eandem fere quam reliquae gentes habent opinionem: Apollinem morbos depellere, Minvervam operum atque artificiorum initia tradere, Iovem imperium caelestium tenere, Martem bella regere. (3) huic, cum proelio dimicare constituerunt, ea, quae bello ceperint, plerumque devovent. cum superaverint, animalia capta immolant reliquasque

15 (1) The other class is the class of knights. When there is a need - that is, when a war breaks out, which usually happened every year before Caesar's arrival, since they themselves would be waging war or defending themselves against attacks – they all commit themselves to the war, and, each man who is especially rich in family prestige or resources surrounds himself with servants and clients accordingly.

16 (1) The whole nation of Gauls is deeply dedicated to religious observance. (2) For this reason, those who are afflicted with serious illnesses or who suffer setbacks in war or are otherwise in danger either conduct human sacrifice or make a vow that they will do so. They employ the Druids to oversee these sacrifices. (3) They do this because they believe that it is not possible to appease the divinity of the gods unless the life of a man is given over in exchange for the life of another. (4) Some of them possess enormous figures, the limbs of which are woven out of twigs. These they fill with people who are still alive. They set these structures on fire and the men, consumed by the flame, are burned alive. (5) They believe that the punishment of those who have been caught in theft or banditry or some other crime is more pleasing to the gods, but when the supply of guilty men runs low, they resort to the punishment of the innocent.

17 (1) They worship Mercury most of all among the gods. There are many images of him; they consider him the inventor of all arts and the protector of all roads and paths, and they believe that he has the greatest power to influence commerce and trade. (2) After him, they worship Apollo and Mars and Jupiter and Minerva. They have essentially the same beliefs about them as others do: Apollo wards off sickness, Minerva invented crafts and the skilled trades, Jupiter holds dominion over the heavens, and Mars rules over warfare. (3) When they have decided to fight a decisive battle, they generally vow everything they will seize in the war to Mars. When they are victorious, they sacrifice the animals they have captured and bring

res in unum locum conferunt. (4) multis in civitatibus harum rerum exstructos cumulos locis consecratis conspicari licet. (5) neque saepe accidit, ut neglecta quispiam religione aut capta apud se occultare aut posita tollere auderet, gravissimumque ei rei supplicium cum cruciatu constitutum est.

18 (1) Galli se omnes ab Dite patre prognatos praedicant idque ab druidibus proditum dicunt. (2) ob eam causam spatia omnis temporis non numero dierum, sed noctium finiunt. dies natales et mens[i]um et annorum initia sic observant, ut noctem dies subsequatur. (3) in reliquis vitae institutis hoc fere ab reliquis differunt, quod suos liberos, nisi cum adoleverunt, ut munus militiae sustinere possint, palam ad se adire non patiuntur filiumque puerili aetate in publico in conspectu patris adsistere turpe ducunt.

19 (1) Viri, quantas pecunias ab uxoribus dotis nomine acceperunt, tantas ex suis bonis aestimatione facta cum dotibus communicant. (2) huius omnis pecuniae coniunctim ratio habetur fructusque servantur. uter eorum vita superaverit, ad eum pars utriusque cum fructibus superiorum temporum pervenit. (3) viri in uxores sicuti in liberos vitae necisque habent potestatem, et cum pater familiae inlustriore loco natus decessit, eius propinqui conveniunt, et de morte si res in suspicionem venit, de uxoribus in servilem modum quaestionem habent, et si compertum est, igni atque omnibus tormentis excruciates interficiunt. (4) funera sunt pro cultu Gallorum magnifica et sumptuosa, omniaque, quae vivis cordi fuisse arbitrantur, in ignem inferunt, etiam animalia; ac paulo supra hanc memoriam servi et clientes, quos ab iis dilectos esse constabat, iustis fune<b>ribus confectis una cremabantur.

the rest of the spoils into one place. (4) In many states you can see heaping piles of these spoils in sacred places. (5) It does not often happen that someone utterly disregards religion and dares to hide some of these spoils for himself or to take away what has been left there; the sentence established for this is the most severe punishment by torture.

18 (1) The Gauls claim that they are all descended from Father Dis and they say that this tradition is handed down by the Druids. (2) For this reason, they count the passage of time not by the number of days, but by the number of nights. Likewise, they mark birthdays and the beginnings of months and years in such a way that the occasion is marked by sundown the night before. (3) In the rest of their habits they differ from nearly everyone else in that they do not allow their sons to approach them in public until they have reached the age when they are able to take on military service; they also say that is shameful for a son who is still a child to stand in view of his father in public.

19 (1) Whatever money husbands receive from their wives in the name of the dowry they make an estimate of and match it with the same amount from their own estates. (2) This is considered a joint account of their shared money and the interest is saved. Whichever of the couple lives longer retains both of their shares as well as any interest that has accrued during the previous years. (3) Husbands hold the power of life and death over their wives just as over their children. When a father of high social status dies, his relatives convene, and if there is anything suspicious about his death, they hold an inquisition of his wives in the same manner as slaves are interrogated. If anything is discovered, they torment and kill the women with fire and all means of torture. (4) Compared with their lifestyle, the funerals of the Gauls are grand and lavish. Everything thought to be dear to them while living is thrown into the fire, even animals. Up until quite recently, at the conclusion of the funeral rites they would also cremate the slaves and clients who were known to be beloved to the deceased.

20 (1) Quae civitates commodius suam rem publicam administrare existimantur, habent legibus sanctum, si quis quid de re p. a finitimis rumore ac fama acceperit, uti ad magistratum deferat neve cum quo alio communicet, (2) quod saepe homines temerarios atque imperitos falsis rumoribus terreri et ad facinus impelli et de summis rebus consilium capere cognitum est. (3) magistratus, quae visa sunt, occultant, quaeque esse ex usu iudicaverunt, multitudini produnt. de re p. nisi per concilium loqui non conceditur.

21 (1) Germani multum ab hac consuetudine differunt. nam neque druides habent, qui rebus divinis praesint, neque sacrificiis student. (2) deorum numero eos solos ducunt, quos cernunt et quorum aperte opibus iuvantur, Solem et Vulcanum et Lunam. reliquos ne fama quidem acceperunt. (3) vita omnis in venationibus atque in studiis rei militaris consistit; a parvis labori ac duritiae student. (4) qui diutissime impuberes permanserunt, maximam inter suos ferunt laudem: hoc ali[i] staturam, ali[i] vires nervosque confirmari putant. (5) intra annum vero vicesimum feminae notitiam habuisse in turpissimis habent rebus. cuius rei nulla est occultatio, quod et promiscue in fluminibus perluuntur et pellibus aut parvis renonum tegimentis utuntur, magna corporis parte nuda.

22 (1) Agri culturae non student, maiorque pars eorum victus in lacte, caseo, carne consistit. (2) neque quisquam agri modum certum aut fines habet proprios, sed magistratus ac principes in annos singulos gentibus cognationibusque hominum, quique una coierunt, quantum et quo loco visum est agri adtribuunt atque anno post alio transire cogunt. (3) eius rei multas adferunt

20 (1) Those states which are thought to govern themselves more appropriately have decreed by law that if anyone learns anything concerning the public interest from his neighbors by rumor or report, he should report it to a magistrate and should not discuss it with anyone else. (2) This is because it is well-known that hasty or inexperienced men can be terrified by false reports and are thus driven to crime or to plot about the most important affairs. (3) The magistrates conceal what seems appropriate to conceal and make known to the public only those things that they have deemed to be useful. Discussion of state affairs is not permitted except in an assembly.

21 (1) The Germans are very different in their way of life. They do not have Druids to oversee religious affairs, nor are they interested in holding sacrifices. (2) They count among the number of their gods only those whom they can actually perceive and by whose influence they are obviously helped: the sun, fire, and the moon. They have never even heard stories about the other gods. (3) Their whole way of life consists in hunting and military exercises; from childhood they are eager to undertake work and hardship. (4) Those who remain virgins the longest earn the highest praise among their cohort; some think that this increases one's stature and some think that it increases bodily strength and vigor. (5) Having sex with a woman before one's twentieth year is considered a great disgrace. There is no secrecy around the human body, since they bathe all together in the rivers and they wear hides or small deerskins as clothing, which leaves much of their bodies bare.

22 (1) They do not practice agriculture in any serious way, and most of their diet consists of milk, cheese, and meat. (2) No man has a tract of land or a property that belongs exclusively to him, but rather each year the magistrates and leaders assign land to the peoples and families who have assembled and determine how much land and what location are appropriate for each; the next year, they are compelled to move to another location. (3)

causas: ne adsidua consuetudine capti studium belli gerendi agri cultura commutent; ne latos fines parare studeant potentioresque humiliores possessionibus expellant; ne accuratius ad frigora atque aestus vitandos aedificent; ne qua oriatur pecuniae cupiditas, qua ex re factiones dissessionesque nascuntur; (4) ut animi aequitate plebem contineant, cum suas quisque opes cum potentissimis aequari videat.

23 (1) Civitatibus maxima laus est quam latissimi circum se vastatis finibus solitudines habere. (2) hoc proprium virtutis existimant, expulsos agris finitimos cedere neque quemquam prope se audere consistere. (3) simul hoc se fore tutiores arbitrantur repentinae incursionis timore sublato. (4) cum bellum civitas aut inlatum defendit aut infert, magistratus, qui ei bello praesint et vitae necisque habeant potestatem, deliguntur. (5) in pace nullus est communis magistratus, sed principes regionum atque pagorum inter suos ius dicunt controversiasque minuunt. (6) latrocinia nullam habent infamiam, quae extra fines cuiusque civitatis fiunt, atque ea iuventutis exercendae ac desidiae minuendae causa fieri praedicant. (7) atque ubi quis ex principibus in concilio dixit se ducem fore, qui sequi velint, profiteantur, consurgunt ii, qui et causam et hominem probant, suumque auxilium pollicentur atque a multitudine conlaudantur. (8) qui ex his secuti non sunt, in desertorum ac proditorum numero ducuntur, omniumque his rerum postea fides derogatur. (9) hospitem violare fas non putant. qui quacumque de causa ad eos venerunt, ab iniuria prohibent sanctosque habent, hisque omnium domus patent victusque communicatur.

They give several reasons for this practice: a fear that they will surrender to complacency and abandon their zeal for battle in favor of agriculture, or that they will become eager to expand their property and the more powerful will drive the less powerful from their property, or that they will build more carefully to avoid having to endure cold or heat, or that greed will arise, and from there factions and quarrels. (4) They also believe that this system keeps the common people content, since each man sees that his own wealth is equal to that of the most powerful.

23 (1) They praise most highly those states which are surrounded by the widest stretches of deserted land, which they create by laying waste to their borders. (2) They consider it a badge of honor that their neighbors have been driven out of their land and have abandoned it and that no one dares to settle near them. (3) They also think that this makes them safer since they do not have to fear a sudden attack. (4) When a state either defends itself against an attack or makes one itself, magistrates are chosen to lead the war, and they have the power of life and death. (5) There is no central office-holder in peacetime, but rather the leaders of the regions and districts work together to administer justice and settle conflicts. (6) Banditry is not considered shameful, provided that it happens outside the borders of one's own state; in fact, they claim that banditry is practiced to keep the youth occupied and discourage laziness. (7) And so one of the leading men will announce in an assembly that he will take charge and that those who are willing to follow him should declare it. Those who approve of both the plan and the man come together and promise to provide assistance, and they are praised by the masses. (8) Those who do not fall in line are considered deserters and traitors, and thereafter they lose the community's trust in all matters. (9) They think it is morally wrong to harm a guest. They consider anyone who has come to them for any reason untouchable, and they protect them from any harm; everyone's home is available to them and provisions are offered freely.

24 (1) Ac fuit antea tempus, cum Germanos Galli virtute superarent, ultro bella inferrent, propter hominum multitudinem agrique inopiam trans Rhenum colonias mitterent. (2) itaque ea, quae fertilissima Germaniae sunt loca circum Hercynium silvam, quam Eratostheni et quibusdam Gr<a>ecis fama notam esse video, quam illi Orcyniam appellant, Volcae Tectosages occupaverunt atque ibi consederunt. (3) quae gens ad hoc tempus his sedibus sese continet summamque habet iustitiae et bellicae laudis opinionem. (4) nunc quoniam in eadem inopia egestate patientia, qua Germani, permanent, eodem victu et cultu corporis utuntur. (5) Gallis autem provinciarum propinquitas et transmarinarum rerum notitia multa ad copiam atque usus largitur; (6) paulatim adsuefacti superari multisque victi proeliis ne se quidem ipsi cum illis virtute comparant.

25 (1) Huius Hercyniae silvae, quae supra demonstrata est, latitudo novem dierum iter expedito patet. non enim aliter finiri potest neque mensuras itinerum noverunt. (2) oritur ab Helvetiorum et Nemetum et Rauracorum finibus rectaque fluminis Danubii regione pertinet ad fines Dacorum et Anartium. (3) hinc se flectit sinistrorsus diversis a flumine regionibus multarumque gentium fines propter magnitudinem attingit. (4) neque quisquam est huius Germaniae, qui se [aut audisse] aut adisse ad initium eius silvae dicat, cum dierum iter LX processerit, aut quo ex loco oriatur, acceperit. (5) multaque in ea genera ferarum nasci constat, quae reliquis in locis visa non sint, ex quibus, quae maxime differant a ceteris et memoriae prodenda videantur, haec sunt.

24 (1) There was once a time when the Gauls surpassed the Germans in courage; they aggressively attacked them, and because of their population density and lack of land the Gauls sent colonies across the Rhine. (2) And so the Volcae Tectosages seized and settled in the most fertile parts of Germany, the area around the Hercynian Forest. (I note that Eratosthenes and some others of the Greeks were familiar with this area by report, although they called it the "Orcynian" Forest.) (3) The Volcae Tectosages inhabit this region to this day, and they have earned an excellent reputation for justice and military glory. (4) Even today they live under the same conditions of scarcity, poverty, and hardship as the Germans, and they follow the same diet and manner of dress. (5) For the Gauls, on the other hand, proximity to the provinces and experience with importing provide many goods, both indulgent and practical. (6) They gradually got used to being defeated, and because they were defeated in so many battles they do not even consider themselves to be the Germans' equals in bravery.

25 (1) The Hercynian Forest, which I mentioned above, is nine days' march across (if travelling light). It is not possible to describe its size any other way because they do not have other units of measure. (2) It begins in the territory of the Helvetii, Nemetes, and Raurici, runs parallel to the straight section of the Danube, and stretches to the territory of the Dacians and the Anartes. (3) From there it turns leftward and through regions away from the river, and because of its great size it reaches the territories of many peoples. (4) There is no one in this part of Germany who can say that he has heard about or seen for himself the edge of the forest - even if he has gone as far as sixty days' journey – or who knows where it begins. (5) It is well-known that many types of animals live here that cannot be found in other places. I will describe the ones which are the most different from other animals and, accordingly, should be catalogued.

26 (1) Est bos cervi figura, cuius a media fronte inter aures unum cornu existit excelsius magisque derectum his, quae nobis nota sunt, cornibus; (2) ab eius summo sicut palmae ramique late diffunduntur. (3) eadem est feminae marisque natura, eadem forma magnitudoque cornuum.

27 (1) Sunt item, quae appellantur alces. harum est consimilis capris figura et varietas pellium, sed magnitudine paulo antecedunt mutilaeque sunt cornibus et crura sine nodis articulisque habent. (2) neque quietis causa procumbunt neque, si quo adflictae casu conciderunt, erigere sese aut sublevare possunt. (3) his sunt arbores pro cubilibus. ad eas se adplicant atque ita paulum modo reclinatae quietem capiunt. (4) quarum ex vestigiis cum est animadversum a venatoribus, quo se recipere consuerint, omnes eo loco aut ab radicibus subruunt aut accidunt arbores, tantum ut summa species earum stantium relinquatur. (5) huc cum se consuetudine reclinaverunt, infirmas arbores pondere adfligunt atque una ipsae concidunt.

28 (1) Tertium est genus eorum, qui uri appellantur. hi sunt magnitudine paulo infra elephantos, specie et colore et figura tauri. (2) magna vis est eorum et magna velocitas; neque homini neque ferae, quam conspexerunt, parcunt. hos studiose foveis captos interficiunt. (3) hoc se labore durant adulescentes atque hoc genere venationis exercent, et qui plurimos ex his interfecerunt, relatis in publicum cornibus, quae sint testimonio, magnam ferunt laudem. (4) sed adsuescere ad homines et mansuefieri ne parvuli quidem excepti possunt. (5) amplitudo cornuum et figura et species multum a nostrorum boum cornibus differt. (6) haec studiose conquisita ab labris argento circumcludunt atque in amplissimis epulis pro poculis utuntur.

26 (1) There is an ox that is built like a stag. A single horn grows from its forehead, between its ears, which is taller and straighter than the horns of animals that are familiar to us. (2) From the top of this horn, branches stretch out wide like hands. (3) The male and the female of the species look the same, as the shape and size of their horns is identical.

27 (1) There are also animals called elk. Their shape and dappled coat are similar to those of goats, but they are a bit larger, do not have horns, and their legs do not have joints or ligaments. (2) They do not lie down to sleep nor are they able to pick themselves up and stand again if they fall down for some reason. (3) They use trees as beds; they lean against them and sleep like that, just barely reclining. (4) Hunters learn where they typically rest by following their tracks. They either dig around the trees at their roots or cut them just enough that the tops appear to be standing solidly. (5) When the elk lean against these as usual, they knock over the weakened trees with their weight and fall down with them.

28 (1) There is a third type of creature called the uri. These are a little bit smaller than elephants and have the appearance of a bull in both color and shape. (2) Their strength and speed are remarkable; they spare neither man nor beast whom they see. The Germans are able to kill them only with great difficulty, by trapping them in pits. (3) The youth train themselves and gain practice with this type of hunting; those who kill the most uri carry around the horns in public as a testament to their skill and earn great praise. (4) However, they cannot be domesticated or tamed, not even if they are captured while still young. (5) The size, shape, and appearance of their horns is quite different from the horns of our cattle. (5) These are highly sought after; the Germans encircle the rim with silver and use them as drinking vessels at their most lavish parties.

29 (1) Caesar postquam per Ubios explorates comperit Suebos sese in silvas recepisse, inopiam frumenti veritus, quod, ut supra demonstravimus, minime omnes Germani agri culturae student, constituit non progredi longius. (2) sed, ne omnino metum reditus sui barbaris tolleret atque ut eorum auxilia tardaret, reducto exercitu partem ultimam pontis, (3) quae ripas Ubiorum contingebat, in longitudinem pedum ducentorum rescindit atque in extremo ponte turrim tabulatorum quattuor constituit praesidiumque cohortium duodecim pontis tuendi causa ponit magnisque eum locum munitionibus firmat. ei loco praesidioque Gaium Volcacium Tullum adulescentem praefecit. (4) ipse, cum maturescere frumenta inciperent, ad bellum Ambiorigis profectus per Arduennam silvam, quae est totius Galliae maxima atque ab ripis Rheni finibusque Treverorum ad Nervios pertinet milibusque amplius quingentis in longitudinem patet, Lucium Minucium Basil[i]um cum omni equitatu praemittit, (5) si quid celeritate itineris atque o<p>portunitate temporis proficere possit. monet, ut ignes in castris fieri prohibeat, ne qua eius adventus procul significatio fiat. sese confestim subsequi dicit.

30 (1) Basil[i]us, ut imperatum est, facit. celeriter contraque omnium opinionem confecto itinere multos in agris inopinantes deprehendit. eorum indicio ad ipsum Ambiorigem contendit, quo in loco cum paucis equitibus esse dicebatur. (2) multum cum in omnibus rebus, tum in re militari potest Fortuna. nam magno accidit casu, ut in ipsum incautum etiam atque imparatum incideret priusque eius adventus ab omnibus videretur, quam fama ac nuntius adferretur. sic magnae fuit fortunae omni militari instrumento, quod circum se habebat, erepto raedis equisque comprehensis ipsum effugere mortem. (3) sed hoc quoque factum est, quod aedificio circumdato silva – ut sunt fere domicilia Gallorum, qui vitandi aestus causa plerumque silvarum ac fluminum petunt propinquitates – comites

29 (1) When Caesar learned from the Ubian scouts that the Suebi had retreated into the forest, he worried about a lack of food since, as I mentioned previously, none of the Germans really practice agriculture. He decided not to advance. (2) Even so, he did not want the barbarians to lose all fear of his return, and he also wished to slow their reinforcements. (3) He withdrew his army and tore down a 200-foot section of the bridge at the far end, where it reached the bank on the side of the Ubii. At the other end of the bridge he built a four-story tower; he stationed a guard of twelve cohorts there to protect the bridge and strengthened the location with additional fortifications. He put the young Gaius Volcacius Tullus in charge of the place and the guard. (4) Caesar himself, when the crops began to ripen, set out to do battle with Ambiorix, traveling through the Ardennes Forest. This is the largest forest in Gaul; it stretches from the banks of the Rhine and the borders of the Treveri all the way to the territory of the Nervii and measures more than 500 miles across. He sent Lucius Minucius Basilus ahead with the whole cavalry (5) to see whether he might be able to march swiftly and use time to his advantage. Caesar warned Minucius that he should forbid the soldiers to light fires in the camp, lest they give away any indication of the Romans' arrival. He said that he would follow up shortly.

30 (1) Basilus did as ordered. He made the march even faster than expected and took many men by surprise in the fields. On their advice he set out for the place where Ambiorix was said to be with a small number of cavalry. (2) Just as in so many other things, Fortune holds sway in war. For it happened by total chance that Basilus caught Ambiorix himself off guard and unprepared, and burst into view of everyone before rumor or report of his approach could reach them. It was another stroke of great fortune that Ambiorix escaped death even though all the military equipment he had with him was seized and his chariots and horses confiscated. (3) He only managed this because his house was surrounded by forest (as the Gauls' houses usually are, since they usually try to live near forest or rivers to avoid the heat). His companions and

familiaresque eius angusto in loco paulisper equitum nostrorum vim sustinuerunt. (4) his pugnantibus illum in equum quidam ex suis intulit, fugientem silvae texerunt. sic et ad subeundum periculum et ad vitandum multum Fortuna valuit.

31 (1) Ambiorix copias suas iudicione non conduxerit, quod proelio dimicandum non existimaret, an tempore exclusus et repentino equitum adventu prohibitus, cum reliquum exercitum subsequi crederet, dubium est. (2) sed certe dimissis per agros nuntiis sibi quemquem consulere iussit. quorum pars in Arduennam silvam, pars in continentes paludes profugit. (3) qui proximi Oceano fuerunt, hi insulis sese occultaverunt, quas aestus efficere consueverunt. (4) multi ex suis finibus egressi se suaque omnia alienissimis crediderunt. (5) Catuvolcus rex dimidiae partis Eburonum, qui una cum Ambiorige consilium inierat, aetate iam confectus, cum laborem belli aut fugae ferre non posset, omnibus precibus detestatus Ambiorigem, qui eius consilii auctor fuisset, taxo, cuius magna in Gallia Germaniaque copia est, se exanimavit.

32 (1) Segni Condrusique, ex gente et numero Germanorum, qui sunt inter Eburones Treverosque, legatos ad Caesarem miserunt oratum, ne se in hostium numero duceret neve omnium Germanorum, qui essent citra Rhenum, unam esse causam iudicaret; nihil se de bello cogitavisse, nulla Ambiorigi auxilia misisse. (2) Caesar re explorata quaestione captivorum, si qui ad eos Eburones ex fuga convenissent, ad se ut reducerentur, imperavit. si ita fecissent, fines eorum se violaturum negavit. (3) tum copiis in tres partes distributis impedimenta omnium legionum Atuatucam contulit. id

relatives briefly withstood the attack of our cavalry in a narrow spot. (4) While they were fighting, one of his followers mounted Ambiorix on his horse, and the forest gave him cover as he fled. And so Fortune was in control, whether it was leading him into danger or helping him avoid it.

31 (1) It is not clear whether Ambiorix intentionally refrained from gathering his troops because he did not think it wise to engage in battle or whether he was hindered by a lack of time and the sudden arrival of our cavalry (since he assumed the rest of our army would follow). (2) In any case, he sent messengers through the countryside and ordered everyone to look out for themselves. Some fled into the Ardennes Forest, some into the expansive marshes. (3) Those who lived closest to the ocean hid themselves in the islands which were regularly created by the tides. (4) Many, when they had departed from their own territory, entrusted themselves and all their possessions to complete strangers. (5) Catuvolcus, who was king over half of the Eburones and who had first entered into this plot with Ambiorix, was worn down with age and could not endure the effort of either war or flight. Denouncing Ambiorix with every curse for being the instigator of the plot, he killed himself by eating from the yew tree, which is abundant in Gaul and Germany.

32 (1) The Segni and the Condrusi, who are counted among the German peoples and who dwell between the Eburones and the Treveri, sent legates to Caesar to beg him not to regard them among his enemies and not to think of all the Germans on this side of the Rhine as united by a single cause. They had no plans for war, they said, and they had given no help to Ambiorix. (2) Caesar confirmed this by questioning some prisoners. He ordered that if any of the Eburones had taken refuge among the Segni and Condrusi in their flight that they should be returned to him. If they did as he ordered, he promised that he would not harm their territory. (3) Then he split his forces into three parts and brought all the baggage to Atuatuca. That is the name of

castelli nomen est. (4) hoc fere est in mediis Eburonum finibus, ubi Titurius atque Aurunculeius hiemandi causa consederant. (5) hunc cum reliquis rebus locum probabat, tum quod superioris anni munitiones integrae manebant, ut militum laborem sublevaret. praesidio impedimentis legionem quartam decimam reliquit, unam ex iis tribus, quas proxime conscriptas ex Italia traduxerat. (6) ei legioni castrisque Quintum Tullium Ciceronem praeficit ducentosque equites ei attribuit.

33 (1) Partito exercitu Titum Labienum cum legionibus tribus ad Oceanum versus in eas partes, quae Menapios attingunt, proficisci iubet, (2) Gaium Trebonium cum pari legionum numero ad eam regionem, quae Atuatucis adiacet, depopulandam mittit. (3) ipse cum reliquis tribus ad flumen Scaldim, quod influit in Mosam, extremasque Arduennae partes ire constituit, quo cum paucis equitibus profectum Ambiorigem audiebat. (4) discedens post diem septimum sese reversurum confirmat, quam ad diem ei legioni, quae in praesidio relinquebatur, frumentum deberi sciebat. (5) Labienum Treboniumque hortatur, si rei p. commodo facere possint, ad eum diem revertantur, ut rursus communicato consilio exploratisque hostium rationibus aliud initium belli capere possint.

34 (1) Erat, ut supra demonstravimus, manus certa nulla, non oppidum, non prae<si>dium, quod se armis defenderet, sed in omnes partes dispersa multitudo. (2) ubi cuique aut valles abdita aut locus silvestris aut palus impedita spem praesidii aut salutis aliquam offerebat, consederat. (3) haec loca vicinitatibus erant nota magnamque res diligentiam requirebat non in summa exercitus tuenda – nullum enim poterat universis <a> perterritis ac dispersis periculum accidere –, sed in singulis militibus conservandis.

a fort. (4) It is more or less in the middle of the Eburones' territory, where Sabinus and Cotta had established camp for the winter. (5) Caesar chose this place for a variety of reasons, particularly because the fortifications built the previous year were intact, which would take some of the burden off his soldiers. He left the fourteenth legion to guard the baggage; this was one of the three legions he had recently raised from Italy. (6) He put Quintus Tullius Cicero in charge of the legion and the camp and assigned two hundred cavalry to him.

33 (1) Once he had divided the army, Caesar ordered Titus Labienus to march with three legions toward the ocean to the territories which border the Menapii. (2) He sent Gaius Trebonius with the same number of legions to lay waste to the region bordering the Atuatuci. (3) Caesar himself decided to go with the remaining three legions toward the Scaldis River, which flows into the Mosa, and the far reaches of the Ardennes forest, where he had heard Ambiroix had gone with some of his cavalry. (4) When he departed, he promised that he would return on the seventh day; he knew that that was the day the corn ration was due to the legion which had been left behind on guard. (5) He urged Labienus and Trebonius to return that same day, if they could do so without endangering the common safety, so that they could discuss their plans, research the enemy's strategy, and come up with a new approach to the war.

34 (1) As I have already mentioned, there was no standing army, no town or garrison that could defend itself with arms; the people had scattered all over the place. (2) Each person hunkered down wherever a hidden valley or wooded spot or impassable swamp offered them some hope of protection or safety. (3) These places were well-known to the neighboring people and the situation required great thoughtfulness from Caesar, not necessarily in protecting the army as a unit (for no danger could befall them if they remained united against the terrified and scattered enemy) but in keeping the individual soldiers safe. However, this problem was

quae tamen ex parte res ad salutem exercitus pertinebat. (4) nam et praedae cupiditas multos longius evocabat et silvae incertis occultisque itineribus confertos adire prohibebant. (5) si negotium confici stirpemque hominum sceleratorum interfici velle[n]t, dimittendae plures manus diducendique erant milites. (6) si continere ad signa manipulos vellet, ut instituta ratio et consuetudo exercitus Romani postulabat, locus ipse erat praesidio barbaris, neque ex occulto insidiandi et dispersos circumveniendi singulis deerat audacia. (7) ut in eiusmodi difficultatibus, quantum diligentia provideri poterat, providebatur, ut potius in nocendo aliquid praetermitteretur, etsi omnium animi ad ulciscendum ardebant, quam cum aliquo militum detrimento noceretur. (8) dimittit ad finitimas civitates nuntios Caesar. omnes evocat spe praedae ad diripiendos Eburones, ut potius in silvis Gallorum vita quam legionarius miles periclitetur, simul ut magna multitudine circumfusa pro tali facinore stirps ac nomen civitatis tollatur. (9) magnus undique numerus celeriter convenit.

35 (1) Haec in omnibus Eburonum partibus gerebantur diesque adpetebat septimus. quem ad diem Caesar ad impedimenta legionemque reverti constituerat. (2) hic quantum in bello Fortuna possit et quantos adferat casus, cognosci potuit. (3) dissipatis ac perterritis hostibus, ut demonstravimus, manus erat nulla quae parvam modo causam timoris adferret. (4) trans Rhenum ad Germanos pervenit fama diripi Eburones atque ultro omnes ad praedam evocari. (5) cogunt equitum duo milia Sugambri, qui sunt proximi Rheno. a quibus receptos ex fuga Tenctheros atque Usipetes supra docuimus. (6) transeunt Rhenum navibus ratibusque triginta milibus passuum infra eum locum, ubi pons erat perfectus

still relevant to the safety of the whole army. (4) For the desire for plunder had lured many of them out too far and the woods, with their confusing and hidden paths, kept them from sticking together in groups. (5) If Caesar wanted to put an end to the affair and wipe out this race of hateful men, he needed to send out more troops and disperse the soldiers more widely. (6) On the other hand, if he wanted to maintain formation, as the well-established and customary discipline of the Roman army demanded, the very location itself would protect the barbarians; not a single one of them lacked the daring to set an ambush or surround the scattered troops. (7) To the extent it was possible in such a difficult situation, whatever could be anticipated was anticipated with care. Even though all the soldiers' hearts burned for revenge, Caesar was more concerned that his men suffer no harm than that they seize the opportunity to inflict damage. (8) He sent messengers to the neighboring states and offered the hope of plunder as incentive for their help destroying the Eburones, since he would rather risk the lives of the Gauls in the woods than endanger a single legionary soldier. As soon as this formidable force had surrounded them, the entire line and the very name of the Eburones would be annihilated as punishment for their horrific crime. (9) A great number of men from all over assembled quickly.

35 (1) This was going on in every part of the Eburones' territory, and the seventh day was approaching – that is, the day by which Caesar had promised to return to the baggage and the legion. (2) From what happened next one can see how much Fortune controls things in war and what great havoc she wreaks. (3) The enemy were scattered and frightened, as I described above, and there was no organized force that could give even a slight cause for fear. (4) Word spread to the Germans across the Rhine that the Eburones were being pillaged, and anyone who wanted to could join in the plunder. (5) The Sugambri, who live closest to the Rhine and who had given protection to the Tenctheri and Uspites during their retreat (as I described above), collected 2,000 cavalry. (6) They crossed the Rhine with boats and rafts about thirty miles below the spot

praesidiumque a Caesare relictum. primos Eburonum fines adeunt. multos ex fuga dispersos excipiunt. magno pecoris numero, cuius sunt cupidissimi barbari, potiuntur. (7) invitati praeda longius procedunt. non hos palus – in bello latrociniisque natos –, non silvae morantur. quibus in locus sit Caesar, ex captivis quaerunt. profectum longius reperiunt omnemque exercitum discessisse cognoscunt. (8) atque unus ex captivis 'quid vos' inquit 'hanc miseram ac tenuem sectamini praedam, quibus licet iam esse fortunatissimos? tribus horis Atuatucam venire potestis. (9) huc omnes suas fortunas exercitus Romanorum contulit. praesidii tantum est, ut ne murus quidem cingi possit neque quisquam egredi extra munitiones audeat.' (10) oblata spe Germani, quam nacti erant praedam, in occulto relinquunt. ipsi Atuatucam contendunt usi eodem duce, cuius haec indicio cognoverant.

36 (1) Cicero, qui omnes superiores dies praeceptis Caesaris summa diligentia milites in castris continuisset ac ne calonem quidem quemquam extra munitionem egredi passus esset, septimo die diffidens de numero dierum Caesarem fidem servaturum, quod longius eum progressum audiebat neque ulla de reditu eius fama adferebatur, (2) simul eorum permotus vocibus, qui illius patientiam p<a>ene obsessionem appellabant, siquidem ex castris egredi non liceret, nullum eiusmodi casum ex<s>pectans, quo novem oppositis legionibus maximoque equitatu, dispersis ac p<a>ene deletis hostibus in milibus passuum tribus offendi posset, quinque cohortes frumentatum in proximas segetes mittit, quas inter et castra unus omnino collis intererat. (3) complures erant in castris ex legionibus aegri relicti. ex quibus, qui hoc spatio dierum convaluerant, circiter trecenti sub vexillo una mittuntur. magna praeterea multitudo calonum, magna vis iumentorum, quae in castris subsederat, facta potestate sequitur.

where Caesar had built the bridge and left behind the garrison. The Sugambri arrived at the edge of the Eburones' territory. They captured many who were fleeing, as well as a great number of cattle, something that barbarians especially prize. (7) Lured by the promise of plunder, they ventured farther out. Neither the swamps nor the forest could deter these men, who were born for war and robbery. They asked some of their prisoners where Caesar was, and learned that he had gone farther ahead and that his whole army had departed. (8) One of the prisoners spoke up: "Why are you chasing after this meager, pathetic booty when you have the chance to become unbelievably rich right now? You could be at Atuatuca in three days. (9) The Roman army has staked its entire fortune there, but they've left such a pathetic garrison that it can't even protect the whole wall, and none of them dare to step foot outside the fortifications." (10) This gave hope to the Germans, who hid the loot they had already plundered. They headed for Atuatuca led by the same prisoner who had provided this information.

36 (1) Although Cicero had diligently restrained his soldiers within the camp through the preceding days in accordance with Caesar's wishes and had not even permitted any of the orderlies to go outside the fortifications, by the seventh day he became uneasy that Caesar would not keep his promise, since he had heard that Caesar had advanced further but had received no report about his return. (2) At the same time, Cicero was being provoked by those who were saying that his willingness to wait basically amounted to a siege, since no one was able to leave camp. He did not anticipate that any trouble could arise within three miles of camp, since he had nine legions and a large contingent of cavalry, while the enemy were scattered and had been nearly wiped out. He sent five cohorts to forage in the closest fields, which were separated from the camp by a single hill. (3) Several of the legionaries who were sick had been left behind in camp. About three hundred of them had recovered in the intervening days and were sent out as a separate unit. Once permission was granted, they were accompanied by many of the orderlies and a large number of the pack-animals which had been left behind in camp.

37 (1) Hoc ipso tempore [et] casu Germani equites interveniunt protinusque eodem illo, quo venerant, cursu ab decumana porta in castra inrumpere conantur, (2) nec prius sunt visi obiectis ab ea parte silvis, quam castris adpropinquarent, usque eo ut, qui sub vallo tenderent, mercatores recipiendi sui facultatem non haberent. (3) inopinantes nostri re nova perturbantur, ac vix primum impetum cohors in statione sustinet. (4) circumfunduntur hostes ex reliquis partibus, si quem aditum reperire possint. (5) aegre portas nostri tuentur. reliquos aditus locus ipse per se munitioque defendit. (6) totis trepidatur castris, atque alius ex alio causam tumultus quaerit. neque quo signa ferantur, neque quam in partem quisque conveniat, provident. (7) alius castra iam capta pronuntiat, alius deleto exercitu atque imperatore victores barbaros venisse contendit. (8) plerique novas sibi ex loco religiones fingunt Cottaeque et Titurii calamitatem, qui in eodem occiderint castello, ante oculos ponunt. (9) tali timore omnibus perterritis confirmatur opinio barbaris, ut ex captivo audierant, nullum esse intus praesidium. (10) perrumpere nituntur seque ipsi adhortantur, ne tantam fortunam ex manibus dimittant.

38 (1) Erat aeger in praesidio relictus Publius Sextius Baculus, qui primum pilum apud Caesarem duxerat, cuius mentionem superioribus proeliis fecimus, ac diem iam quintum cibo caruerat. (2) hic diffisus suae atque omnium saluti inermis ex tabernaculo prodit. videt imminere hostes atque in summo esse rem discrimine. capit arma a proximis atque in porta consistit. (3) consequuntur hunc centuriones eius cohortis, quae in statione erat, paulisper

37 (1) At this particularly unfortunate moment the German cavalry arrived and immediately tried to break into camp through the Decuman Gate at full gallop. (2) Because there were trees in the way on that side no one saw them until they were already right at the camp; it happened so quickly that not even the merchants who kept shop under the rampart had a chance to escape. (3) Our men were caught off guard and overwhelmed by the sudden turn of events, and the cohort on duty scarcely withstood the first attack. (4) The enemy encircled the camp to see if they could find any point of access on the other sides. (5) With effort, our men were able to protect the gates; the place essentially defended the remaining entrances itself, thanks to its location and the other fortifications. (6) Fear ran through the whole camp as they asked each other what caused the commotion. They could not decide where to take the standards or where they should gather. (7) Someone announced that the camp had already been captured, and someone else claimed that the army and its commander had been destroyed and the victorious barbarians were approaching. (8) Most of the men began to imagine frightening, superstitious things because of where they were; they saw in their mind's eye the disaster of Sabinus and Cotta, who had been slaughtered in this same stronghold. (9) Everyone was terrified, and seeing them in such fear confirmed the barbarians' belief that there was no guard within the camp, as they had heard from that prisoner. (10) They tried to force their way in and encouraged each other not to let such a great fortune slip from their grasp.

38 (1) Publius Sextius Baculus (who had reached the rank of chief centurion under Caesar and whom I have mentioned in the context of earlier battles) had been wounded and was left behind in the garrison; he was now on his fifth day without food. (2) Because he was anxious about his own safety (and that of everyone else), he left his tent despite being unarmed. He saw that the enemy were bearing down and that the camp was in a dire situation. Baculus seized some weapons from those who were nearby and positioned himself in the gate. (3) Some of the centurions from the cohort that was on guard followed him, and for a short time they were able to hold off the

una proelium sustinent. (4) relinquit animus Sextium gravibus acceptis vulneribus. deficiens aegre per manus tractus servatur. (5) hoc spatio interposito reliqui sese confirmant tantum, ut in munitionibus consistere audeant speciemque defensorum praebeant.

39 (1) Interim confecta frumentatione milites nostri clamorem exaudiunt, praecurrunt equites. (2) quanto res sit in periculo, cognoscunt. hic vero nulla munitio est quae perterritos recipiat. modo conscripti atque usus militaris imperiti ad tribunum militum centurionesque ora convertunt. (3) quid ab his praecipiatur, ex<s>pectant. nemo est tam fortis, quin rei novitiate perturbetur. (4) barbari signa procul conspicati oppugnatione desistunt, redisse primo legiones credunt, quas longius discessisse ex captivis cognoverant, postea despecta paucitate ex omnibus partibus impetum faciunt.

40 (1) Calones in proximum tumulum procurrunt. hinc celeriter deiecti se in signa manipulosque coniciunt. eo magis timidos perterrent milites. (2) alii cuneo facto ut celeriter perrumpant, censent – quoniam tam propinqua sint castra, etsi pars aliqua circumventa ceciderit, at reliquos servari posse confidunt –, (3) alii ut in iugo consistant atque eundem omnes ferant casum. (4) hoc veteres non probant milites, quos sub vexillo una profectos docuimus. itaque inter se cohortati duce Gaio Trebonio equite Romano, qui iis erat praepositus, per medios hostes perrumpunt incolumesque ad unum omnes in castra perveniunt. (5) hos subsecuti equites calonesque

attack by working together. (4) However, Baculus sustained serious wounds and fainted; although his strength was failing, his fellow soldiers were just barely able to save him by carrying him away. (5) Because Baculus had bought them some time, the rest of the soldiers composed themselves enough that they dared to take their position on the fortifications and to make a show of resistance.

39 (1) Meanwhile, after the foraging had been completed, our soldiers heard a shout in the distance, and the cavalry ran ahead. (2) They recognized how much danger they were in. There was no fortification there to give cover, and they were frightened. Those who had just recently been conscripted and were inexperienced in battle turned to the military tribunes and the centurions and awaited their instructions. (3) There is no one so brave that he is not unnerved by a new situation. (4) The barbarians spotted our standards from far away and backed off the siege. At first, they thought that the legions (which, according to the prisoners, had marched farther away) had returned; but then, looking scornfully at their small number, the enemy attacked from all sides.

40 (1) The orderlies rushed forward to the closest hill. They were driven quickly from this position and pushed their way into the formations and maniples, and in doing so terrified the frightened soldiers even more. (2) Some suggested that they form a wedge to break through more quickly; since the camp was so close by, they reasoned, even if some of them were surrounded and killed, they were confident that the rest could be saved. (3) Others argued that they should take a stand on the ridge and endure the same fate all together. (4) The veteran soldiers (who, as I have described, had set out together as a single detachment) did not approve of this idea. And so, urging each other on, under the leadership of the Roman knight Gaius Trebonius, who had been put in charge by Caesar, they charged right through the enemy and made it to the camp with every last one of them unharmed. (5) The cavalry and orderlies followed them in the same charge and were saved by the courage of

eodem impetu militum virtute servantur. (6) at ii, qui in iugo constiterant, nullo etiamnunc usu rei militaris percepto neque in eo, quod probaverant, consilio permanere, ut se loco superiore defenderent, neque eam, quam profuisse aliis vim celeritatem viderant, imitari potuerunt, sed se in castra recipere conati iniquum in locum demiserunt. (7) centuriones, quorum nonnulli ex inferioribus ordinibus reliquarum legionum virtutis causa in superiores erant ordines huius legionis traducti, ne ante partam rei militaris laudem amitterent, fortissime pugnantes conciderunt. (8) militum pars horum virtute summotis hostibus praeter spem incolumis in castra pervenit, pars a barbaris circumventa periit.

41 (1) Germani desperata expugnatione castrorum, quod nostros iam constitisse in munitionibus videbant, cum ea praeda, quam in silvis deposuerant, trans Rhenum sese receperunt. (2) ac tantus fuit etiam post discessum hostium terror, ut ea nocte, cum Gaius Volusenus missus cum equitatu in castra venisset, fidem non faceret adesse cum incolumi Caesarem exercitu. (3) sic omnium animos timor praeoccupaverat, ut p<a>ene alienata mente deletis omnibus copiis equitatum se ex fuga recepisse dicerent neque incolumi exercitu Germanos castra oppugnaturos fuisse contenderent. quem timorem Caesaris adventus sustulit.

42 (1) Reversus ille, eventus belli non ignorans, unum, quod cohortes ex statione et praesidio essent emissae, questus – ne minimum quidem casu locum relinqui debuisse – multam Fortunam in repentino hostium adventu potuisse iudicavit, (2) multo etiam amplius quod p<a>ene ab ipso vallo portisque castrorum barbaros avertisset. (3) quarum omnium rerum maxime admirandum videbatur, quod Germani, qui eo consilio Rhenum transierant, ut Ambiorigis fines depopularentur, ad castra Romanorum delati optatissimum Ambiorigi beneficium obtulerant.

the soldiers. (6) But those who had taken up a position on the ridge still had no sense of military strategy and could not do as they had planned (that is, to use the height to their advantage in defending themselves), nor could they imitate the strength and speed they saw displayed by the others. When they tried to retreat into the camp they wound up in a dangerous position. (7) The centurions, some of whom had been promoted from the lower ranks in other legions to higher ranks in this one because of their courage, died fighting bravely rather than forfeit their glorious reputation for fighting. (8) Some of the soldiers courageously forced the enemy back and defied expectations by making it back to camp safely; some were surrounded by the barbarians and perished.

41 (1) The Germans gave up on besieging the camp, since they saw that our men were already taking a stand on the fortifications. They retreated across the Rhine with the plunder they had hidden in the forest. (2) But even after the enemy departed, everyone was still so afraid that when Gaius Volusenus (who had been sent out with the cavalry) arrived at the camp that night, he could not convince anyone that Caesar was nearby and that his army was unharmed. (3) Fear so thoroughly overtook their spirits that, as if they had all lost their minds, they insisted that all the other forces had been cut off and the cavalry had arrived in retreat; if the army were safe, they claimed, the Germans would not have attacked the camp. The arrival of Caesar relieved this fear.

42 (1) Caesar was not unaware of the risks of war. When he returned, his only critique was that the cohorts had been sent away from their post and the garrison; they should not have allowed even the slightest opportunity for disaster. He judged that Fortune had greatly influenced matters with the sudden arrival of the enemy, and even more so by turning the barbarians away from the rampart and gates of the camp. (3) What seemed most astonishing of all was the fact that the Germans who had crossed the Rhine to waste the territory of Ambiorix had actually done him a most generous favor when they were diverted to the Roman camp.

43 (1) Caesar rursus ad vexandos hostes profectus magno coacto <equitum> numero ex finitimis civitatibus in omnes partes dimittit. (2) omnes vici atque omnia aedificia, quae quisque conspexerat, incendebantur, pecora interficiebantur, praeda ex omnibus locis agebatur. (3) frumenta non solum a tanta multitudine iumentorum atque hominum consumebantur, sed etiam anni tempore atque imbribus procubuerant, ut si qui etiam in praesentia se occultassent, tamen his deducto exercitu rerum omnium inopia pereundum videretur. (4) ac s<a>epe in eum locum ventum est tanto in omnes partes diviso equitatu, ut [non] modo visum ab se Ambiorigem in fuga circumspicerent captivi nec plane etiam abisse ex conspectus contenderent, (5) ut spe consequendi inlata atque infinito labore suscepto, qui se summam a Caesare gratiam inituros putarent, p<a>ene naturam studio vincerent, semperque paulum ad summam felicitatem defuisse videretur, (6) atque ille latebris aut silvis aut saltibus se eriperet et noctu occultatus alias regiones partesque peteret non maiore equitum praesidio quam quattuor. quibus solis vitam suam committere audebat.

44 (1) Tali modo vastatis regionibus exercitum Caesar duarum cohortium damno Durocortorum Remorum reducit concilioque in eum locum Galliae indicto de coniuratione Senonum et Carnutum quaestionem habere instituit et de Accione, (2) qui princeps eius consilii fuerat, graviore sententia pronuntiata more maiorum supplicium sumpsit. (3) nonnulli iudicium veriti profugerunt. quibus cum aqua atque igni interdixisset, duas legiones ad fines Treverorum, duas in Lingonibus, sex reliquas in Senonum finibus Agedinci in hibernis conlocavit frumentoque exercitui proviso, ut instituerat. in Italiam ad conventus agendos profectus est.

43 (1) Caesar set out again to harass the enemy. He collected a great number of cavalry from the neighboring states and sent them in every direction. (2) Every neighborhood, every structure his men laid eyes on was burned, the cattle were slaughtered, plunder was rustled up from every corner. (3) Their corn was not only eaten up by the huge number of pack-animals and men but also matted down by the heavy seasonal rains. As a result, anyone who had managed to hide for the time being was still likely to die of starvation when Caesar's army left. (4) A large contingent of cavalry was sent out in all directions, and it frequently happened that the prisoners would look around as if they had spotted Ambiorix in flight and they could swear he was just out of sight. (5) This raised the cavalry's hopes of catching Ambiorix, and they put in a monumental effort. Since they believed this would earn them the highest esteem in Caesar's eyes, they zealously pushed past their natural limits, and it always seemed like great success was just out of their reach. (6) As for Ambiorix himself, he escaped, fleeing from his hiding places in the woods and thickets and seeking out other territories and regions under cover of night. His guard consisted of not more than four cavalrymen; to these alone did he dare entrust his life.

44 (1) After devastating the area in this way Caesar led his army (minus two cohorts) to Durocortorum, among the Remi. He summoned a Gallic assembly to meet there and decided hold an inquiry regarding the conspiracy of the Senones and Carnutes. (2) He pronounced a very serious sentence against Acco, who had been the leader of the plot, and punished him according to the custom of our ancestors. (3) Some others feared the same punishment and fled, and Caesar decreed them banished. He sent two legions to spend the winter on the borders of the Treveri, two to the Lingones, and six to Agedincum, in the territory of the Senones. When he had secured the army's grain supply, he set out for Italy to hold assizes, as was his custom.

COMMENTARY BOOK V

Chapters 1–2: Caesar's Preparations for Britain

Caesar orders that preparations be made for a second expedition to Britain. He orders repair work and new construction to replenish the fleet, badly diminished by a storm during the previous year's invasion. His soldiers complete this work with great speed and capability.

Chapter 1

(1) **In the consulship of Lucius Domitius and Appius Claudius…:** 54 BCE. Lucius Domitius Ahenobarbus, brother-in-law of Cato the Younger, had a long-standing hostility toward Caesar and sided with the senatorial faction against him in 49; he was pardoned by Caesar after his defeat at Corfinium but eventually rejoined the Pompeians and was killed shortly after Pharsalus in 48. Appius Claudius Pulcher also went east with Pompey in 49 and died in Greece that year. Notably, as censor, Appius had ordered the expulsion of the historian Sallust from the senate.

Caesar: Caesar scrupulously avoids referring to himself in the first person when describing his military activities. However, he frequently refers to the Roman troops using the first person plural possessive adjective ('our men'); cf. 5.3.5 (*nostri exercitus*), 5.9.3 (*nostros*), and 5.11.9 (*nostro adventu*) below.

for Italy: i.e. Cisalpine Gaul (where, we learn at 5.1.5, he is conducting assizes)

new ships … the old ones: the Roman invasion of Britain in the previous year had largely been a disappointment for Caesar. Among other embarrassments, Caesar's fleet was badly damaged by a storm. Twelve ships were lost, and many others were badly damaged (4.29); with great effort and haste the Romans were able to repair enough ships to make the trip back to the continent before the fall weather made crossing more difficult or impossible (4.36). The diminished fleet was insufficient for a return expedition; hence the repair work and new construction detailed here.

(2) **the Mediterranean Sea:** lit. 'our sea' (*mari nostro*)

because of the frequent changes of the tide: according to Holmes (1914) *ad loc.*, this explanation is incorrect; rather, the "comparative smallness of the waves in the Channel is due to the shallowness of the water and its contraction within narrow limits."

(3) **equipped with oars:** *actuarias* is derived from *ago, agere* (to drive or propel). Caesar means that the ships should be fitted with oars so they can be propelled swiftly instead of relying solely on sails, as the Gallic ships did.
(5) **When the assizes in Nearer Gaul were finished:** *conventus* can refer to any gathering, but by the late Republic it had also taken on the technical meaning of 'assizes', or the regular meetings between a body of Roman citizens living in a particular province and their governor (in this case, Caesar as proconsul). The *conventus* were typically held at fixed intervals; Caesar seems to have scheduled his for the end of the fighting season, when his legions were settled in winter quarters (cf. *BG* 1.54, 8.46).

Illyricum: located along the east coast of the Adriatic Sea. Caesar was granted the proconsulship of Illyricum as well as Cisalpine Gaul under the *lex Vatinia* of 59 BCE.

raids by the Pirustae: the Pirustae seem to have occupied the mountainous region corresponding with modern-day Montenegro and were generally identified among the Pannonian peoples (cf. Strabo 7.5.3). This is their only appearance in Caesar's works.

Latin
(7) *qui doceant*: relative clause of purpose (A&G 531.2).
(9) *qui litem aestiment poenamque constituant*: another relative clause of purpose

Chapter 2
(2) **I described:** When Caesar refers to himself as the work's author, he uses the first-person plural (*demonstravimus* here). He meticulously avoids referring to himself in the first person when describing himself as commander (cf. 5.1.1 above).
(3) **Portus Itius:** the identification of Portus Itius remains unknown. It seems to have been located in the country of the Morini (cf. 5.24.2 below); while it is certainly in the general vicinity of Cape Grisnez, a mere 34 km across the strait from Dover, its precise location is elusive. Caesar probably launched his first British expedition from Boulogne, but this small harbor could not have accommodated the over 800 ships Caesar claims to have sailed in the second expedition. Wissant, Calais, Sangatte, Ambleteuse, and Dunkirk have all been suggested.
(4) **the Treveri**: the Treveri dwelled on the near side of the Rhine, in the Moselle basin; around 16 BCE the Romans established *Augusta*

Treverorum ('the city of Augustus among the Treveri') in what is now Trier (whose French name, Trèves, reflects the influence of the Treveri). The names of their leaders, Indutiomarus and Cingetorix, suggest Celtic origins, though Tacitus reports that they claimed German descent (*Germania* 28). Prior to this episode in Book 5 they also make brief appearances as either troublemakers or half-hearted allies (*BG* 2.24, 3.11, 4.6, and 4.10). The revolt of the Treveri led by Indutiomarus will occupy Caesar for much of 54 BCE (and Book 5).

were not obeying his authority: this was not the first occasion on which the Treveri had caused Caesar difficulty. In 57 BCE, they had offered Caesar support in his campaign against the Belgae, only to desert from battle against the Nervii (2.24).

Latin

(2) **of the type I described above:** *cuius* is in the genitive case because of attraction to its antecedent (*eius generis*) rather than the accusative we might expect (A&G 306a).

neque multum abesse ab eo, quin paucis diebus deduci possint: lit. "and not much was absent from this <possibility>, that they were able to be launched within a few days." *Quin* is regularly used to introduce subjunctive clauses that follow a main verb or expression of hindering, refusing, delaying, etc. when that main idea is being negated (A&G 558).

(3) *quid fieri velit*: indirect question (A&G 574)

Chapters 3–4: Caesar and the Treveri

Caesar arrives among the Treveri to address various issues, including reports that they have been harassing nearby groups. He is drawn into a dispute between Indutiomarus and Cingetorix, rivals for preeminence among the Treveri.

Chapter 3

(1) **cavalry:** Caesar has mentioned previously the high repute of the Treveran cavalry (*…equites Treveri, quorum inter Gallos opinio est virtutis singularis*, "The Treveran cavalry, who have a reputation among the Gauls for their outstanding courage", 2.24).

(2) **Indutiomarus and Cingetorix:** both names are of Celtic origin, suggesting that the Treveri are of Celtic descent rather than German, as they claimed (cf. Tacitus, *Germania* 28).

(4) **Ardennes forest:** the Ardennes forest is a hilly, densely forested region covering some 4300 square miles, primarily in southeastern Belgium.

Remi: the Remi were a powerful Belgic people situated in the northern Champagne Plain, toward the southern end of the Ardennes forest; their capital, Durocortorum, later took its name (modern Reims) from this group. The Remi were important allies of Caesar throughout his tenure in Gaul and were among the few groups that maintained loyalty to Caesar during the rebellion of Vercingetorix (cf. 7.63).

Latin

(5) *quoniam ... non posse<n>t*: causal clauses introduced by *quoniam* are regularly indicative, but *possent* here is subjunctive as the verb of a subordinate clause in implied indirect discourse (governed by an implicit expression of speech by the *principes* who are defending their actions; A&G 540.2b, 580).

(6–7) *sese ... permissurum*: a long passage of implied indirect discourse; we are meant to understand that this is the content of the message delivered by the *legati* on Indutiomarus' behalf and that it is governed by an implicit *dicit, demonstrat,* vel sim.

(6) *sese*: reflexive referring back to Indutiomarus as the original author of the message, rather than to the envoys who are actually reporting it.

(7) *si Caesar permitteret ... venturum ... permissurum*: future condition in indirect discourse (A&G 589a).

Chapter 4

(1) **his plan:** that is, Indutiomarus' plot to revolt against Caesar.

Latin

(2) *uti ... maneret*: indirect command governed by *hortatus est* (also called substantive clause of purpose; A&G 563).

(3) *nihilo ... setius*: colloquial expression for 'nevertheless' (*nihilo* is an ablative of comparison).

Chapters 5–7: The Return of Dumnorix

As Caesar prepares to sail for Britain, he is distracted and delayed by the Aeduan aristocrat Dumnorix, who is plotting intrigue against the Romans.

Chapter 5

(2) **in the country of the Meldi:** the location here is uncertain. This is Caesar's only mention of the Meldi, if indeed they are named here; various manuscripts record *Medi, Melui, Hedui,* and *Belgae*. The second century CE geographer Claudius Ptolemy places the Meldi near Iatinum (modern Meaux, its name derived from the group described here), on the Matrona (Marne) river. Strabo and Pliny do not give an exact location, but both identify the Meldi as neighbors of the Parisii, who dwelled on the Sequana (Seine).

Latin

(4) *cum ipse abesset*: circumstantial cum-clause (lit. 'when he himself was absent'; A&G 546)

Chapter 6

(1) **Dumnorix:** this is not Caesar's first encounter with the Aeduan Dumnorix. At the beginning of Caesar's tenure in Gaul Dumnorix had made an alliance with Orgetorix of the Helvetii and Casticus of the Sequani; they planned to each seize the kingship in their respective states and then together take control of all Gaul (*BG* 1.3). This plan was unsuccessful. Casticus' fate is unknown, but Orgetorix was either killed in an uprising or committed suicide (1.4); Dumnorix was only spared by Caesar thanks to the intervention of his brother Diviciacus, whose loyalty toward the Romans Caesar noted (1.18). However, as is made clear in this passage, Caesar still did not put much stock in Dumnorix' trustworthiness.

whom I discussed earlier: *BG* 1.3, 9, 18-20.

(3) **he was afraid:** the subjunctive (*timeret*) is used here in a causal clause in implied indirect discourse (cf. 5.3.5 above). Here, the subjunctive indicates that this is Dumnorix' claim, and the narrator makes no claim for its veracity.

(6) **an oath:** *ius iurandum* (lit. 'law to be sworn') is generally translated as 'oath'. This term is used to refer to the oath taken by elected officials and other public magistrates or the oaths taken in courts of justice, as well as in the context of foreign treaties (as in this example); the Roman military oath, however, was called the *sacramentum*.

Latin

(1) *magni animi, magnae ... auctoritatis*: genitives of quality (A&G 345).
(3) *quod ... diceret*: Holmes (1914) *ad loc.* disagrees that the mood of *diceret* is explained by the same reasoning as *timeret* (above, 5.6.3) and suggests that it has simply been attracted to the subjunctive of *timeret* (A&G 593); otherwise, he argues, we should have expected *partim quod, ut dicebat, religionibus impediretur*.
(4) *coepit*: governs several infinitives (*sevocare, hortari, territare, interponere,* and *poscere*). *fieri* and *esse*, on the other hand, are governed by the indirect discourse implied by *metu territare*.
(6) *ex usu:* 'in the best interest'

Chapter 7

(1) **the Aeduan state:** situated between the Loire and Saône rivers, the Aedui had long been important allies of Caesar and the Romans, and they feature prominently in Books 1 and 2 of the *BG.* While he recognized the danger posed by Dumnorix, Caesar also knew that insulting the Aedui by treating one of their aristocracy badly would be strategically unsound. The murder of Dumnorix may well have contributed to the disaffection that led the Aedui to join the revolt of Vercingetorix in 52.
(9) **they surrounded ... and killed:** although Caesar presents Dumnorix' death rather matter-of-factly here, the historian Mommsen recognized the chilling effect his murder would have had on the Gallic aristocracy: "That the most esteemed knight of the most powerful and still the least dependent of the Celtic cantons should have been put to death by the Romans, was a thunder-clap for the whole Celtic nobility; every one who was conscious of similar sentiments – and they formed the great majority – saw in that catastrophe the picture of what was in store for himself (*History of Rome* Vol. 4, 261)."

Latin

(1) *quibuscumque rebus posset:* relative clause of characteristic (A&G 534)

Chapters 8–11: Caesar Sails for Britain

Caesar sails for Britain, leaving Labienus in charge of three legions and some of the cavalry on the mainland. He is temporarily driven off course but lands safely by midday. Once disembarked, the Romans are attacked by the Britons, who have organized under one Cassivellaunus.

Chapter 8

(1) **Labienus**: Titus Labienus served as Caesar's legate in Gaul and is frequently singled out for mention in the *BG* for the particular trust and responsibility Caesar granted him (e.g., among many, *BG* 1.10, 4.38, 7.34, 56–59). As recognition for his distinguished service, Caesar granted Labienus the governorship of Cisalpine Gaul in 51 (*BG* 8.52). Labienus nevertheless defected to the Pompeian cause during the civil war. It is probably with some sense of irony that Caesar depicts Labienus as leading Pompey's men in swearing loyalty to their commander before Dyrrachium (*BC* 3.13). According to Appian, after Labienus' death at Munda in 45 his head was brought to Caesar (*B Civ.* 2.105).

(5) **Caesar reached Britain:** The precise location of Caesar's landing remains in question. Holmes (1914) *ad loc.* interprets Caesar's description to mean that he arrived in Britain near the location of his landing the previous year (somewhere in East Kent, perhaps between Walmer and Deal), though not necessarily in the exact same place. However, recent excavations at Ebbsfleet have revealed what appears to be a first-century BCE encampment, suggesting that Caesar may have landed at nearby Pegwell Bay on the Isle of Thanet; the topography of this site is consistent with Caesar's description.

Latin

(1)–(2) Chapter 8 opens with a long, complex sentence best broken into multiple sentences in the English translation. There is a moderate degree of *hypotaxis* (subordination) for Caesar. The constructions can be mapped as follows (the subject, words modifying the subject, and main verbs are underlined and subordinate clauses are indented):

> His rebus gestis, (*ablative absolute*)
>
> Labieno in continenti cum tribus legionibus et equitum milibus duobus relicto, (*ablative absolute*)
>
> > ut portus tueretur et rei frumentariae provideret, (*purpose clause*)

quaeque in Gallia gererentur (*indirect question governed by cognosceret*)

cognosceret, consiliumque pro tempore et pro re caperet, (*purpose clause continued*)

<u>ipse</u> cum quinque legionibus et pari numero equitum,

quem in continenti relinquebat, (*relative clause*)

solis occasu naves <u>solvit</u>

et leni Africo <u>provectus</u>,

media circiter nocte vento intermisso, (*ablative absolute*)

cursum <u>non tenuit</u>

et longius <u>delatus</u> aestu

orta luce sub sinistra Britanniam relictam <u>conspexit</u>.

(4) *vectoris gravibusque navigiis*: although I have translated this clause as a concessive ablative absolute, one could plausibly make the case for interpreting these ablatives as instrumental (A&G 408; cf. Holmes (1914) *ad loc.*).
(6) *cum ... convenissent*: concessive cum-clause (A&G 549); I have taken some liberty with the translation here, expressing the idea more than the syntax.

Chapter 9
(1) **ten cohorts:** a legion consisted of ten cohorts; since Caesar does not simply say that he left behind a legion, we may infer that the ten cohorts were comprised of troops selected from Caesar's five legions.
Quintus Atrius: Quintus Atrius is otherwise unknown.
(3) **chariots:** chariots (*esseda*) were a crucial piece of battle equipment for the Britons and were particularly effective against Caesar's legions, who were inexperienced in this type of warfare and were caught off guard by it during the first expedition to Britain (BG 4.33). On British use of chariots in battle, see also Diodorus Siculus, *Library of History* 5.29.1–2 and Strabo, *Geography* 4.5.2.
to the river: generally identified as the Stour.
(4) **they occupied a place that was well-fortified...:** Holmes (1914) *ad loc.* locates this camp in Bigbury, a mile or so from modern Canterbury.

(7) **the Seventh Legion:** the Seventh Legion may have had a particular grudge against the Britons, as they had been ambushed and suffered casualties while collecting food during the previous campaign (*BG* 4.32).

Latin
(1) *qui ... essent*: relative clause of purpose (A&G 531.2).
praesidio navibus: the 'double dative' construction (A&G 382), consisting of a dative of purpose (here, *praesidio,* 'as a guard') and a dative of interest (*navibus*, 'for the ships'). Note that the same construction is repeated in this same section (*praesidio navibus Quintum Atrium praefecit*).

Chapter 10
Latin
(2) *qui nuntiarent*: relative clause of purpose (A&G 531.2).

Chapter 11
(3) **workmen:** according to the fourth-century CE military treatise *De Re Militari,* attributed to Vegetius, "blacksmiths, carpenters, butchers, and deer and boar hunters" made particularly useful soldiers due to their unique skill sets (*fabros ferrarios carpentarios macellarios et cervorum aprorumque venatores convenit sociare militiae*, 1.7). We may reasonably assume there were a number of men in Caesar's legion trained in various crafts upon whom Caesar would call in just such a situation.
(8) **Cassivellaunus:** nothing is known about Cassivellaunus' activities prior to this episode beyond what Caesar himself tells us here. His resistance to Caesar's invasion became legendary in Britain; he is depicted in Gregory of Monmouth's *Historia Regum Britanniae* under the name Cassibelanus and in the medieval Welsh Triads as Caswallawn.
Tamesis: the Thames.

Latin
(5) *res erat multae operae ac laboris*: lit. 'the matter was one of great work and effort'; *multae operae* and *laboris* are genitives of quality (A&G 345).
(7) *praesidio navibus*: double dative (cf. 9.1 above).

Chapters 12–14: Geographical/Ethnographical Digression on Britain
Caesar describes the topography and inhabitants of Britain.

Chapter 12

(1) **The interior part…:** the geographical or ethnographical digression was a common feature of Greek historiography (see, e.g., Thucydides on Sicily, Herodotus on Egypt and Scythia). Because the earliest histories by Romans have only survived in fragments, it is difficult to say for certain what role geography and ethnography played in Roman authors before Caesar; however, Caesar's contemporary Sallust featured geographical digressions in his histories, suggesting continuity between the Roman historians and their Greek predecessors. It is worth noting that Caesar's contemporaries did not call the *The Gallic War* a 'history', but rather a *commentarius*, a genre which, strictly speaking, should be free of adornment and elaboration. The inclusion of digressions like this (or on the Hercynian Forest in Book 6) may have been among the factors that led Aulus Hirtius (who completed Book 8 of the *BG* after Caesar's death) and Cicero to reflect that Caesar's writings had left little room for development by later historians. On the *BG* and the *commentarius* genre, see Introduction, pp. 19–20.

born from the island itself: that is, the Britons believed they were autochthonous, having sprung forth from the land itself rather than having arrived in Britain from elsewhere (like those who crossed over from Belgium, as described in the next sentence). As descendants of Aeneas, who fled Troy, the Romans did not claim autochthony, but this was a central component of many local myths in the Greek world. According to the 5th century historian Hellanicus, the Athenians, Arcadians, Aeginetans, and Thebans were autochthonous; indeed, the myth of Athenian autochthony played an important role in Athenian political identity in the 5th and 4th centuries (see, e.g., Isocrates, *Panegyricus* 24–25). Beyond Europe, Herodotus claims that the Libyans and Ethiopians were autochthonous (4.109).

(4) **bronze or gold coins:** the earliest British coins were modeled on coinage from Gaul and date to the mid-second century BCE.

(5) **Tin:** *plumbum album* is tin, as opposed to *plumbum nigrum,* which is lead.

in the inland regions: Caesar seems to be incorrect about this, as the tin mines are in Cornwall, a peninsula at England's southwestern tip.

(6) **as pets:** *animi voluptatisque causa,* lit. 'for the sake of spirit and pleasure'. I presume Caesar means the Britons kept these animals as pets.

If true, this was a point of commonality with the Romans; the hare seems to have been a popular courtship gift, and the tradition of keeping geese is attested as early as the *Odyssey*, in which Penelope speaks warmly of her pets (19.536–7).

Chapter 13

(1) **The island...:** Caesar's description of the geography of Britain is not precisely accurate, but surprisingly close to reality given that no Roman had yet sailed around the island or traveled its full extent on land. Caesar does not specify his sources by name, but from his description we can understand that he relied on a combination of written sources (*nonnulli scripserunt,* 13.3), reconnaissance missions (*percontationibus rep[p]eriebamus*, 13.4), and his own first-hand experience (*videbamus*, 13.4). Krebs (2018a) outlined the more 'scientific' aspects of Caesar's geography of Britain (in comparison with the 'descriptive' geography of Gaul) and suggested that the mapping of Britain represented just the first step in Caesar's broader ambition to map the entire world.

(2) **The island Hibernia:** Ireland. This is the first certain reference to Ireland in extant Greek or Roman texts, though it is likely that the island was described in works of the Hellenistic geographers, most of which survive only in fragments. See Freeman (2001) for a comprehensive study of Ireland in classical antiquity.

(3) **Mona:** the Isle of Man

(4) **water-clock measurements:** Caesar probably refers here to the water clock or clepsydra (lit. 'water thief', from the Greek κλέπτειν, *kleptein,* 'to steal' and ὕδωρ, *hydor,* 'water'). The version used by the Romans had been refined by the Alexandrian inventor Ctesibius in the third century BCE.

(7) **two thousand miles in circumference:** Assuming that Caesar's "two thousand miles" refers to nautical miles in the roughly triangular shape he has described, this is a reasonable estimate; including the many coves and inlets and bays and headlands and peninsulas that make up Britain's coastline would obviously drive this number much higher (the United Kingdom's Ordnance Survey measures the coastline of Great Britain at 11,073 miles).

Chapter 14

(1) **most civilized:** Caesar's ethnography of the Britons is consistent in tone and substance with other ancient ethnographies, which often focused on other cultures' respective degrees of 'civilization' and 'barbarity', particularly in

relation to the author's own culture and often in morally loaded terms that would have no place in 'modern' ethnographic studies (e.g., the reference here to those dwelling in Kent as the 'most civilized by far' of the Britons). Skinner (2012) gives a detailed overview of the topic with extensive bibliography.

(2) **stain themselves with woad:** *Isatis tinctoria,* or woad, is a flowering plant native to the Caucasus and central Asia but also cultivated throughout Europe in antiquity. Its leaves could be used to produce a blue dye. Although it has today been replaced by artificial blue dye for most purposes, *Isatis tinctoria* is still cultivated in China and a herb produced from its root is commonly used in traditional Chinese medicine.

(3) **They share ... wives:** without knowledge of his source for this information it is difficult to determine Caesar's accuracy here. Formal polyandry was once thought to be extraordinarily rare, though a recent study by Hames and Starkweather (2012) has challenged that assumption.

Latin

(2) *horribiliores ... aspectu*: ablative of specification (A&G 418)
capillo ... promisso: ablative of quality (A&G 415)

Chapters 15–19: Battle with the Britons

Caesar's narrative resumes where he left off in Chapter 11, before the digression on Britain. The Romans initially struggle to adapt to the Britons' fighting tactics but eventually momentum shifts in favor of the Romans. Caesar leads his troops into Cassivellaunus' territory.

Chapter 15

(4) **first cohorts:** the first cohorts of the legions were comprised of the most experienced soldiers

new type of fighting: Caesar's troops had encountered the British charioteers in battle the year before (and Caesar describes their tactics in detail at *BG* 4.33), so we might assume that these men had not been on that expedition; on the other hand, Caesar specified that they were the first (i.e. most experienced) cohorts of the legions. Emphasizing the novelty of the Britons' fighting tactics might be a bit of artful misdirection on Caesar's part to justify the Romans' failure to achieve a swift victory.

(5) **Quintus Laberius Durus:** a military tribune, otherwise unknown. Military tribunes and other junior officers are often singled out for praise, or their deaths marked by name. This allowed Caesar to depict himself as

a magnanimous general while also implicitly benefitting from the refracted glory of his subordinates. The 'centurions' contest' (5.44 below) is an excellent example of this. As Welch (1998) notes, Caesar's higher-ranking legates do not receive such uniformly panegyric treatment, perhaps because their role as Caesar's closer social equals and plausible rivals required starker distinction between them and the *summus imperator*. A folk-etymological tradition holds that Julliberrie's Grave, a Neolithic long barrow overlooking the Stour, is named for the fallen tribune through a corruption of his name combined with 'Julius'.

Latin
(3) *intermisso spatio*: an implicit 'temporis' should be understood here (lit. 'with an interval [of time] interrupting', that is, 'after a short time'). Compare with *intermisso loci spatio* in 15.4 below.
(4) *subsidio*: dative of purpose (A&G 531.2)

Chapter 16
(1) **to abandon formation:** *ab signis discedere,* 'to move away from the standards'. Holmes (1914) *ad loc.* suggests that this should not be taken literally and that the standards stand in by metonymy for the idea of proper formation (cf. 5.17.2 below).
(3) **Thus, this style of cavalry battle...:** commentators have found this sentence difficult to explain, and some editors bracket it as a later interpolation; the objection seems to be that *equestris proelii ratio* should refer to a type of battle fought exclusively with cavalry, while the Britons are obviously using chariots as well. Caesar did, in fact, have a more precise way of referring to chariot fighting; he gives a detailed description of the Britons' tactics at 4.33, introduced with the phrase *genus hoc est essedis pugnae* ("this style of fighting is chariot-based"). If 5.16.3 were authentic, it seems reasonable that Caesar would have used a similar phrase here.

Latin
(1) *Toto hoc in genere pugnae*: a tricky phrase, as the literal translation ('in this whole type of fight') makes little sense. One solution is to understand *toto* as an example of hypallage, modifying the 'idea' of *pugnae* even though it agrees grammatically with *genere*. This is how I arrived at the translation **The whole battle...** which I think best conveys Caesar's sense here.
dimicaretur: impersonal passive (A&G 208d)

Chapter 17

(2) **Gaius Trebonius:** Gaius Trebonius (cos. 45) was tribune of the plebs in 55 BCE, when he proposed the *lex Trebonia*, which granted the outgoing consuls Crassus and Pompey five-year proconsular commands in Syria and the Spains, respectively. After his service in Gaul from 54–49 he remained a loyal Caesarian through the war with Pompey, but in 44 Trebonius took part in the conspiracy to assassinate Caesar; he was tasked with distracting Mark Antony while the murder took place. He departed to assume the proconsulship of Asia shortly thereafter and was assassinated in Smyrna by Publius Cornelius Dolabella in the following year.

they could not break formation: *ab signis legionibusque non absisterent,* lit. 'they could not depart from the standards and legions'. Cf. 5.16.1 above.

Latin

(3) *finem sequendi fecerunt*: lit. 'they made an end of pursuing', but the infinitive sounds more natural in English than the gerund.

Chapter 18

(1) **only one place:** it is unclear where Caesar and his troops crossed the Thames. Holmes' tentative identification of Brentford as the location more or less satisfied scholars in the 20th century.

Chapter 19

(1) **As I mentioned earlier:** at 5.17.5

(3) **As a result...:** *reliquebatur ut,* lit. 'It remained that... '

despite the difficulty of the march: *quantum labore atque itinere legionarii milites efficere poterant,* lit. 'what the legionary soldiers were able to accomplish in their labor and marching'.

Latin

(1)–(2) Chapter 19 opens with an unusually long (though not overly complex) sentence best broken into multiple sentences in the English translation.

Chapters 20–22: The Britons Surrender

The Trinovantes negotiate terms of surrender to Caesar, and other groups follow suit. Under pressure, Cassivellaunus eventually surrenders as well.

Chapter 20

(1) **the Trinovantes:** the Trinovantes (or Trinobantes) dwelled on the north side of the Thames in modern-day Essex and Suffolk. Caesar tells us they were one of the most powerful groups in Britain (*prope firmissima earum regionum civitas*), but we do not know much about their activities before Caesar's invasion except that their king (identified in some manuscripts by the name Imaneuntis) had recently been overthrown by Cassivellaunus, and the expelled king's son Mandubracius had sought Caesar's protection in Gaul (see below).

Mandubracius: son of the overthrown king of the Trinovantes, Mandubracius seems to have fled to Gaul seeking Caesar's protection sometime before the expedition of 54 BCE. He may have earned Caesar's protection in his lifetime, but his historical reputation suffered from it; under the name 'Afarwy' he is denounced as one of the 'Three Dishonoured Men' in the Welsh Triads, explicitly for inviting Caesar into Britain.

Latin

(1) [*Galliam*]: redundant and probably a gloss on *continentem*

[*inianuvetitius*]: some manuscripts name Mandubracius' father here, as Inianuvetitius or Imaneuntis

(3) *qui praesit ... obtineat*: relative clause of purpose (A&G 531.2)

Chapter 21

(1) **The Cenimagni, Segontiaci, Ancalites, Bibroci, and Cassi:** nothing else is known for certain about these peoples and they do not appear elsewhere in the *The Gallic War*.

(2) **Cassivellaunus' stronghold:** the precise location is unknown; plausible guesses include modern St. Albans, Hexton, and Weathampstead.

Chapter 22

(1) **which I noted above:** at 5.14.1

four kings: Cingetorix, Carvilius, Taximagulus, and Segovax are otherwise unknown. This Cingetorix is clearly not Cingetorix the Treveran, whom Caesar favored in his dispute with Indutiomarus in 5.3–4.

camp by the shore: that is, the fortifications the Romans constructed on the beach in Chapter 11.

(2) **Lugotorix:** otherwise unknown.

(3) **Commius of the Atrebates:** the Atrebates were a Belgic group situated near modern Arras, in the Artois region. They participated in the rebellion against Caesar in 57 BCE, contributing 15,000 men (2.4); along with the Nervii and the Veromandui, they were defeated by Caesar at the Sambre river (2.23). Commius had been made king of the Atrebates by Caesar after their defeat.

(4) **Caesar had decided…** Caesar's concern about Gallic uprisings in his absence proved valid, as this is indeed what happened (see Chapter 26 below). It is fully plausible that this was part of Caesar's calculation, though one might wonder whether Caesar the narrator has given it special emphasis with foreshadowing here to underscore the shrewdness of Caesar the commander.

this conflict could easily drag on: it was by now late August or early September and Caesar perceived that pursuing a more crushing defeat of the Britons could be difficult and costly (or perhaps impossible). Caesar's abrupt change of heart may have also been influenced by another, more personal circumstance, for according to Seneca Caesar was in Britain when he received news of his daughter Julia's death (*De Consolatione ad Marciam* 14). Not only was this a tragic personal loss, it had political implications, as well; Julia was married to Pompey, Caesar's rival and triumviral colleague with whom he had an increasingly strained relationship (see Introduction, pp. 9–10).

tribute: since no garrison was left behind in Britain, it is unclear for how long the Britons actually paid tribute to Rome prior to Claudius' conquest in 43 CE. The hostages obtained from Cassivellaunus provided some leverage, at least through 50 while Caesar remained in Gaul. Cicero's complaints to Atticus, however, suggest that the British expedition was viewed in Rome as generally unprofitable; in a letter from October 54, he griped that the only booty the Romans would extract from Britain was substandard slave labor (*ad Att.* 4.17).

he strictly forbade: *interdicit atque imperat*, lit. 'he forbade and commanded'; the addition of *imperat* seems intended to strengthen the force of *interdicit.*

Latin

(4) *quid ... vectigalis ... penderet*: *vectigalis* is a partitive genitive (A&G 346); *penderet* is subjunctive as the verb in an indirect question (A&G 574)

(5) *ne ... noceat*: indirect command (also called substantive clause of purpose; A&G 563)

Chapters 23–24: Caesar's Return to Gaul

With some difficulty, Caesar returns to Gaul with all of his troops and hostages. He stations his legions in winter-quarters throughout Gaul, spreading them out more than usual to accommodate a poor harvest. Several individuals who will figure prominently in the rest of Book Five are introduced in Chapter 24.

Chapter 23

(6) **the equinox:** around September 20.

second watch: second watch began around 9 p.m.

at dawn he reached land: sunrise near Boulogne in late September is around 7 am; the crossing thus took around ten hours.

Latin

(4) *desideraretur ... caperent ... reicerentur:* subjunctive verbs of the substantive clause of result introduced by the impersonal *sic accidit* (A&G 569)

Chapter 24

(1) **Samarobriva:** modern Amiens, in northern France.

(2) **Gaius Fabius:** a legate who makes multiple appearances in the *The Gallic War*. He reappears later in Book 5, coming to the aid of Q. Cicero's besieged camp along with Marcus Crassus. Fabius is later deployed by Caesar against the Menapii at 6.6, and again at Gergovia in Book 7; we also know from Hirtius' continuation of the *The Gallic War* that Fabius was tasked with reinforcing Caesar against the Suessiones (8.6) and later rescued the camp of Caninius Rebilus from Dumnacus of the Andes (8.26–31).

the Morini: a Belgic people inhabiting the area around modern Pas-de-Calais, bordering the English Channel. The Morini likely controlled Portus Itius, whence Caesar launched the expedition of 54 (cf. 5.2.3), though its precise location is unknown. The Morini make several appearances in the *BG*. They contributed 25,000 men to the revolt of the Belgic peoples in 57 (2.4.9)

and joined the alliance of the Veneti against Caesar in 56 (3.9.10); along with the Menapii, they were the final group subdued in that conflict (3.28). In 55, as Caesar was preparing his first British expedition and eyeing the territory of the Morini as a launching point, they apologized for their role in the previous rebellions and gave hostages (4.20–21); however, induced by the possibility of plunder (*spe praedae adducti,* 4.37.1) they turned on Caesar again but were subdued by Labienus (4.38). The Morini make a final appearance in Book 7, contributing 5,000 men to Vercigetorix' revolt (7.75–6).

Quintus Cicero: younger brother of the orator Marcus Tullius Cicero. He began his political career as plebeian aedile in 65 BCE and was elected praetor in 62. After three years as governor of Asia, he served as Pompey's legate in Sardinia in winter 57/6 and then with Caesar in Gaul from 54–51. Like his brother, Quintus sided with Pompey during the civil war and was pardoned by Caesar in the aftermath of Pharsalus; also like his brother, he fell victim to the proscriptions and was killed in 43. Based on their surviving correspondence (the three books of letters *ad Quintum fratrem* and four additional short letters from Quintus in the *ad Familiares*), the brothers' relationship seems to have been generally warm, and Quintus served as Marcus' legate in Cilicia in 51/50; Marcus, however, was not immune to the fraternal impulse to deliver (sometimes hectoring) advice to his younger brother. Quintus was an enthusiastic writer, spending his down time in Gaul composing poetry and translating Sophocles into Latin. The brothers may have collaborated to produce poetic accounts of the second British expedition; their letters suggest that Marcus wrote an epic *De expeditione Britannica* while Quintus may have been working on a *fabula praetexta* (historical drama); see Kruschwitz (2014). Quintus is also credited with authorship of a short guide to political campaigning (*Commentariolum Petitionis,* or the 'Little Handbook of Electioneering'), though this attribution is sometimes contested.

the Nervii: one of the most powerful Belgic peoples, the Nervii inhabited what is now the central region of Belgium. Tacitus says that the Nervii, along with the Treveri, claimed Germanic descent (*Germania* 28; cf. 5.2.4 above), and the geographer Strabo also refers to them as Germanic (4.3). The Nervii play a central role in Book Two as fearsome combatants in the Belgic uprising of 57 BCE. Caesar even provides a brief ethnography of the group in which he emphasizes their ferocity and pride (2.15). He had good reason to show them respect, since they very nearly defeated him at the Battle of the Sabis (2.16–27). Although Caesar claims at 2.28.1 to have nearly wiped out

the Nervii (*prope internecionem gente ac nomine Nerviorum*), they return as formidable foes who join forces with Ambiorix in 5.38.

Lucius Roscius: Luscius Roscius Fabatus was a loyal Caesarian. His first political office was tribune of the plebs in 55 BCE and he was elected praetor in 49. In that year, he advanced the *lex Roscia*, which granted Roman citizenship to Transpadana; through this law, Caesar hoped to secure the loyalty of the groups in this part of Cisalpine Gaul whose support could aid him in the war against Pompey. Fabatus also served as an intermediary in Caesar's attempts to negotiate with Pompey and the senate. After Caesar's death, he aligned himself with Mark Antony and was killed in the Battle of Forum Gallorum in April 43.

the Esuvii: the Esuvii (or Esubii or Sesuvii) probably dwelled in and around modern Normandy. They make two other appearances in the *BG*: in Book Two, they are listed among the Belgic states subdued by Publius Crassus (2.34.7) and in Book Three Crassus sends the prefect Titus Terrasidius to negotiate with them for provisions (3.7.4).

Titus Labienus: see 5.8.1 above

the Remi: see 5.3.4 above

the Treveri: see 5.2.4 above. It is unsurprising that Caesar assigned Labienus to spend the winter near the territory of the Treveri, given that (at this time) he was one of Caesar's trusted subordinates and there was potential for unrest among the Treveri. As Caesar notes with a hint of foreshadowing at the end of the first Treveran episode (5.3–4), Indutiomarus remained fiercely resentful of Caesar's decision to support his rival Cingetorix.

(3) **Marcus Crassus:** Marcus Licinius Crassus, elder son of the Marcus Licinius Crassus who had partnered with Caesar and Pompey in the so-called 'First Triumvirate'.

Lucius Munatius Plancus: consul in 42 BCE (with the triumvir Marcus Aurelius Lepidus) and censor in 22 BCE, Lucius Munatius Plancus survived the civil wars of the first century BCE thanks to his remarkable political adroitness; Velleius Paterculus, who did not admire him for this, remarked that he was "a traitor, as if infected with it" (*morbo proditor*, 2.83.1). Plancus remained loyal to Caesar through the civil war with Pompey and was rewarded with the proconsulship of Gallia Comata in 44. After Caesar's assassination, he participated in the negotiations among Antony, Lepidus, and the senatorial faction in 43; his support of the future triumvirs Antony and Lepidus was rewarded with the consulship of 42. Although Plancus initially sided with Antony during the triumviral conflicts, supporting his

interests as governor of Asia in 40 and proconsul of Syria in 36, he shifted his allegiance to Octavian sometime before Actium. According to Suetonius (*Aug.* 7), it was Plancus who proposed the title 'Augustus' for Octavian in 27. Plancus' funeral inscription at his tomb in Gaeta names him as the founder of Raurica and Lugdunum (modern Lyons).

Gaius Trebonius: see 5.17.2 above

(4) **the Eburones:** the ill-fated Eburones were a Belgic people, among a group that Caesar refers to as the 'Germans' (*...qui uno nomine Germani appellantur,* 2.4.10). They dwelled between the Meuse and the Rhine; the modern name of the town and abbey Averbode might derive from the group's name. The Eburones were dependents of the Treveri (*Treverorum clientes* 4.6.4), and it was through the influence of the Treveran Indutiomarus that the leaders of the Eburones, Ambiorix and Catuvolcus, orchestrated the uprising that would ultimately lead to the group's annihilation (cf. 5.26.2 below).

Ambiorix and Catuvolcus: joint leaders of the Eburones. Catuvolcus largely drops out of the narrative after this, but Ambiorix has a central role in the revolt sparked by Indutiomarus and in the destruction of Sabinus and Cotta's legions (5.26-27).

(5) **Quintus Titurius Sabinus:** nothing is known of the legate Sabinus' career beyond his role in the Gallic Wars. He contributed to the suppression of the Belgic revolt in 57 BCE (2.5, 9–10) and in the following year distinguished himself with a victory over the Venelli. (3.11, 17–19). However, he will best be remembered for his role in the devastation of the legion under his command in this book. The stark difference between Caesar's approving depiction of Sabinus in Book Three and his scapegoating of the legate in Book Five furnishes more questions than answers in the debate over serial or unitary composition (see Introduction, pp. 21–22). Perhaps Caesar praised Sabinus in Book Three despite fully knowing his disastrous end in Book Five; he may have wished to emphasize Sabinus' dramatic reversal of fortune and thus did not want to turn the reader against him prematurely, or he may have exaggerated Sabinus' competence to justify his later decision to put him in command of a legion. On the other hand, he makes artful use of foreshadowing *within* this book (e.g., Indutiomarus' anger at 5.4.4) and, we might imagine, would have done so *across* books as well if they were composed together, and the praise in Book Three might be genuine and ignorant of later events.

Lucius Aurunculeius Cotta: aside from a few brief mentions of his earlier activities in Gaul (2.11, 4.22, 4.38), Cotta is best known for his

failure to prevent disaster from befalling the legion under his and Sabinus' command during the revolt of Ambiorix in this book (5.26–37).

Latin
(2) *ducendam*: gerundive expressing purpose (A&G 500)
(8) *quoad ... cognovisset*: subjunctive verb of a temporal clause indicating Caesar's expectation (A&G 553)

Chapter 25: The Revolt of Tasgetius
Tasgetius, whom Caesar had installed as king of the Carnutes (apparently despite the Carnutes' objections), is assassinated. Caesar sends Lucius Plancus to address the situation.

Chapter 25
(1) **Among the Carnutes there was a well-born man named Tasgetius:** *Erat in Carnutibus summo loco natus Tasgetius* This phrase is reminiscent of the '*est locus...*' epic formula for introducing digressions, and signals to the reader a shift from the main narrative. Cf. the 'Centurions' Contest' at 5.44 below and epic parallels at *Il.* 2.811, 6.152, 13.32, *Aen.* 1.159 and 1.530. See Gerrish (2018) on epic resonances in this book of the *BG*.

the Carnutes: a Gallic people who occupied a large territory between the Seine and the Loire; their name is reflected in the modern town of Chartres. The Carnutes are later described as dependents of the Remi (*quorum erant in clientela,* 6.4.5); it is not clear whether this had always been the case or whether Caesar had assigned the Carnutes to the supervision of the loyal Remi after the assassination of Tasgetius.

well-born: *summo loco natus*; lit. 'born to the highest station'. Cf. the description of Vertico as *loco natus honesto* at 5.45.2

Tasgetius: unknown outside this episode, Tasgetius seems to have been installed by Caesar as king of the Carnutes around 57 BCE (if he was in his third year of rule when he was killed, as Caesar tells us at 5.25.3).

(2) **courage and goodwill toward him:** *pro eius virtute atque in se benevolentia.* Unusually high praise from Caesar. *Constantia* is not ascribed to any other individuals in the *BG*, and *virtus* is granted to only a handful of other named individuals: the legates Quintus Cicero (5.48.6) and Titus Labienus (7.59.6), the centurions Vorenus and Pullo (5.44.), the military tribune Gaius Volusenus (3.5.2), and Valerius Troucilius of the Helvii, a second-generation Roman citizen who served Caesar as an interpreter and

envoy (1.46.4). Commius of the Atrebates is the only other Gallic leader characterized by *virtus* (4.21.7); it is perhaps worth noting that Commius, like Tasgetius, had been installed as king by Caesar. Barlow (1998)'s discussion of Caesar's characterization of Gallic leaders is supplemented with a useful appendix listing the Gallic, German, and British leaders who appear in the *BG* and the distinguishing features Caesar attributes to them.

(3) **He was ruling for the third year...** Hering preserves the text of manuscript α, which leaves us without a subject for *interfecerunt*. This poses a problem of interpretation as well as translation – who assassinated Tasgetius? His personal enemies are a sensible guess, but the dative/ablative *inimicis* cannot be the subject of *interfecerunt*. Consequently, my translation here follows what I believe to be the sense of the sentence rather than the syntax; this is presumably what Holmes (1914) had in mind, as well, when he followed β here, emending *inimicis* to *inimici*.

(4) **Lucius Plancus:** whom Caesar had sent with Marcus Crassus and Gaius Trebonius to winter among the Belgae at 5.24.3

(5) **winter quarters ... as a winter camp:** *in hiberna perventum locumque hibernis esse munitum*. Somewhat redundant; Meusel omits it entirely, and Holmes (1914) concurs with this judgment. While it does not entirely solve the issue of redundancy, I think *hibernis* can plausibly be construed as a dative of purpose (A&G 382.2); note similar uses by Caesar at *BG* 1.30.3 (*locumque domicilio. . .deligerent*) and 7.16.1 (*locum castris deligit*).

Latin

(4) *cognoverit*: subjunctive verb of a subordinate (relative) clause in indirect discourse (A&G 580)

(5) *perventum:* really *perventum (esse)*, this is the impersonal passive (lit. 'there was arriving'; A&G 208d)

Chapters 26–27: Ambiorix and Catuvolcus Revolt

Encouraged by the bitter Indutiomarus, Ambiorix and Catuvolcus lead an attack on the camp of Sabinus and Cotta. When the Romans fend off the initial attack, Ambiorix shows a remarkable change of heart and tells the legates that the Gauls are planning a simultaneous attack on multiple winter camps; he advises that they should depart immediately and offers safe passage through his territory.

Chapter 26

(2) **Indutiomarus the Treveran:** who had been simmering with resentment and perhaps waiting for an opportunity to antagonize the Romans since Caesar had supported his rival in a dispute over leadership earlier that year (5.3–4).

Latin

(1) *ventum est:* impersonal passive (A&G 208d)

(4) *uti ... prodiret*: indirect command governed by *conclamaverunt* (also called substantive clause of purpose; A&G 563)

vellent ... sperarent: subjunctive verbs of subordinate (relative) clauses in indirect discourse (A&G 580)

Chapter 27

(1) **Gaius Arpinius:** the *eques* ('knight') Gaius Arpinius is otherwise unknown.

Sabinus: for consistency and clarity I will refer to Quintus Titurius Sabinus and Lucius Aurunculeius Cotta throughout by their familiar *cognomina* ('nicknames') Sabinus and Cotta, even where Caesar addresses them by *praenomen* ('first name') and *nomen* ('family name'), as here.

Quintus Iunius: otherwise unknown.

(2) **the Atuatuci:** the Atuatuci (or Adtuatuci) were a Germanic people dwelling near the Meuse. According to Caesar, they were descended from the Cimbri and Teutones, remnants of a guard left behind on the march toward Italy (2.29). The Atuatuci participated in the Belgic uprising of 57 BCE (2.4 and 16); they were besieged and defeated by the Romans, and Caesar reports that 4,000 of the Atuatuci were killed and 53,000 sold into slavery (2.29–33).

(7) **history of hospitality:** Ambiorix refers here to the formal institution of 'hospitality' (*hospitium*) rather than 'hospitality' in the more general, colloquial sense (i.e. hosting a guest generously). Traveling in the ancient world could be a dangerous enterprise, and those who ventured away from home on public or private business often relied on formal and informal contacts to provide safety, lodging, and provisions along the way. Practices of hospitality are attested as early as the Homeric poems, in which the Greek notion of *xenia* (often translated as 'guest-friendship') features. The Romans observed both *hospitium publicum* ('public hospitality') and *hospitium privatum* ('private hospitality'). *Hospitium publicum* was established

formally between states, on the model of Greek *proxenia*; *hospitium privatum*, the type of *hospitium* Ambiorix probably refers to here, could be arranged between individual Romans and foreigners and, like *xenia*, would be handed down within a family. Besides safety while traveling, *hospitium privatum* could also be a source of legal protection or political advantage.
(10) **an oath:** cf. 5.6.6 above
(11) **by doing these things**: a loose translation of *quod cum faciat*, lit. 'the fact that, when he did these things... '; probably a causal cum-clause (A&G 549)

owed to Caesar: *pro eius meritis*; lit. 'in exchange for his [sc. *Caesaris*] deserved things'.

Latin
(1) *missu Caesaris:* lit. 'by the sending of Caesar'. *Missu* is an ablative of specification or accordance (A&G 418a)

ventitare: the frequentative form of *venire*, emphasizing (along with *consuerat*) the regularity with which Quintus Junius had interacted with Ambiorix in the past (*iam ante*).
(2)–(11) a long passage of indirect discourse governed by *locutus est*.
(3) *coactu civitatis*: ablative of specification or accordance (A&G 418a)
minus ... iuris: partitive genitive (A&G 346)
(5) *alterae*: an archaic form of the dative instead of the more usual *alteri* (cf. Terence, *Phorm*. 928 and *Andr*. 983).

subsidio: dative of purpose (A&G 531.2)

Chapters 28–31: Sabinus and Cotta Quarrel

The Roman camp is divided over how to respond to Ambiorix' information. Cotta advises that they remain in camp unless instructed otherwise by Caesar, while Sabinus argues for a swift departure. After a contentious debate Cotta cedes to Sabinus and the legion spends the night preparing to march

Chapter 28

(1) **obscure and humble:** *ignobilis atque humilis*; this is the only use of *ignobilis* in the *The Gallic War*.
(2) **a fierce quarrel:** as Grillo (2016) notes, Caesar follows both historiographical and epic tradition here with Sabinus and Cotta's version of the 'quarreling generals' *topos*; in this type-scene, two commanders argue

over the best course of action and ultimately choose the path that leads to destruction. Cf. Polydamas and Hector in *Iliad* 18, Nicias and Alcibiades in Book 6 of Thucydides, Paullus and Varro at Cannae in Polybius, Book 3.

Latin

(3) *discedendum*: impersonal passive (A&G 208d)

iniussu Caesaris: ablative of specification or accordance (A&G 418a); cf. 5.27.1 and 3 above

(4)–(6) indirect discourse governed by *docebant*

(4) *testimonio*: dative of purpose (A&G 531.2)

Chapter 29

(3) **the death of Ariovistus:** Ariovistus was a leader of the Suebi who had been recognized by the senate during Caesar's consulship in 59 BCE as "king and a friend of the Roman people" (*rex atque amicus*, *BG* 1.35.2); however, in the following year found himself at odds with Caesar over his treatment of the Aedui (1.31). Sabinus' implication seems to be that Ariovistus died by Roman hands, although this is not depicted in the BG; Ariovistus escaped after being defeated in battle (1.53) and does not appear again in the narrative until Sabinus' speech.

Latin

(1)–(7) an extended passage of indirect discourse

(3) *magno ... dolori*: dative of purpose (A&G 382)

(6) *esset ... perventuros* and *consentiret ... esse ... positam*: future conditions in indirect speech (A&G 589). Note that there is no formal distinction between future more vivid and less vivid conditionals in indirect statement.

Chapter 30

(1) **Cotta and the centurions:** it is already a mark against Sabinus that he advises overruling Caesar's orders (*iniussu Caesaris,* 5.28.3) and substituting his own judgment; here, Caesar emphasizes Sabinus' wrongheadedness by indicating that not only Cotta, but also the most experienced centurions (*primis ordinibus*, lit. 'men of the first rank') disagreed with his plan.

Sabinus shouted: this is the first instance of direct speech (*oratio recta*) in Book Five and only the second of the *BG*'s twelve examples; the anonymous standard-bearer of the Tenth Legion makes a brief exhortation

at 4.25.3. The BG's speeches grow longer and more complex in the later books, culminating in one Critognatus' lengthy speech to the besieged at Alesia at 7.77 (in which, among other things, he advises that they resort to cannibalism to survive the siege). Caesar's more extensive use of direct speech in the later books has been cited as evidence for serial composition and the evolution of his literary techniques over time. See futher discussion in Introduction, pp. 37–38; cf. Grillo (2018) and Rasmussen (1963) on Caesar's use of *oratio recta*.

(2) **from you, Cotta:** Sabinus does not address Cotta by name here, but his shift from the second person plural address (*vincite, vultis, vobis*) to the second person singular (*te*) implies that these remarks are directed specifically at his opponent.

Latin

(2) *qui ... terrear*: relative clause of characteristic (A&G 534)

Chapter 31

(3) **yielded:** *dat ... manus*; lit. 'gave his hand'. *Manus* frequently takes on a metaphorical meaning to refer to power or authority (e.g., *manu mittere*, from which the English 'manumission' derives).

(4)–(6) **The rest of the night...** By this point in the Sabinus and Cotta episode the reader (or listener) may have noticed a remarkable shift in tone from earlier chapters in Book Five, in which potentially dramatic events like the defeat of Cassivellaunus were depicted in a comparatively colorless way; the Sabinus and Cotta episode seems to represent a marked departure from the conventions of the *commentarius* (see Introduction, pp. 19–21). Sabinus' speech in Chapter 30 contributes to the dramatic effect, as does the depiction here in Chapter 31 of the soldiers' anxious night. Caesar's description of the argument stretching into the night and men nervously packing and 'psyching themselves up' until dawn is reminiscent of *Iliad* 10, in which the Greeks and Trojans each hold late-night meetings (*Il.* 10.1–253 and 299–301). The nighttime setting is also a crucial element of ambush type-scenes in epic (e.g., the Doloneia in *Iliad* 10) and the reader's awareness of this trope also may have contributed to the sense of growing dread here. See Dué and Ebbot (2010) on the Iliadic model and Gerrish (2018) on this scene in particular.

Latin

(1) *consurgitur*: impersonal passive (A&G 208d)

(3) *quid ... posset* and *quid ... reliquere cogeretur*: indirect questions (A&G 574) governed by an implicit verb of wondering or debating (I have supplied **debated** in the translation).

(6) *sic ... ut ... esset persuasum:* result or consecutive clause (A&G 537); *esset persuasum* is impersonal passive (A&G 208d; cf. *BG* 2.10.5 and 3.2.5)

Chapters 32–37: Disaster Befalls the Legion

The Romans are ambushed. Panic overwhelms the unprepared Romans, to the advantage of the enemy. Sabinus tries to negotiate surrender to Ambiorix but is tricked once again. He is killed by Ambiorix' men and Cotta dies in battle. Trapped with no hope of victory or escape, the rest of the legion commits suicide.

Chapter 33

(1) **heat of the moment:** *in ipso negotio*; lit. 'during the affair itself'.

(3) **form a circle:** *in orbem consisterent*. A defensive tactic employed when fighting an enemy with greater numbers. Caesar's men use the same tactic against the Morini at 4.37.2 (*cum illi orbe facto sese defenderent*).

(6) **the inevitable happened when...:** *accidit – quod fieri necesse erat –, ut...* I have tried to maintain Caesar's sense here rather than hewing closely to the Latin syntax, for the impersonal substantive clause of result (*accidit ... ut*; A&G 569.2) can be awkward in English.

broke formation: *ab signis discederent*; see 5.16.1 above

weeping: *fletu*. Despite modern stereotypes of the Roman army as 'tough' and hypermasculine, depictions of soldiers weeping in fear or distress are not unusual in historiography. Cf. *BG* 1.39.4; Livy 25.8; Tacitus *Histories* 2.29.1 and 4.46.5 and *Annals* 1.24.3. See Rey (2015) on the effects of weeping in Roman culture (with particular focus on gendered differences in the socially permissible types of crying).

Latin

(1) *qui ... providisset*: relative causal clause (A&G 540c)

trepidare ... concursare. ... disponere: historical infinitives (A&G 463)

ut ... viderentur: result or consecutive clause (A&G 537)

(2) *qui ... cogitasset ... fuisset*: relative causal clause (A&G 540c), nicely parallel with the depiction of Sabinus in 5.33.1

(3) *quid ... faciendum esset*: indirect question (A&G 574)

ut ... relinquerent ... consisterent: indirect command governed by *pronuntiari* (also called substantive cause of purpose; A&G 563).

Chapter 34

(2) **deserted ... by their leader:** that is, they had been 'deserted' by Sabinus in his failure to anticipate the ambush.

Latin

(1) indirect discourse governed by *pronuntiari*

(3)–(4) indirect discourse governed by *pronuntiari*

Chapter 35

(2) **their open flank:** that is, the right side, unprotected by the soldiers' shields (which were carried on the left arm).

(5) **the eighth hour:** about 2 pm.

(6) **Titus Balventius:** otherwise unknown.

chief centurion: *primum pilum.* The chief centurion (*primipilus* or *primus pilus*) probably served a one-year term; from this position he could possibly advance to camp prefect (*praefectus castrorum*) or tribune of the urban cohorts (*cohortes urbanae*).

javelin: *tragula.* The tragula was a type of javelin or dart with an attached strap by which it was flung.

(7) **Quintus Lucanius:** otherwise unknown.

(8) **sling bullet:** The *funda* is properly the actual sling (usually made of leather), but presumably Cotta has been struck by a projectile and not the sling itself. The slingers ('funditores') were a crucial element of both Greek and Roman warfare, and they could hurl rocks or purpose-made sling bullets (*glandae*) with deadly precision. In this case, however, the blow was not fatal, since Cotta reappears in the next chapter.

Latin

(4) *vellent*: the protasis of a future condition set in the past can appear in the subjunctive without suggesting that it is a contrafactual condition (A&G 516f).

(6) *Tito Balventio*: dative of reference, specifically disadvantage (A&G 376)

magnae auctoritatis: genitive of quality (A&G 345).

Chapter 36

(1) **Gnaeus Pompey:** clearly not Caesar's triumviral colleague, but rather a Gallic native who obtained citizenship through Pompey's patronage and, as was customary, adopted his patron's name; cf. *BG* 1.47.4.

Latin

(1) *rogatum*: supine expressing purpose (A&G 509)

(2) *quod ... pertineat:* this clause forms the subject of *posse*

ipsi vero nihil nocitum iri: *nocitum iri* is the future passive infinitive, used impersonally (A&G 208d), and *nihil* is a Greek accusative (also called accusative of specification; A&G 397b).

(3) *ut ... excedant ... conloquantur*: indirect command governed by *communicat* (also called substantive clause of purpose; A&G 563).

Chapter 37

(3) **let out a howl:** *ululatum tollunt*. Caesar seems to emphasize the 'barbarity' of the enemy here (cf. Livy 5.35.5). The term *ululatus* is often used to describe the shrieks of mourning; the frenzied cries of worshippers of Bacchus are also described this way (e.g., Catullus 63.24, Ovid, Met. 3.528, 705, 725).

(5) **the standard-bearer Lucius Petrosidius:** Lucius Petrosidius is otherwise unknown. The standard-bearer (*aquilifer*) of the legion carried the 'eagle' (*aquila*), a silver or bronze eagle mounted on a tall pole that was the most prized of the legions' standards. Losing the *aquila* was a great mark of shame; hence, the heroism of Lucius Petrosidius' action here in ensuring the safety of the standard over his own.

(6) **committed suicide:** a horrific outcome described in characteristically unemotive language (cf. the death of Dumnorix at 5.7.9). Although the prominence of a few famous examples (e.g., Cato, Brutus, Mark Antony) creates the impression that the Roman military had a deep tradition of preserving one's honor by committing suicide rather than surrendering, Rauh (2015) has suggested that this phenomenon is exaggerated; the documented examples generally involve individual leaders and are concentrated in the context of the first-century civil wars. A group suicide in a foreign war was unusual, and, as here, seems to have been a last resort in the face of imminent slaughter (rather than grounded in a sense of humiliation or shame). Cf. Polybius on the aftermath of Lake Trasimene 3.84.8–10 and Livy on the Roman troops besieged by Hannibal at Casilinum (23.19.6).

(7) **a few men escaped:** although these survivors made it to Labienus' camp, word of Sabinus and Cotta's demise would evidently not reach Caesar until after the rescue of Quintus Cicero's camp (5.52)

Latin

(1) *ut ... faciant*: indirect command governed by *imperat* (also called substantive clause of purpose; A&G 563).

Chapters 38–43: Ambiorix Besieges the Camp of Q. Cicero

Buoyed by the disaster of Sabinus and Cotta, Ambiorix musters support from the Eburones, Nervii, Atuatuci, and their dependents and besieges the camp of Quintus Cicero. The Nervii attempt to entrap Cicero with a similar ruse as Ambiorix used against Sabinus, but Cicero is not tricked.

Chapter 38

(1) **the Atuatuci:** see 5.27.2
(2) **the Nervii:** the strength of the Nervii was apparently not as reduced as Caesar had thought (or at least claimed) at 2.28.1.
(4) **wintering with Cicero:** Quintus Cicero had been dispatched by Caesar to winter with his legion among the Nervii (5.24.2).

Latin

(2) *ne ... .dimittant*: indirect command governed by *hortatur* (also called substantive clause of purpose; A&G 563).

liberandi ... ulciscendi occasionem: lit. 'chance of freeing ... and avenging', but the infinitive sounds more natural in English than the gerund.
(4) *nihil ... negotii*: lit. 'nothing of trouble'; partitive genitive (A&G 346)

Chapter 39

(1) **the Ceutrones...:** none of these groups are otherwise known.
(2) **The inevitable happened again:** *h[u]ic quoque accidit – quod fuit necesse –, ut ... interciperentur.* Caesar alludes here to the ambush of Sabinus' men and closely echoes language in that passage (*accidit – quod fieri necesse erat –, ut ...*, 5.33.6). As in that passage, I have tried to maintain Caesar's sense in my translation rather than hewing closely to the Latin syntax, since the impersonal substantive clause of result (A&G 569.2) can be awkward in English.

Latin
(2) *qui ... discessissent*: relative causal clause (A&G 540c)

Chapter 40
(1) **to Caesar:** who was still at Samarobriva (cf. 5.24, 46-7)
(2) **towers:** towers (*turres*) were a critical element on both sides of siege warfare, and the Romans constructed both stationary and movable towers as battle demanded. In a defensive situation, as here, stationary towers were built at regular intervals to fortify a town or camp. Movable towers could either be dismantled and carried (*turres plicatiles*) or wheeled (*turres ambulatoriae*) and strategically positioned to attack.
(3) **the trench:** camps were typically fortified by both a palisade (*vallum*) and a ditch or trench (*fossa*).
(6) **fire-sharpened stakes:** when necessary, the Romans would improvise to supplement their regular weapons, and used fire to harden and sharpen these wooden stakes, which could then be thrown at the enemy like a javelin. Cf. *BG* 7.81.4; Sallust, *Catiline* 56.3; Tacitus, *Annals* 4.51.

mural javelins: a heavy pike about two meters long with a wooden shaft and sharp iron tip, the *pilum* was one of the legionaries' crucial pieces of equipment. The *pilum* would generally be deployed by hurling it against the enemy from a distance before charging forward to attack with the *gladius* (sword). The relative softness of the iron shank may have been a tactical feature, as the bending of the shank would have made it difficult to remove a *pilum* from a shield once pierced. The *pila* described here may have been heavier than the *pila* usually carried by the legionaries and specifically designed to be flung down from a height, such as the fortified towers being constructed.

The towers were fitted with floors... The *turres contabulatae* were wooden towers with multiple stories (as many as ten stories; cf. *BG* 8.41.5). The tops of the towers were fortified with *pinnae* (battlements or parapets) and *loricae* (woven breastwork; they take their name from *lorum*, a thong). The *pinnae* and *loricae* would protect the soldiers as they stood atop the towers and hurled down the *muralia pila* and other projectiles against the enemy. Caesar gives a similar description of the Roman fortifications at *BG* 7.72.

Latin
(1) *pertulissent*: subjunctive for the future perfect indicative of a future condition in implied indirect discourse (A&G 589, 592.2)

(4) *a nostris ... resistetur*: impersonal passive (A&G 208d) with ablative of agent (A&G 405)
(7) *tenuissima valetudine*: ablative of quality (A&G 415)

Chapter 41

(2) **the same things:** like Ambiorix, the leaders of the Nervii assure the Romans of safe passage through their territory if they should abandon their winter camp (cf. 5.27). Cicero's tart reply suggests that, unlike the credulous Sabinus, he has seen through the ruse.
(5) **accommodating their winter quarters:** in the view of the Nervii, the Romans' encampment of a standing military force within their borders represents the action of an occupying force, not friends or allies. Besides the symbolic appearance of occupation, the presence of a Roman army was probably a drain on local resources, as well, even if it did provide some opportunity for trade and commerce.

Latin

(5) *quicquam ... praesidii*: partitive genitive (A&G 346)
hoc ... animo: ablative of quality (A&G 415)
ut ... recusent ... nolint: substantive clause of result (A&G 571c)
(7)–(8) indirect discourse introduced by *respondit*

Chapter 42

(3) **dig up ... and carry it in their cloaks:** a verb of carrying must be supplied here, since *exhaurire* only makes sense with *manibus* (an example of zeugma).
(4) **three miles in circumference:** *milium pedum XV*, or fifteen thousand feet; a Roman mile measured approximately five thousand Roman feet.
(5) **grappling-hooks:** *falces*. The *falx* was a sickle-shaped hook used in siege warfare to pull down the enemy's wall (or try to pull down the enemies stationed on the wall)

protective covers: *testudines*. This apparatus takes its name from the Latin word for 'tortoise' (*testudo*) because of its resemblance to the turtle's protective shell. The *testudo* was a sort of portable hut that provided cover to soldiers as they tried to compromise the enemy's defenses (e.g., filling in the trench); battle-rams could be wheeled into place under cover of the *testudo* as well. The *testudines* were probably made of flame-resistant materials like rawhides and had a sloped cover so that items dropped on them from above

would slide off. The same name is given to the battle formation in which soldiers clustered together in a closely-packed group and used their shields to form a tortoise shell-like protective cover.

Chapter 43

(1) **red-hot bullets made of softened clay:** *ferventes fusilli ex argilla glandes*. *Fusilis* properly means 'molten' or 'liquid', but in this case probably describes the pliable state of the super-heated clay bullets. Holmes (1914) *ad loc*. supposes that the slings (*fundis*) may have been lined with metal to protect them against these scorching-hot bullets.

(3) **towers and covers:** *turres testudinesque*. The moveable versions of the *turres* and *testudines* described above (5.40.2 and 42.5)

Latin

(5) *habuit eventum ... ut... vulnaretur atque interficeretur*: lit. 'It had the outcome that ... were wounded and killed'; result clause (A&G 537)

(6) *se introire vellent*: indirect question introduced by *vocibus* (A&G 586)

5.44: The Centurions' Contest

Caesar punctuates his narrative of the siege of Q. Cicero's camp with a brief vignette showcasing the courage and spirit of two centurions, Titus Pullo and Lucius Vorenus.

Chapter 44

(1) **In this legion were...:** *erant in ea legione fortissimi viri*: the first of several epic 'resonances' in this passage. Cf. 5.25 above (*Erat in Carnutibus summo loco natus Tasgetius,* "Among the Carnutes there was a well-born man named Tasgetius...").

who were nearing the first rank: i.e., the rank of chief centurion (*primipilus*) of a legion. Cf. 5.35.6 above.

Titus Pullo and Lucius Vorenus: Lucius Vorenus is otherwise unknown. Titus Pullo is possibly to be identified with the 'T. Puleione' at *BC* 3.67.5, who is similarly described as defending a camp "most bravely" (*fortissime*). This T. Puleio had apparently betrayed C. Antonius (*cuius opera proditum exercitum C. Antoni demonstravimus*) at some point and is now fighting with the Pompeians; however, the episode referred to is not found in the *BC*.

(2) **for rank**: *de loco*: *locus* has many meanings beyond geographical place, including 'rank' in the military context or "office" in the political sphere.

(3) **"Why do you hesitate, Vorenus?":** Pullo's challenge to Vorenus recalls the battle taunts familiar from epic. Heroes frequently taunt their opponents, but they also use similar goading to encourage their comrades (e.g., Agamemnon to Menestheus at *Il.* 4.338–48 and to Diomedes at 4.370–400).

(4) **broke into the fighting:** another possible echo of the epic tradition here, as Pullo's plunge into the most densely packed part of the enemy line recalls the heroic *aristeia*, in which a fighter throws himself into battle and displays exceptional courage (e.g., Diomedes at *Il.* 5.633–654, Achilles in *Il.* 21). This type-scene sometimes, though not always, ends with the hero's death, and its use here allows Caesar to heighten the drama of the scene.

(7) **dart:** the *verutum* was a light, slim, tapered dart, generally used by the archers and skirmishers among the auxiliaries (in contrast with the *iaculum* and *telum*, which were employed by the light infantry, and the *pilum*, a heavier javelin used by the *hastati* and *principes*, the first two lines of infantry.

(8) **This setback:** *hic casus*: i.e., the dart becoming stuck in his sword-belt.

obstructed his hand when he was trying to draw his sword: the *balteus* was typically worn slung over the shoulder. Perhaps the force of the strike slid the belt out of position around Pullo's shoulder, making it difficult for Pullo to reach his sword, or perhaps it was simply difficult to reach around the impaled dart with his free hand.

(9) **His rival Vorenus:** *inimicus* denotes a personal rival or foe, in contrast with *hostis* (an enemy-in-arms; usually, but not always, a foreign enemy).

(13) **he tripped and fell into a hollow:** *in locum deiectus inferiorem concidit*: lit. 'cast down into a rather low place, he fell'.

(14) **Fortune:** *Fortuna* wears many faces in *The Gallic* War, as it did in Roman thought more generally. It sometimes conveys the sense of 'good fortune' (e.g., *BG* 4.26: *hoc unum ad pristinam fortunam Caesari defuit,* "This one thing prevented Caesar from recapturing his earlier good fortune"; see Fowler 1903 for other examples). Its use here is more akin to the Greek τύχη, with its connotations of capriciousness and variability (especially when paired with *utrumque versavit*). In the context of the indecisive outcome of the centurions' 'contest', we are perhaps meant to understand that Caesar's men are so uniformly courageous that even the most exacting judge cannot distinguish between them. See Introduction, pp. 30–32.

Latin

(3) *quem locum probandae virtutis tuae*: lit. 'what opportunity of proving your courage', but the infinitive sounds more natural in English than the gerundive (cf. 5.44.6 below).

(5) **Nor, indeed, did Vorenus stay...:** While *ne ... quidem* typically applies the negative force to the word in between (in this case, *Vorenus*), this does not obtain here ("Not even Vorenus remained..." does not make sense in context). Despite the word order, the clause should probably be more closely construed with *continet* than *Vorenus*.

(6) *neque dant regrediendi facultatem*: lit. 'no opportunity of retreating', but the infinitive sounds more natural in English than the gerund (cf. 5.44.3 above).

5.45–52: Caesar Rescues the Camp of Q. Cicero

Caesar learns of the crisis at Cicero's camp and summons additional legions out of their winter camps. Caesar himself arrives and saves the day.

Chapter 45

(2) **Vertico:** Vertico aids Q. Cicero again at 5.49 but does not appear elsewhere in the *The Gallic War*.

well-born: *loco natus honesto*: lit. 'born in an honorable rank', probably meaning that Vertico's family was among the nobility.

(4) **The slave carried the letter...:** *has ille iaculo inligatas effert*: it is unclear exactly how the note was concealed 'in' or 'on' the javelin. Hodges suggests that it was "perhaps concealed in the shaft, or placed under the detachable head"; Holmes (1914) *ad loc.* proposes that the letter could have been concealed by wrapping twine around it "as if the javelin had been spliced."

Chapter 46

(1) **the eleventh hour:** *hora undecima*: around five o'clock in the afternoon.

the Bellovaci: the Bellovaci were a powerful Belgic people whose territory was situated in the Thérain valley, around modern Beuvais (the name of which derives from the group's name; cf. Claudius Ptolemy 2.9.4, Strabo 4.3.5). They appear in Book 2, in which they are first subdued by Caesar, and Book 7, in which they reluctantly contribute two thousand men to Vercingetorix' revolt (7.75); The Bellovaci also feature in Book 8, which narrates their rebellion against Caesar in 51 BCE.

the quaestor Marcus Crassus: see 5.24.3 above.

(2) **as soon as he received the message:** *cum nuntio*: lit. 'with the message', or 'with the messenger', but Caesar seems to mean that Crassus left as soon as he received Caesar's order.
(3) **Gaius Fabius:** see 5.24.2 above
the Atrebates: see 5.22.3 above

Latin
(3) *qua sibi iter faciundum sciebat*: passive periphrastic with dative of agent (A&G 374a)

Chapter 47
(1) **around the third hour:** *hora circiter tertia*: around eight in the morning.
advance party: *antecursoribus,* or 'forerunners' in the most literal sense; that is, the advance party or scouts sent out ahead of the main group.
(2) **Samarobriva:** see 5.24.1

Latin
(4) **When he heard...:** an unusual degree of *hypotaxis* (subordination) for Caesar. The constructions can be mapped as follows (the main clauses are underlined and subordinate clauses are indented):

Labienus

interitu Sabini et caede cohortium cognita (*ablative absolute*)

cum omnes ad eum Treverorum copiae venissent (*subjunctive cum-clause)*

veritus ne (*participle introducing fear clause*)

si ex hibernis fugae similem profectionem fecisset (*protasis of future less vivid conditional*, A&G 514 B.2.b; *pluperfect represents secondary sequence within fear clause*)

hostium impetum sustinere non posset

praesertim quos recenti victoria efferi sciret (*relative causal clause*; A&G 535 e)

litteras Caesari remittit

quanto cum periculo legionem ex hibernis educturus esset (*indirect question*)

rem gestam in Eburonibus perscribit,

docet

omnes equitatus peditatusque copias Treverorum tria milia passuum longe ab suis castris consedisse (*indirect statement*)

Chapter 48

(4) **in Greek:** *Graecis ... litteris*. Strictly speaking this should mean 'in Greek letters' rather than 'in the Greek language' (for which we might expect the adverb *Graece*), but Caesar must mean the latter. Since the Gauls were familiar with the Greek alphabet (cf. *BG* 1.29 on the Helvetii and 6.14 on the Druids), simply transliterating a message written in Latin (which was also familiar to many Gauls) into Greek letters would be insufficient disguise. The 2nd century CE Macedonian writer Polyaenus records in his treatise on *Strategemata* ('Stratagems') that Caesar's message said simply: "Caesar to Cicero: be strong and await help" (Καῖσαρ Κικέρωνι θαρρεῖν. προσδέχου βοήθειαν, 8.23.6).

(5) **javelin:** *tragulam*. Cf. 5.35.6.

Latin

(3) *uti ... deferat*: indirect command governed by *persuadet* (also called substantive clause of purpose; A&G 563).

Chapter 49

(2) **that same Vertico I mentioned above:** at 5.45.2

(7) **by narrowing the passageways as much as possible:** *angustiis viarum, quam maxime potest, contrahit*. Caesar's plan is to compress the camp so that the Roman forces appear more meagre than they are, which in turn will falsely inflate the confidence of the Treveri. In its most basic sense, *via* means 'road' or 'path'; here it specifically refers to the passageways that divided the camp. Roman camps were generally organized according to a basic square template: a 'Main Street' (*via principalis*) ran from the Left Main Gate (*porta principalis sinistra*) to the Right Main Gate (*porta principalis dextra*); the 'Praetorian Street' (*via praetoria*; so-called because it ran through the *praetorium* or headquarters building) ran perpendicular to the *via principalis* from the Praetorian Gate (*porta praetoria*) to the Decuman Gate (*porta decumana*). There would have been several additional passageways running each way, parallel to the *via prinicpalis* or *via praetoria*.

Latin

(1) *qui ... deferat*: relative clause of purpose (A&G 531.2)

(6) *magni periculi*: genitive of quality (A&G 345).

Chapter 50

(5) **create the appearance of fear:** continuing the tactic of deception begun in Chapter 49, Caesar tries to foster arrogance in the enemy by creating the impression of disarray in the Roman camp; perhaps the Treveri will be provoked into making a rash move.

Latin

(3) *si ... posset ... si ... non posset*: these are not contrafactual conditions; the imperfect subjunctive is perhaps explained as a future condition 'thrown back into past time' (A&G 516f)

(5) *concursari ... agi*: impersonal passives (A&G 208d)

Chapter 51

(5) **Caesar killed ... and stripped:** *tum Caesar ... occidit ... atque exuit.* note the subtle shift in emphasis here; while the past several chapters have focused on the actions of Caesar's soldiers as they carry out his orders, Caesar is the singular grammatical subject of the triumphant verbs that round out this chapter (*in fugam dat; occidit; exuit*).

Chapter 52

(5) **an assembly:** *contione*. Generally speaking, *contio* can refer to any assembly, but in its more specific use the *contio* is an assembly of Romans convened by a public official or a general. In the political sphere, magistrates used the opportunity to bring potential measures before the people and to try to gain support for them (or dissuade the audience from their opponents' measures). The *contio* was for informational and deliberative purposes only; elections and formal legal proceedings took place in the *comitia*. In the military sphere, as in this passage, a general could call for a *contio* to address his troops.

Latin

(3) *quanto ... quanta ... sint administratae*: indirect questions (A&G 574)

(6) *sit acceptum*: subjunctive verb of a subordinate (causal) clause in implied indirect discourse (A&G 580; indirect discourse implied by *consolatur et confirmat*)

relinquatur: subjunctive verb of a subordinate (causal) clause in indirect discourse governed by *docet* (A&G 580)

Chapter 53

(1) **by the Remi:** *per Remos*. Some readers have taken this to mean 'through the territory of the Remi' (i.e. *per fines Remorum*) but I am inclined to agree with Holmes (1914) *ad loc.* in understanding something more like 'through the efforts of the Remi' (*per opera Remorum*). As Holmes notes, there are only two occasions when Caesar uses *per* with the name of a group to express 'through the territory of', and in those cases context makes the meaning unambiguous (*BG* 1.6.1 and 1.9.1).

(3) **Fabius:** Gaius Fabius, who had come to the aid of Cicero's camp along with the quaestor Marcus Crassus (5.46.1)

(6) **the quaestor Lucius Roscius:** Lucius Roscius was last seen being sent to winter quarters among the Esuvii (5.24.2). The Esuvii dwelled in what is now Normandy, making Roscius a strategic target for the Armoricae or 'maritime states' (on which see below).

Armoricae: The Armoricae or Aremoricae were peoples who dwelled near the coast between the Seine and the Loire; the name is thought to derive from the Celtic word meaning 'maritime'.

Latin

(4) *quid ... consilii*: partitive genitive (A&G 346)

caperent ... fierent: subjunctives in indirect questions (A&G 574)

(5) *acciperet*: subjunctive in a *quin*-clause (A&G 558)

Chapter 54

(2) **Senones:** the Senones were a powerful Gallic state dwelling in the upper Seine river basin; their capital, Agedincum, derives its modern name (Sens) from the group's name. Aggrieved by Caesar's interference in their affairs, in 53 BCE the Senones joined the Carnutes in a conspiracy under the leadership of one Acco (6.2–5, 44); they later joined with Vercingetorix in the revolt of 52 BCE.

Cavarinus: Cavarinus is unknown before this episode. Although he is driven into exile by his countrymen he returns to the narrative of the *BG* in Book 6, where he appears with Caesar leading a Senonian cavalry detachment.

Moritasgus: this Moritasgus is otherwise unknown. He seems to share a name, however, with a Celtic healing god who is identified with Apollo in two inscriptions from Alesia (*CIL* XIII 11240 and 11241).

(5) **I am not sure...:** a rare interjection of Caesar the narrator editorializing on the events of the narrative. The roundabout phrasing here (*idque adeo*

haud scio mirandumne sit) creates a bit of a straw man; there is surely no one who finds it surprising that the Gauls would chafe under Roman domination, but suggesting it gives Caesar an excuse to remind his audience that he has achieved victories against a formidable foe.

Latin
(4) *esse ... repertos*: the infinitive (with the subject accusative *aliquos ... principes*) functions here as the subject of *valuit* and *attulit* (A&G 452)

Chapter 55
(2) **the war with Ariovistus:** see 5.29.3

the migration of the Tenctheri: in the previous year (55 BCE), the Tenctheri, who along with the Usipetes had been driven out of their own territory by their fellow Germans the Suebi, crossed the Rhine and in turn pushed the Menapii out of their territory (*BG* 4.1, 4, 16).

Latin
(1) *mitterent ... sollicitarent ... pollicerentur ... dicerent*: subjunctives in a *quin*-clause (A&G 558).

Chapter 56
(1) **the Carnutes:** see 5.25.1
(2) **the customary way for Gauls to declare war:** the custom described here of torturing and sacrificing the last soldier to arrive when summoned may be an example of the practices Caesar refers to in his digression on the Gauls in Book 6 (see especially 6.16).
(3) **Cingetorix ... whom I mentioned earlier as having made a promise to Caesar:** at 5.3.3.

Latin
(1) *si ... coepisset*: subjunctive for the future perfect indicative of a future conditional in indirect discourse (A&G 589). Note that there is no formal distinction between future more vivid and less vivid conditionals in indirect statement.

Chapter 58
(7) **for a short time after this:** *pauloque ... post id*. The narrator seems aware that this peace will be short-lived. This might point toward the

composition of Books 5 and 6 together during the winter of 53/2 BCE, as has been suggested (see Introduction, pp. 28–29) or may simply indicate that it was not completed during the brief intermission of winter 54/3 and that Caesar continued to write or revise it after hostilities resumed in 53.

COMMENTARY BOOK VI

Chapters 1–4

Caesar anticipates further unrest and spends the winter season (54/3 BCE) preparing accordingly. He quickly subdues an uprising of the Senones and turns his attention toward the anticipated war with the Treveri.

Chapter 1

(1) **Caesar had many reasons...** As he opens Book 6, Caesar alludes to the turmoil of the previous year (54 BCE), in which he had faced widespread discontent and the costly uprising of Ambiorix.

Marcus Silanus: grandson of a consul of 109 BCE (Marcus Junius Silanus) and brother-in-law of the triumvir Marcus Aemilius Lepidus. His path after Caesar's assassination was dramatically winding. Initially he joined with Lepidus and then went to aid Antony at Mutina. After the formation of the triumvirate in 43 he ran afoul of the triumvirs and fled to the protection of Sextus Pompey in Sicily. Restored in the pact of Misenum, he served in Greece under Antony but switched allegiances to join Octavian before Actium; he was later rewarded with the consulship of 25 BCE (serving with Augustus as co-consul).

Gaius Antistius Reginus: the identification of Gaius Antistius Reginus is unclear. The *gens Antistia* was a notable plebeian family whose recent members included Pompey's first wife (whom he divorced under orders from Sulla), but it is not known where this Antistius fits into the family tree.

Titus Sextius: Titus Sextius served under Caesar in Gaul and probably also in the civil war with Pompey. In 44 BCE he succeeded the historian Sallust as governor of Africa Nova. In retaliation for his support of Antony at Mutina, the senate ordered Sextius to surrender two legions to Italy and one to Quintus Cornificius, governor of Africa Vetus. After the establishment of the triumvirate, he took Africa Vetus by force and ruled both Africas with the triumvirs' consent until the Perusine War, at which point they were transferred to Octavian's lieutenant Gaius Fuficius Fango; he reclaimed the provinces on Antony's behalf during the Perusine War but ultimately handed them over to Lepidus in 40.

(2) **since Pompey was staying near the city...** Pompey's proconsular province was the Spains (Citerior and Ulterior), but he installed legates to

govern Spain in his stead and spent the year close to Rome. He could not legally enter the city without resigning his military command (*imperium*) but needed to remain close enough to maintain his political presence, especially since Caesar's popularity among the Roman people remained high (thanks to the reports of his successes in Gaul). Pompey thus remained close enough to the city to engage in public life but without surrendering his *imperium*, observing the letter (if not the spirit) of the law.

the troops he had levied from Cisalpine Gaul as consul: i.e. in 55/4 BCE.

(4) **which he had lost with Sabinus:** i.e. Quintus Titurius Sabinus (see 5.24.5 and 27.1). Caesar refers here to the legion that was tricked and ambushed by Ambiorix in the previous year (5.24–37).

Latin

(2) *sacramento rogavisset*: *sacramento rogare* is a technical term for 'to swear a [military] oath'.

Chapter 2

(1) **When Indutiomarus was killed, as I have described…:** Indutiomarus, the Treveran noble whose implication of Caesar in a local dispute for power set in motion the turmoil of 55 and provided a useful pretext for Ambiorix' intervention, was captured and killed by Labienus' cavalry (5.58).

Treveri: see 5.2.4

(2) **Ambiorix:** see 5.24.4. Ambiorix, whose revolt against Caesar consumed much of 54 BCE (and thus accounts for most of Book 5), was last seen traveling among various groups trying to build a coalition to exploit the momentum gained by his devastation of the legion under Sabinus and Cotta (5.38–9).

(3) **the Nervii** and **Atuatuci:** see 5.24.2 and 5.27.2, respectively.

the Menapii: the Menapii were a Belgic people residing with a significant recent history of resisting Roman intervention in Gaul. In 57 BCE, they contributed 9000 men to the Belgic confederacy against Caesar (*BG* 2.4), and in 56 they were among the groups that allied with the Veneti against Caesar (3.9). Along with the Morini, the Menapii continued to resist Caesar after the rest of the allied states had been subdued and were punished with the devastation of their fields and settlements (3.28–9). In 55, the Menapii were driven out of their territory by the invading Usipetes and Tenctheri (4.4); when Caesar sailed for Britain later that year he assigned Sabinus and

Cotta to keep the Morini and Menapii in check (4.22), and the Romans once again laid waste to the territory of the Menapii.

the Senones: see 5.54.2

the Carnutes: see 5.25.1

Chapter 3

(4) **summoned a council:** Caesar generally convened a council of Gallic leaders early in the spring; cf. 4.6.5 and 5.24.1 (in which the council for 54 BCE was held after the invasion of Britain).

Lutetia: modern Paris. The original site, on the Ile de la Cité, was captured and destroyed by Labienus during the revolt of Vercingetorix in 52 BCE (*BG* 7.57–8).

the Parisii: the Parisii lived on the banks of the Sequana (Seine) River. In 52 BCE they were among the states that joined the alliance of Vercingetorix (7.4); as a result, their town Lutetia was destroyed by Labienus (5.57–8, see above).

(5) **in the previous generation:** lit. "in the memory of their fathers (*patrum memoria*)".

Chapter 4

(1) **Acco:** a leader among the Senones, Acco is otherwise unknown.

(2) **the Aedui:** see 5.7.1

(5) **the Remi:** see 5.3.4

their dependents: cf. 5.25.1

Chapters 5–10

The war against the Treveri is renewed. Caesar makes a pre-emptive strike against the Menapii. The Treveri attack the camp of Labienus, who uses a clever ruse to escape. Caesar arrives in the territory of the Treveri and crosses the Rhine for the second time. The Suebi prepare to defend themselves against the Roman incursion.

Chapter 5

(2) **Cavarinus:** see 5.54.2. Cavarinus had been appointed king of the Senones by Caesar but was rejected by them and fled to Caesar's protection when he discovered a plot to assassinate him.

Cavarinus' hot temper or the hatred he had incurred: the Senones were presumably not pleased that Cavarinus had anticipated their attempt on

his life and had found refuge with the Romans, and from Caesar's description of Cavarinus' temperament toward his former subjects (*iracundia*), leaving him behind would probably have created more problems than it prevented.

(4) **the Eburones:** see 5.24.4

hospitality: on the formal institution of hospitality (*hospitium*), see 5.27.7

(6) **Labienus:** see 5.8.1.

Latin

(3) *pro explorato habebat:* lit. 'considered it as something that had been investigated/researched'.

Chapter 6

(1) **Gaius Fabius:** see 5.24.2

Marcus Crassus: see 5.24.3

(4) **Commius of the Atrebates:** see 5.22.3. Commius had been installed by Caesar as king of the Atrebates after Caesar's victory over the group in 57 and had remained loyal and useful to Caesar since then, even helping Caesar negotiate the surrender of Cassivellaunus (5.22). Notably, Commius is one of only two Gallic leaders to whom Caesar ascribes *virtus* (4.21.7; the other is Tasgetius at 5.25.2).

Latin

(3) *si ... recipissent*: subjunctive for the future perfect indicative of a conditional in indirect discourse (A&G 589)

Chapter 7

(1) **wintering within their borders:** Caesar had assigned Labienus to winter quarters among the Treveri during the previous year (5.24); Labienus was one of Caesar's most trusted lieutenants and, as the uprising of Indutiomarus the year before had confirmed, the Treveri were increasingly resentful of Caesar's presence in Gaul.

(5) **a river that was difficult to cross:** commentators have disagreed about the identification of this river; suggestions include the Moselle, the Mouzon, and the Ourthe.

(6) **Labienus announced publicly to a council:** Holmes (1914) *ad loc.* skepticism of the reading *consilio* here is probably well-founded. A council of war (*consilium*) would necessarily be held out of enemy earshot and most likely

not open to the entire camp; however, the point of Labienus' ruse (emphasized by *palam*, 'publicly') was that the Gallic cavalry in his camp *would* hear his 'plan' and relay it to the Treveri, who would be tricked into believing the Romans were retreating. Hecker's emendation *consulto* ('intentionally, by design') makes good sense.

(8) **centurions of the first rank:** *primis ordinibus* (cf. 5.30.1 and 5.44.1).

more loudly and frantically than was typical for the Romans: *maiore strepitu et tumultu quam p. R. fert consuetudo*; lit. 'with greater noise and commotion than the custom of the Roman people allowed'.

Latin

(2) *missu Caesaris:* lit. 'by the sending of Caesar'. *Missu* is an ablative of specification or accordance (A&G 418a)

(4) *aliquam dimicandi facultatem*: lit. 'some opportunity of fighting' but the infinitive sounds more natural in English than the gerund

(5) *difficili transitu flumen*: ablative of quality (A&G 415)

(8) *quid sui sit consilii*: lit. 'what of a plan there was'; *consilii* is partitive genitive (A&G 346) and *sit* is subjunctive in an indirect question (A&G 574).

Chapter 8

(1) **It was a waste of time:** *longum esse.*

(3) **"You have the opportunity...":** one of just twelve examples of direct speech in the *BG* (see note on 5.30.1). Labienus' exhortation that the soldiers fight as if Caesar were watching them in person allows Caesar to demonstrate the loyalty and devotion his men felt toward him without having to claim this outright in his own authorial voice. See Introduction, pp. 37–38 as well as Rasmussen (1963) and Grillo (2018) for discussion and further bibliography on the direct and indirect speeches in the commentaries.

(6) **contrary to their expectations:** *praeter spem*

assemble in formation facing the enemy and **attacking them:** *signa ad hostem converti* and *infestis signis ad se ire*, lit. 'turn the standards toward the enemy' and 'coming at them with hostile standards'. The standards probably stand in by metonymy for the idea of proper formation (cf. 5.16.1 and 5.17.2).

Latin

(1) *ut ... non audeant ... non dubitant*: substantive clauses of purpose governed by *pati* (A&G 563c)

(5) *praesidio*: dative of purpose (A&G 531.2)
(7) *auxilio*: dative of purpose (A&G 531.2)

Chapter 9

(2) **the Germans had sent help:** Caesar does not seem to take into consideration the fact that the Germans had fled without actually providing aid once they heard about Labienus' rout of the Treveri.
(3) **where he had crossed with his army before:** Caesar alludes here to his crossing of the Rhine in 55 BCE (*BG* 4.17). The precise locations of his crossings are uncertain; Holmes (1914) *ad loc.* ventured a (tentative) guess that both crossings took place somewhere between modern Koblenz and Andernach.
(4) **familiar and well-established:** i.e. from the campaign of 55.
(6) **the Ubii:** a Germanic people dwelling on the east bank of the Rhine. Longtime foes of the Suebi (*BG* 4.3), the Ubii were the only Germans across the Rhine to make a treaty of friendship with Caesar (*amicitiam fecerant*, 4.16.5), which they did to secure protection against the Suebi; Caesar did, in fact, come to their aid (4.19). In 38 BCE the Ubii moved to the west bank of the Rhine (through the assistance of Agrippa) to escape further harassment by the Suebi.
(8) **the Suebi:** a Germanic people dwelling east of the Rhine, the Suebi are described by Caesar as the "largest and most warlike of all the German peoples" (*Sueborum gens est longe maxima et bellicosissima Germanorum omnium*, *BG* 4.1.3). They first appear in the *BG* as antagonists of the Treveri and allies of Ariovistus (1.37, 51–54) and, as described at 6.9.6 above, had a long history of antagonizing the Ubii.

Latin
(7) *petunt atque orant, ut sibi parcat* and *ne ... pendant*: indirect commands (also called substantive clause of purpose; A&G 563).

Chapter 10

(5) **the Bacenis:** it is unclear precisely where the Bacenis Forest was located. Moberly (1878) *ad loc.* suggests that Caesar's description of the forest as forming a 'natural wall' or 'barrier' (*pro nativo muro*) is consistent with the Thüringer Wald, a forested mountain range in the modern German state of Thuringia.
the Cherusci: a Germanic people not otherwise mentioned in the *BG*.

Latin

(2)–(3) *imperat, ut ... deducant ... conferant* and *mandat ut ... mittant ... cognoscant*: indirect commands (also called substantive clause of purpose; A&G 563).

(5) *appellatur*: the shift back to the indicative here probably indicates that this is Caesar's own knowledge, not part of the scouts' report.

Chapters 11–20

Digression on the political structure and factions, class system, and religious and ritual practices among the Gauls.

Chapter 11

(1) **Since we have arrived at this point:** Caesar here opens a lengthy excursus on the peoples and regions of Gaul and Germany. The Gallic half of the digression consists of numerous components: the political structure and factions among the Gauls (11–12), the two ranking classes among the Gauls, the Druids (13–14) and the knights (15), religion and ritual practices among the Gauls (15–20). On the role of digressions in the *BG* and ancient historiography more generally, see Introduction, p. 34–36 and commentary at 5.12.1.

Latin

(3) *redeat*: this subjunctive might plausibly be explained as either a relative clause of result (A&G 537.2) or a relative clause of characteristic (A&G 534). I have opted for the former interpretation in my translation, since Caesar's point seems to be that their jurisdiction over important matters is the *result* of their high esteem among their countrymen rather than a merely concurrent circumstance.

Chapter 12

(1) **the Sequani:** the Sequani were a Gallic people who inhabited the upper Arar (saône) river basin. The Sequani were longtime rivals of the Aedui, who were particularly favored by Caesar and Rome (see note on 6.12.3 below). They were among the groups targeted by Ariovistus in 58 BCE and were afforded some protection by Caesar's intervention (*BG* 1.31–54). However, they remained resentful of Caesar's elevation of the Aedui and later joined the revolt of Vercingetorix, contributing 12,000 men (7.75).

(3) **But after numerous victories in battle...:** Caesar refers here to conflicts

between the Sequani and Aedui in the late 60s BCE, and in particular to the Battle of Magetobriga in 63, at which the combined forces of the Sequani, the Arverni, and the Suebi (under the leadership of Ariovistus) massacred the defeated Aedui. With the druid Diviciacus as their representative, the Aedui traveled to Rome to seek relief (see section 5 below); this set the precedent for Caesar's intervention against Ariovistus in 58 BCE (*BG* 1.31–54).
(5) **Diviciacus:** Diviciacus (sometimes Divitiacus) of the Aedui is the only druid to be known by name.

Chapter 13
(3) **the Druids:** Caesar's description of the Druids (13–14) is the oldest surviving account of this group; they are also described by the elder Pliny (*Natural History* 16.249). After the invasion of Britain by the emperor Claudius the Druids began to be characterized in more pejorative terms by Roman authors, perhaps to justify the Romans' brutal conquest of the island; for example, Suetonius calls their religion "savage and brutal" (*religionem dirae immanitatis*). See Aldhouse-Green (2010) for an overview of the evidence for and lifestyle of the ancient Druids.
(11) **discovered in Britain:** modern scholars have disagreed on the origins of Druidism, both in terms of its geographical origin (whether in Britain, as Caesar claims here, or on the mainland) and its age (dating from as early as the Neolithic to as late as the 3rd century BCE). Spence (1971) 166–71 and Holmes (1914) *ad loc.* summarize a variety of arguments.

Latin
(1) *nullo concilio*: *nullo* is an archaic form of the dative (rather than the expected classical form *nulli*). Moberly (1878) *ad loc.* deduces this based on analogy with *alterae* at 5.27.5. Caesar does not use *adhibeo* with a dative elsewhere in the *BG*, preferring the absolute usage (for example, *fratrem adhibit*, *BG* 1.20.5) or *ad* + accusative (e.g., *neque hos ad concilium adhibendos censeo,* 7.77.3); the dative usage is less common in classical Latin but it would be difficult to make sense of an ablative here.
(4) *magno ... sunt ... honore*: ablative of quality (A&G 415)
(7) *est interdictum*: impersonal passive (lit. 'there was forbidding/barring', A&G 208d)

Chapter 14
(3) **it is not right:** *neque fas esse*. Caesar's use of the term *fas* here is apt,

as it originated in the religious sphere (although it comes to be used more generally to mean 'right' or 'possible').

in Greek: cf. 5.48.4. It is less clear here than in the earlier example whether Caesar means 'the Greek language' or 'Greek characters'. In the case of Caesar's coded dispatch to Quintus Cicero in Book 5, the point of writing in the Greek *language* was to conceal the message despite local familiarity with Greek *characters*. The Druid writing referred to here is specifically *not* their secret teaching, but rather all their other public and private transactions, so concealment may not be the point. On balance, however, I am inclined to think it is more likely that Caesar refers to writing in the Greek language here.

(4) **they do not want those who learn it...** The Druids' belief that the practice of writing leads to the decline of memory and wisdom echoes the claim presented in Plato's *Phaedrus*. Plato's Socrates recounts the myth of Theuth and Thamus. The god Theuth, the inventor of writing, asked Thamus (at that time king of the Egyptians) to spread his new art among humankind. Thamus warns Theuth that his new invention may *seem* likely to improve memory, but it will in fact *diminish* the learner's ability to remember, for "they will trust to the external written characters and not remember of themselves. The specific which you have discovered is an aid not to memory, but to reminiscence, and you give your disciples not truth, but only the semblance of truth; they will be hearers of many things and will have learned nothing; they will appear to be omniscient and will generally know nothing; they will be tiresome company, having the show of wisdom without the reality" (*Phaed.* 275b, transl. Jowett).

(5) **souls do not perish...** once again, we can detect echoes of Greek philosophy in Caesar's description of the Druids' beliefs, as the conception of the transmigration of the soul is central to Pythagorean doctrine (although it probably did not originate with Pythagoras). Diodorus Siculus (5.28.6) claimed that the Druids encountered Pythagoreanism in their contact with the Greeks who lived in Massilia (modern Marseilles), but Iamblichus and Origen later contend that it was the Greeks who inherited this tradition from the Druids.

(6) **the way the universe works:** *de rerum natura.* This phrase is also the title of the philosopher Lucretius' didactic poem *De Rerum Natura*, which gives an accounting of the Epicurean philosophical worldview. The *DRN* was probably in circulation (if not published) by the mid-50s BCE; Krebs (2013) has argued that at least some portions of the poem reached Caesar in Gaul through correspondence with the brothers Cicero. From Quintus Cicero's

correspondence with his brother Marcus Tullius Cicero, it seems that he was familiar with Lucretius' work (Cic. *Q. fr.* 2.9.3), and may have brought the text with him when he joined Caesar's staff in 54; Caesar also corresponded himself with Marcus about literary topics while in Gaul and seems even to have read drafts of Cicero's work (c.f. Cic. *Q. fr.* 2.15.5). Krebs makes a convincing case for Caesar's awareness of the *DRN* after 54 by identifying numerous possible allusions to the poem in books 5–7 of the *BG* (including this passage).

Latin

(4) *ut ... remittent*: subjunctive verb in a substantive clause of result introduced by the impersonal *accidit* (A&G 569)

Chapter 15

(1)–(2) **each man who is...** *atque eorum ut quisque est genere copiisque amplissimus, ita plurimos circum se ambactos clientesque habet.* I have rendered this phrase rather liberally in my translation to avoid the awkwardness of the correlatives (*ut ... ita*) in English

(2) **servants:** *ambactos. Ambacti* seems to be a Gallic word. Holmes (1914) *ad loc.* surmises that this refers to paid servants; they are contrasted with *clientes*, so they are probably lower-ranking in social status than clients, but they are also not slaves (for which Caesar would have used *servos*).

Chapter 16

(2) **conduct human sacrifice:** *pro victimis homines immolant* (lit. 'sacrifice humans in place of [typical] sacrificial victims'). Accusations of human sacrifice were something of a 'barbarian' topos in ancient literature. Caesar's account takes a more neutral, 'anthropological' tone than later, more polemical accounts (cf. Tacitus, *Annals* 14.30) and refrains from expressing any explicit value judgment on the Druids' practices here.

(4) **enormous figures:** *immani magnitudine simulacra*. The term *simulacra* and the reference to limbs (*membra*) suggests some sort of human- or god-shaped effigy, made (at least in part) of wicker-work (*contexta viminibus*).

Latin

(5) *qui ... sint comprehensi:* relative clause of characteristic (A&G 534)

Chapter 17

(1) **Mercury:** scholars generally agree that the Gauls did not actually

worship the Roman god Mercury himself, but that Caesar has applied the Roman name to the equivalent local god. Spencer (1848) *ad loc.* suggests that Caesar refers to Odin or Wodan here. Cf. Tacitus, *Germania* 9.
(2) **essentially the same beliefs:** Caesar here seems to acknowledge that the Gauls did not actually worship the Roman gods (as noted on Mercury above), but rather that there are significant similarities in the attributes and realms of the local gods and the gods of the Roman pantheon. Holmes (1914) *ad loc.* is, perhaps, overly tart, but his assessment is sensible: "It is hardly necessary to tell the reader that the Celts had their own names for the five great gods whom Caesar called Mercury, Apollo, Mars, Jupiter, and Miverva. The Celtic names, if Caesar knew them, would have meant nothing to his Italian readers; but the Celtic gods whom he called by Roman names appeared to him to correspond, more or less closely, with the five great Roman gods."

Latin
(5) *ut ... auderet:* subjunctive verb of an impersonal substantive clause of result governed by *accidit* (A&G 569.2)

Chapter 18
(1) **Father Dis:** as with the gods described in Chapter 17, Caesar most probably applies the name of a Roman god to a local deity whose attributes remind him of the Roman Dis. In the Roman context, Father Dis (*Dis Pater*) was a god of the underworld and the dead, commonly equated with Pluto or his Greek equivalent Hades. Since Dis is associated with the underworld, the Gauls' claim to be descended from him might be a claim to authochthony (cf. the commentary on the Britons' origin myth at *BG* 5.12).
(2) **they count ... by the number of nights:** cf. Tacitus, *Germania* 11.
the occasion is marked by sundown the night before: *ut noctem dies subsequatur*, lit. 'the day follows upon the night'. I understand the 'day' here to mean the day of celebration.

Chapter 19
(3) **wives:** the plural here suggests (though does not confirm) the practice of polygamy among at least the aristocracy (*inlustriore loco natus*).
in the same manner as slaves: e.g., interrogation by torture. Under Roman law, citizens could give sworn testimony under oath, but testimony delivered by slaves was only considered reliable and valid if obtained by means of torture.

(4) **even animals:** a practice perhaps unsettling to the modern reader, but not unfamiliar in the ancient world (cf. *Iliad* 23.171-174).

Latin
(4) *quae vivis cordi fuisse arbitrantur*: the 'double dative' construction (A&G 382), consisting of a dative of purpose (here, *cordi,* 'for the heart/pleasure') and a dative of interest (*vivis*, 'for the living').

Chapters 21–24
The customs of the Germans and how they differ from the Gauls.

Chapter 21
(2) **the sun, fire, and the moon:** Solem et Vulcanum et Lunam, lit. 'Sol, Vulcan, and Luna'. I have chosen to translate here with the generic names of the natural elements rather than the proper names; I think this better emphasizes Caesar's point that the Germans worship the natural phenomena that benefit them materially.
(4) **some think that this increases...:** cf. Tacitus, *Germania* 20: "The youth learn about sex late, and so their virility is still abundant" (*sera iuvenum venus, eoque inexhausta pubertas*).
(5) **since they bathe all together...:** cf. *BG* 4.1.10. This and several other details are similar to Caesar's brief description of the Suebi in the beginning of Book 4.

Latin
(1) *qui ... praesint*: relative clause of purpose (A&G 531.2).

Chapter 22
(1) **They do not practice agriculture...:** cf. 4.1.8.
(2) **No man has a tract of land...:** cf. 4.1.7.

Chapter 23
(1) **They praise most highly...:** cf. 4.3.
(6) **Banditry:** *latrocinia.* Roving gangs of bandits (*latrones*) could pose a serious risk to travelers in the Roman world. Bandits, like gladiators, were typically figured as 'outsiders' in Roman thought, and the title *latro* even came to be used as a term of political abuse; Caesar's emphasis on the Germans' tolerance of banditry may be meant to highlight their position on the periphery

of the Roman world and alienation from traditional Roman values. On banditry in the Roman world see Shaw (1984) and Grünewald (2004).

(9) **morally wrong to harm a guest**: if the discussion of banditry had an 'othering' effect, it is somewhat balanced here by Caesar's description of the Germans' strict observance of the code of hospitality, a value shared with the Greeks and Romans; cf. 5.27.7.

Latin

(4) *qui ... praesint ... habeant*: relative clause of purpose (A&G 531.2)

Chapter 24

(2) **Volcae Tectosages:** the Volcae Tectosages were a Gallic people who dwelled between the Pyrenees and Narbo (Narbonne). Their counterpart, the Volcae Arecomici, inhabited the region around modern Nîmes. Caesar's Volcae were the descendants of a confederation that invaded Macedonia in the third century BCE, pushing into the Balkans and eventually Anatolia (those that settled there became known as Galatians).

Hercynian Forest: the Hercynian Forest, as Caesar describes in Chapter 25, once stretched in an unbroken expanse from the Rhine across what is now Germany; the ancient sources are unclear about how far east it extended.

Eratosthenes: Eratosthenes of Cyrene (c. 276–194 BCE) was one of the great thinkers of the intellectual community in Ptolemaic Alexandria. He was appointed head librarian of Alexandria's famous Library by Ptolemy III Euergetes and served as a tutor to Ptolemy's children. Although the polymath Eratosthenes had a vast scholarly output encompassing mathematics, geography, literature, and philosophy, today he is best known for calculating the Earth's circumference to a surprisingly reasonable degree of accuracy by measuring shadows in two locations on the summer solstice.

(5) **proximity to the provinces:** that is, the Roman provinces of Cisalpine and Transalpine Gaul. Cf. Caesar's description of the Belgae: "The bravest of all these [groups] are the Belgae, because they live the furthest from the refinement and culture of the [Roman] province, and they rarely interact with traders or import the sorts of goods that would soften their natures" (*Horum omnium fortissimi sunt Belgae, propterea quod a cultu atque humanitate provinciae longissime absunt, minimeque ad eos mercatores saepe commeant atque ea quae ad effeminandos animos pertinent important*, *BG* 1.1.3). As Emily Allen-Hornblower (2014) notes: "Caesar's positive assessment of those Gauls who remain detached from Roman influence (and particularly

those who resist the Germans) and their *virtus* is not without ambivalent implications regarding Rome's degeneracy (687)." At 4.2.1, Caesar notes that the Suebi do interact with traders, but only to sell goods, not to import them. See also Riggsby (2006) 83–96.

Chapters 25–28

Description of the Hercynian Forest and the fantastical beasts that dwell there.

Chapter 25

The digression on the Hercynian Forest and its peculiar, fantastical creatures struck some early readers as so anomalous that it should not be ascribed to Caesar himself (e.g. Klotz (1910)). However, starting from the assumption that this passage *is* Caesarian, more recent scholarship has explored ways in which this strange digression contributes to Caesar's overall rhetorical and narrative aims: see creative and compelling readings by, e.g., Krebs (2006), Riggsby (2006), and Allen-Hornblower (2014).

(2) **the Helvetii, Nemetes, and Raurici:** the Helvetii played a major role in Caesar's first year in Gaul, and the campaign against the Helvetii occupies the first half of Book One (*BG* 1.1–30). The Helvetii were joined in this venture by the Raurici, a neighboring Celtic people. The Nemetes were a Germanic people situated on the Rhine.

the Dacians and Anartes: the Dacians and Anartes dwelled in the region that is now Romania. The Dacians are now perhaps best known for their defeat at the hands of the emperor Trajan in the 2nd century CE in a campaign commemorated in the detailed relief that winds around Trajan's Column in Rome.

Latin

(4) *qui ... dicat ... aut ... acceperit*: relative clause of characteristic (A&G 534).

(5) *quae ... visa non sint*: relative clause of characteristic (A&G 534).

Chapter 26

This chapter begins Caesar's vivid depiction of the Hercynian Forest's marvelous creatures, which, based on these descriptions, we have to assume Caesar probably never saw for himself. As Moberly (1878) *ad loc.* tartly notes: "Conjecture is wasted on this and the next chapter."

(1) **ox that is built like a stag:** "This animal was probably the reindeer, which, however, as the reader knows, has two antlers", Holmes asserts (1914, *ad loc.*).

Chapter 27

(1) **their legs do not have joints:** Pliny the Elder gives a similar (if slightly confused) account; his description of something called the achlis matches Caesar's description of the elk exactly, but Pliny seems to believe these are two different animals and that it is the achlis, not the elk, that possesses unarticulated legs (*Natural History* 8.16).

Chapter 28

(1) **uri:** probably the aurochs, a now-extinct species of wild cattle that inhabited a wide range extending from Britain and mainland Europe to northern Africa and perhaps as far east as India.

Chapters 29–33

The main narrative resumes with Caesar's decision not to pursue the Suebi. He turns his attention back to the pursuit of Ambiorix. Caesar divides the army among himself, Labienus and Trebonius and leaves Quintus Cicero in charge of the garrison at Atuatuca.

Chapter 29

(1) **as I mentioned previously:** Chapter 22

(3) **Gaius Volcacius Tullus:** otherwise unattested, and does not appear elsewhere in the *BG*; perhaps a son of Lucius Volcacius Tullus, consul of 66 BCE.

(4) **Lucius Minucius Basilus:** served under Caesar both in Gaul and during the civil war with Pompey. He was praetor in 45 BCE and was deeply offended at being rewarded by Caesar with cash rather than command of a province the following year (Cassius Dio 43.47.5); this may explain why he joined the conspiracy to assassinate Caesar in 44 (cf. Cicero *Ad Fam.* 6.15).

Latin

(5) *si quid ... possit*: indirect question governed by an implied verb of seeking or investigating

Chapter 30

(2) **Fortune:** cf. 5.44.14. Given the potential embarrassment to Caesar of Ambiorix' daring escape here, we might not be surprised that he attributes the enemy's survival to fate rather than the failure of Caesar's surrogate.

Latin

(2) *accidit ... ut ... incideret ... videretur*: subjunctive verbs in a substantive clause of result introduced by the impersonal *accidit* (A&G 569)

Chapter 31

(2) **Ardennes forest:** cf. 5.3.4.

(3) **the islands:** this area is probably to be identified with the modern province of Zeeland, in the Netherlands; much of the region lies below sea level, hence the creation of islands by the changing tides.

(5) **Catovulcus:** introduced at 5.24.4. Although Caesar notes that he initially entered into the plot against Caesar together with Ambiorix (*una cum Ambiorige*), Catovulcus plays a less prominent role in the narrative than his more aggressive colleague Ambiorix.

yew tree: the yew tree (*Taxus* ba*ccata*) is an evergreen conifer commonly found in western Europe, as Caesar reports. Nearly the entire plant (all except the red flesh of its berries) is poisonous to humans and other animals if ingested, and no antidote exists. Florus reports that a group of Cantabrians committed suicide with an extract of the yew-tree to evade capture by besieging Romans in 22 BCE.

Chapter 32

(1) **the Segni and the Condrusi:** the Segni do not appear elsewhere in the *BG*. The Condrusi are named among the Belgic peoples that joined in the revolt against Caesar in 57 BCE (*BG* 2.4).

(3) **Atuatuca:** this is the first mention of Atuatuca by name in the *BG*. Its precise location is unclear, though we learn from what follows that this place is to be identified with the ill-fated winter camp established by Sabinus and Cotta during the previous year.

(4) **Sabinus and Cotta:** see 5.26—37.

(5) **the Fourteenth legion:** the Fourteenth was probably originally conscripted by Caesar in 57 BCE. This is the legion that was destroyed with Sabinus and Cotta in 54; it was quickly reconstituted by Caesar with fresh levies. During the civil war with Pompey, the Fourteenth was present at the

battles of Illerda, Dyrrhachium, and Pharsalus. The legion (or a re-reconstituted version of it) went on to great achievements under the principate, participating in Claudius' conquest of Britain in 43 CE and leading the suppression of the revolt of Boudicca, queen of the Iceni, in 60/61.
(6) **Quintus Tullius Cicero:** cf. 5.24.2.

Latin
(1) *oratum*: supine expressing purpose (A&G 509).
oratum ne ... duceret ... neve ... iudicaret: indirect command (also called substantive clause of purpose; A&G 563).
(2) *si ... convenissent ... si ... fecissent* subjunctives for the future perfect indicative protases of future conditions in implied indirect discourse (A&G 589, 592.2).
ut reducerentur: indirect command (also called substantive clause of purpose; A&G 563).

Chapter 33
(1) **Titus Labienus:** see 5.8.1.
the Menapii: see 6.2.3.
(2) **Gaius Trebonius:** see 5.17.2.
the Atuatuci: see 5.27.2.
(3) **the Scaldis River:** Caesar's description is problematic. The Scaldis is generally identified with the modern Scheldt River; however, the Scheldt does not flow into the Meuse (*Mosam*), as Caesar describes here. Some commentators have resolved the inconsistency by reading *Sabim* (the Sambre, which does join the Meuse); Holmes (1914) *ad loc.* retains the reading *Scaldim* and points out that Caesar simply might have been working from unreliable information (which does not seem out of the question when one considers the Hercynian Forest description).
(4) **the legion which had been left behind:** the Fourteenth, left at the fort Atuatuca under the command of Quintus Cicero in the previous chapter.

Chapters 34–41

Word spreads among the Germans that the Eburones are being pillaged and Atuatuca is vulnerable, and the Sugambri attack Quintus Cicero's garrison. Although there is some dissent among the troops, the camp is successfully defended. The Germans retreat over the Rhine, and Caesar returns to Atuatuca.

Chapter 34

(5) **If Caesar wanted…:** *si … velle[n]t.* In my opinion, Hering is right to mark this form as dubious, and, assuming Caesar as the subject, I have translated as *vellet* here. Although *vellent* is the more common reading (*velet* appears in two manuscripts described by Holmes as "inferior"), *vellet* makes far more sense in context; it is not clear who the plural subject of *vellent* would be, and there is a parallel *vellet* in the second half of the sentence, the reading of which is undisputed.
(6) **maintain formation:** *continere ad signa manipulos.* The standards probably stand in by metonymy for the idea of proper formation (cf. 5.16.1, 5.17.2, 6.8.6).
(8) **as punishment for their horrific crime:** *pro tali facinore.* i.e. the ambush and slaughter of the legion under Sabinus and Cotta.

Chapter 35

(2) **Fortune:** cf. 5.44.14 and 6.30.2. As with Ambiorix' escape in Chapter 30 above, Caesar here seems to invoke Fortune's capriciousness to deflect potential criticism of himself, his lieutenants, or his troops and guide the reader to understand that the ensuing attack on the Roman garrison and resulting losses were due to misfortune rather than mismanagement (or at least, not his *own* mismanagement; cf. 6.42.1-2).
(5) **as I described above:** the Sugambri, who lived on the east bank of the Rhine, had given refuge and made an alliance with the Usipetes and Tenctheri after their attack on the Menapii (*BG* 4.16-18).
(8) **One of the captives spoke up:** the relative rarity of direct speech in Caesar's commentaries has been noted above (see 5.30.1).

Latin

(9) *praesidii tantum*: partitive genitive (A&G 346); the *tantum* is equivalent to something like *tam parvum*, emphasizing the inadequacy of the garrison.

Chapter 36

Latin

(1) *qui ... continuisset ... passus esset*: relative clause of characteristic with concessive force (A&G 535e).

(2) *frumentatum*: supine expressing purpose (A&G 509).

Chapter 37

(1) **Decuman Gate:** see 5.49.7 for a description of the layout of the typical Roman camp.

(2) **merchants:** Roman camps were essentially small cities, and their population consisted not only of soldiers but also numerous non-combatants serving in various capacities. Camps attracted merchants (*mercatores*) who set up tents outside the encampment. *Mercatores* engaged in both buying and selling; they sold goods like clothing and food from their stalls and may have purchased items of loot from the soldiers to resell in another venue. Caesar's description of the merchants' set-up "under the rampart" (*sub vallo*) suggests that the *mercatores* were not permitted to set up shop within the walls of the camp.

Latin

(2) *recipiendi sui facultatem*: lit. 'an opportunity of retreating' but the infinitive sounds more natural in English than the gerund

Chapter 38

(1) **Publius Sextius Baculus:** unknown outside the *BG*, Publius Sextius Baculus had earned Caesar's admiration (*fortissimo viro, BG* 2.25) for his heroic conduct on multiple occasions. Baculus had survived serious wounds fighting the Nervii in 57 BCE (*BG* 2.25) and distinguished himself again during an attack on Servius Galba's winter quarters at the beginning of the following year (3.5).

chief centurion: cf. 5.35.6

(2) **Baculus seized some weapons...:** Baculus' brave stand here has some echoes of the Homeric *aristeia*, in which a fighter throws himself into battle and displays exceptional courage (e.g., Diomedes at *Il.* 5.633–654, Achilles in *Il.* 21). As with the 'centurions' contest' at 5.44, Caesar exploits the drama of this episode and increases the anticipation around Baculus' fate by using this type-scene, since the epic *aristeia* often (but not always) ends with the hero's death (cf. 5.44.4). It is also worth noting that, as is frequently the

case in the *BG*, the individual singled out for the heroic treatment here is a centurion; Caesar's depiction of the higher-ranking legates is typically less lavish than that of the tribunes and centurions (cf. 5.15.5 and Welch 1998).

Chapter 40

(2) **form a wedge:** *cuneo facto*. The *cuneus* (or ἔμβολον) was a wedge-shaped formation employed by both infantry and cavalry in which the soldiers arranged in a triangular or trapezoidal formation followed the leaders who were concentrated at the tip. According to Asclepiodotus, the author of a first century BCE treatise on military tactics, the wedge formation was invented by the Scythians and then adopted by the Thracians (*Tact.* 7.2–3). This was a favored tactic of Epaminondas of Thebes and Philip and Alexander of Macedon, and was later adopted by the Romans; Frontinus says that the wedge formation was part of the Romans' successful strategy at Pydna (2.3.20).

(4) **Gaius Trebonius:** see 5.17.2.

Chapter 41

(2) **Gaius Volusenus:** one of few ranking officers to be praised for *virtus* by Caesar (*BG* 3.5.2; cf. commentary on 5.25.2), Gaius Volusenus had been in Gaul with Caesar since at least 57 BCE and in 55 was sent to survey the southeastern coast of Britain in advance of the first expedition across the channel (4.21). Volusenus later served under Caesar in the civil war with Pompey. He was targeted by two brothers from the Allobroges who had abandoned their allegiance to Caesar and hoped to curry favor with Pompey by killing him, but they abandoned their plan when the task seemed too difficult (*Bellum Civile* 3.59–60).

Chapters 42–44

With Atuatuca secured, Caesar sets out once more in pursuit of Ambiorix, who escapes again. Caesar holds an inquiry into the plot and executes Acco as its ringleader. He sends the army to winter quarters and sets out for Italy to hold assizes.

Chapter 42

(1) **Fortune:** cf. 5.44.14, 6.30.2. 6.35.2

Chapter 43

(4) **Ambiorix:** Ambiorix will not be mentioned again by Caesar; his escape remains one of the few great embarrassments of Caesar's Gallic campaigns. Caesar is forced to settle for the execution of Acco, upon whom he puts full blame for the uprising (conveniently, since Acco is the one whom he had managed to apprehend; see Ch. 44 below). In his continuation of the *BG*, Aulus Hirtius describes Caesar's renewed attack on Ambiorix' territory in 51 BCE, but says that Caesar had given up hope of capturing Ambiorix himself and trusted that Ambiorix' own nature would ultimately alienate those who would give him safe harbor (*BG* 8.24). Ambiorix' fate is unknown.

Chapter 44

(1) **Durocortorum:** modern Reims; cf. 5.3.4.

(2) **the custom of our ancestors:** i.e. execution, probably by flogging, followed by beheading

(3) **Caesar decreed them banished:** *aqua atque igni interdixisset*, lit. 'forbade them from water and fire'. This legal formula indicated a form of exile that, in effect, forced the penalized party to leave Roman territory by denying them sustenance and safety within the Roman world. The *aquae et ignis interdictio* was typically enacted by proposal of a tribune of the plebs and seems to have been in use from at least the late third century BCE onward. On the complexities of Roman exile, see Kelly (2006).

the Lingones: the Lingones were a Gallic people whose territory was between the Senones and Sequani. They remained generally loyal to Caesar, supplying him with food (*BG* 1.40) and declining to join in Vercingetorix' revolt against Caesar in 52 BCE (7.63).

Agedincum: modern Sens; cf. 5.54.2.

to hold assizes, as was his custom: cf. 5.1.5. If Books 5 and 6 were indeed composed together (see Introduction, pp. 28–29), the ring composition neatly binds the two books.

INDEX

Printed and bound by CPI Group (UK) Ltd, Croydon, CR0 4YY

09/06/2025

14685811-0001